THIS IS CUBA

THIS IS CUBA

An American Journalist
Under Castro's Shadow

David Ariosto

ST. MARTIN'S PRESS ✠ NEW YORK

THIS IS CUBA. Copyright © 2018 by David Ariosto. All rights reserved. Printed in the United States of America. For information, address St. Martin's Press, 175 Fifth Avenue, New York, N.Y. 10010.

www.stmartins.com

Designed by Kelly S. Too

Library of Congress Cataloging-in-Publication Data is available upon request.

ISBN 978-1-250-17697-4 (hardcover)
ISBN 978-1-250-17698-1 (ebook)

Our books may be purchased in bulk for promotional, educational, or business use. Please contact your local bookseller or the Macmillan Corporate and Premium Sales Department at 1-800-221-7945, extension 5442, or by email at MacmillanSpecialMarkets@macmillan.com.

First Edition: December 2018

10 9 8 7 6 5 4 3 2 1

To Steph, Bel, Elizabeth, Mom, and Dad

CONTENTS

AUTHOR'S NOTE

This book encapsulates nine years of reporting on Cuba, a year and a half of which I spent living and working as a photojournalist in Havana. It is based on my own story and the stories of others, drawing on a mix of interviews, memories, and experiences meant to elicit a better understanding of a nation that has so often captured imaginations and been thrust—or has thrust itself—onto the global stage. While officials cited in this book are usually identified by their full names, in some cases I use only the first names of people who expressed concerns for their own safety and well-being. In keeping with the Cuban tradition, I also refer to former presidents Fidel Castro and Raul Castro on second reference by their first names, Fidel and Raul, respectively.

This book is not intended to be a comprehensive portrayal of the island in all its facets and complexities but rather a glimpse of Cuba through my own eyes, a once-naïve American journalist who, after years of reporting on and about the island, has hopefully wised up . . . at least a bit.

This is Cuba.

LAST CALL WITH CASTRO

I sipped an amber rum. Habana Club. Seven years. No ice. He palmed a Bucanero beer, half wrapped in a flimsy white paper napkin. Curls of Cohiba smoke wafted between us, giving the room a translucent look and an acrid taste. Castro was having a drink. And so was I. It was a Friday evening in late November 2010, and we were ensconced on opposite ends of a small subterranean saloon on the western outskirts of Havana. It was my last night in Cuba.

Jammed in the crevices of my back pocket was a one-way ticket to Miami, scheduled for the following morning, the first leg of a connecting flight to New York City. For the past year and a half, Havana had been home during my stint as a photojournalist for CNN on an island still forbidden to most Americans. But now I was ready to leave—forever, I thought. My father, who lived in the pinelands of southern New Jersey, had been sick following acute kidney failure, which punctuated my own recognition that life in Castro's Cuba didn't much suit me anymore. So I had found a job as an editor in New York, exchanged my house on the Caribbean for a studio apartment on Manhattan's Upper East Side, and traded the *guayabera* for a suit and tie; Cuban heat for a wintry chill. Crazy, it seemed, but Gotham was beckoning.

Then again, this *was* my last night in Havana. Better make the most of it.

"Do you know who that is?" whispered Antonina, a server in La Fontana, the private, family-run restaurant, or *paladar*, to which that smoky bar was attached.

"No," I replied. "Who?"

There was usually a breezy familiarity in the way she spoke, imbued with a Caribbean warmth and that marbles-in-your-mouth accent for which much of Cuba is known. The banter was usually light. The topics rarely serious.

But tonight was different. Antonina seemed different, the burden of her words a bit heavier than usual. Inside that *paladar*, a steady crop of regulars had shuffled in. Rum and cigars, coupled with a live singer or guitarist, usually helped to lighten the mood. But tonight, a palpable tension gripped the air. And the staff seemed to feel it. It was a sensation to which many had grown accustomed.

Situated on a leafy street a few blocks from Havana's rocky northern coast, La Fontana had opened in 1995 when authorities still investigated private restaurants for their numbers of tables and chairs (more than twelve could provoke a raid). Its clandestine feel—there was no sign outside and a surrounding stone wall all but hid the restaurant from view—was part of a broader bid for its very survival. And it looked it. The Castro government had almost never regarded privatization kindly, granting business licenses only when economic forces compelled a drip of liberalizing reform. But in the aftermath of the Soviet collapse, a financial crisis had ensued. For decades, Cuba had relied on subsidies from Moscow. In their absence, it teetered on the brink of collapse. Absent his old Kremlin ally, Fidel looked inward for answers and reluctantly allowed a few private restaurants to surface in a fraught attempt to gin up local commerce. La Fontana's two owners, Horacio Reyes-Lovio and Ernesto Blanco, were among the beneficiaries of the new tone and would soon become successful restaurateurs—a dangerous prospect on an island dominated by Communist hard-liners who had spent their careers fending off "yanqui capitalists." New concentrations of wealth were forming that could undermine the Revolution. So the two businessmen kept their profiles low and were quietly, if not begrudgingly, allowed to thrive. Perhaps even government officials were loath to shut down one of the few haunts where they could still score a decent meal.

By the time I arrived in Havana, in June 2009, that old *paladar* had been transformed into a favorite hangout for politicians, their staffs, and foreign businesspeople alike. It was a place to eat, drink, and—in my case—write, mostly from the vantage point of a still somewhat naïve American journalist. A fixture there, I'd often scratch out pages alone atop one of the few polished wooden tables in back, filling a leather-bound notebook with run-on sentences, notes, and smears of blue ink. They were random observations, mostly. A sort of blind attempt to piece together this confounding puzzle of a nation that I now called home. His approach. Her look. Their meeting. A dribble of insight that seeped through the censors of state-run newspapers.

After a few months and what amounted to a few notebooks full of mostly useless pages, I had gotten to know the restaurant's staff. One was Antonina, whose frankness and sharp tongue seemed matched only by her curiosity. It was the former that made us friends and the latter that would drive her to leave the island as a refugee. But before she did, her occasional rum-topped whispers would help fill in my own knowledge gaps, chasms really, when it came to Cuba. Men like Ricardo Alarcon, then president of Cuba's National Assembly, were among La Fontana's well-heeled patrons who often chatted and sipped mojitos with a hardy crop of familiar faces. I'd try without much luck to listen in, attempting to discern with whom he was meeting and what they were discussing. Business could be conducted this way, and the eavesdropping went both ways.

But tonight, my last night, I wondered why Antonina was so serious and to whom she had so subtly pointed. Passing behind me with a tray of empty glasses, she leaned into my ear.

"That's Alejandro," she whispered, brushing back the unkempt strands of raven-colored hair that dropped in front of her face.

By "Alejandro," Antonina had meant Alejandro Castro Espín, a colonel within Cuba's powerful Interior Ministry and a member of the Castro family, whose inherited importance seemed to be outpacing much of the rest of the Castro clan's. It was President Raul Castro's only son who now sat across from me at the bar. How could I not have realized that before? Of course, in November 2010, the extent of Alejandro's importance was not yet clear. He had yet to broker secret deals in Ottawa and Toronto with top Obama advisers Ben Rhodes and Ricardo Zúñiga, nor had he presided over a spy-for-spy negotiation that would lay the groundwork for détente. What *was* clear was that Alejandro was already a player and a de facto top adviser to his father. More importantly, he was rumored to be gaining in power atop the senior echelons of the very agency tasked with Cuba's surveillance and counterintelligence; his ministry spied on journalists and dissidents alike. And by apparent coincidence, in my final hours in Cuba he sat across from me, slouched over a beer.

"*Coño!*" exclaimed Rafa—employing his favorite Cuban expletive—when I later told him of the encounter. Rafael, or "Rafa" for short, was a driver at CNN, and his eyes bulged as he pronounced just the *ño* in that typical Cuban habit of dropping whole syllables. Though he quickly recuperated, casually popped his shoulders, and gave me this simple—though at the time nonsensical—explanation:

"*This is Cuba.*"

I had come to loathe that line, which was by now all too familiar—a favorite amongst those who seemed intent on explaining the unexplainable. In literal terms it meant little. Yet it also perfectly encapsulated everything about Cuba that was maddening, unknowable, and completely out of your hands. Even Cubans without a basis for comparison seem to know, perhaps by way of the trickle of information that seeps in from outside, that their island is somehow different.

"This is Cuba."

That Alejandro Castro Espín, one of the very men responsible for the sort of paranoid patina that coats the island, just so happened to be seated at my go-to bar on my last night in Havana . . . yeah, "This is Cuba" seemed apt.

As for Alejandro, he appeared reticent, reserved, and almost brooding over his beer. With a close-cropped mustache and goatee, and clad in a button-down shirt, the forty-five-year-old Castro scion had the look of middle management. Smart, though privileged, his ascent had been rapid as he sought to burnish his own revolutionary credentials. Alejandro had lost vision in one eye during a military deployment to Angola and yet nonetheless later earned a doctorate in political science, giving him the added chops he may have needed to author a 2009 book, titled *The Empire of Terror*. It derided corporate influence on U.S. governance and was tantamount to an anti-American manifesto. But those who knew Alejandro considered him more sophisticated than that. His old professor Carlos Alzugaray, a former Cuban diplomat posted to the European Union, later told me that his former pupil may have published that book to reinforce his qualifications, and thus curry favor with the old guard. Veterans of the Revolution and the island's one-party system remained skeptical of Cuba's approaching political and economic transition. They may have needed some reassuring. Much of the politburo and many of the military chiefs were in their golden years, indelibly imprinted with Socialist traditions and Communist rhetoric, which they certainly weren't about to abandon. Though a generational shift was under way, conventional wisdom suggested that deference to these old Cold Warriors—who had spent their careers opposing Americans—was a safe bet for anyone with political aspirations.[1]

"When you talk about U.S. imperialism, you have to hit them hard," Alzugaray told me.[2] Even Fidel had needed their tacit buy-in to rule.

Alejandro seemed to understand that, having spent his life immersed in traditions cultivated by his uncle Fidel and father, Raul, who had officially assumed the presidency only in 2008, the year before I arrived. More gatekeeper than puppet master within Cuba's intelligence services, the young colonel's climb within the intelligence apparatus dovetailed with his dad's newfound power. Though the muscle was Raul's, the younger Castro controlled the flow of information. And while precisely who else had their hands on Cuba's levers of power would remain capricious and shrouded in secrecy, drinkers and waitstaff in La Fontana all seemed to know to pay attention when the young Castro walked in.

Alejandro, however, didn't look like the offspring of leftist firebrands. Though he was garrulous and passionate by reputation, here he appeared quiet and lost in thought. From his eyes sparkled gloomy fires, imbued with the sort of melancholy common to so many restless aristocrats. And they seemed to grow colder and darken as the night wore on.

"*Oye!*" yelled a squat man seated beside him. "Do you want another?" he asked Alejandro, giving that universal hand-wave that signaled a request for more beer.

"No, thank you," he replied. With his back propped against the wall, the colonel kept the room in front of him. And every now and then he glared in my direction. His pupils, by now habituated to the saloon's darkness, flitted about the room, alternating between his warmish beer and me.

I should say something, I thought. How could I not?

But what exactly does one say to the man whose agency is charged with spying on you? How does that conversation begin?

As I sat there sipping my rum and planning my approach, the

bartender—an impressively tattooed woman named Jacqueline—
sensed my intention and beat me to the punch.

"*Oye!* Alejandro!" she bellowed, snatching another frosty glass
from below the bar. "Do you know David? He's with CNN."

Conversation ground to a halt. Alejandro put down his glass.
They all just looked at me.

"Uh . . . *hola,*" I said.

The men hardly moved. They just stared. And after an agonizingly
long pause, the Colonel tipped his head in my direction. It was an
acknowledgment and as much of an opening as I'd get. It seemed
enough, and so I went in for a proper introduction.

"I'm—"

"I know who you are," he interrupted, slowly adjusting his gaze
as he peered over his beer.

In the eyes of many in government, I was an instrument of
their enemy: an American journalist with mediocre Spanish whose
country had endeavored to remove the Castros from power, slapping
Cuba with an economic trade embargo—which authorities refer to
as *el bloqueo* (the blockade)—that had lasted for more than half a
century.

But how did he know me?

My thoughts searched back to hundreds of stories I had filmed
and written about over the years, which included dissident protests,
political prisoners, and black-market trade, any number of which
could have piqued government interest. But none of it made me
unique. The island's foreign press corps may have lacked a deep
bench, yet few of its journalists shied away from investigative stories.
Of course, with a government as tightly wound as this one, scoops
were relatively rare.

Nothing came to mind—until something did.

Though not quite a scoop, it had all started on a sunny Friday
afternoon more than a year earlier, on November 6, 2009, with a

woman whose long brown hair and bohemian attire seemed to accentuate her solemn gaze.

Yoani Sánchez was on her way to a march.

The thirty-four-year-old dissident blogger had become one of the Castros' most visible critics. And over the course of just two years, she had developed a sizeable foreign following through her blog, *Generación Y*. In fact, her writings about the hardships of Cuban life and her criticism of its government had earned her international acclaim. In 2008, *Time* magazine listed Yoani as among the world's one hundred most influential people.[3] Posing as a German tourist, she'd sneak into hotel internet cafés to upload her latest musings or deliver them on thumb drives to Cuban exiles living in South Florida. But that day, which had been hotter than most, she was heading to a march against violence in the Cuban capital with fellow bloggers. As temperatures soared and the bloggers approached the march, a pair of "burly" state security agents cut them off.[4]

What happened next would offer a snapshot of what reporting was like in a place where freedom of speech and assembly are not only severely curtailed, but where authorities seem to take pride in their own opacity. According to Yoani and fellow bloggers, the agents didn't want them to attend the march and were intent on preventing them from reaching it.

The situation would quickly devolve. A third security agent joined the men and the three promptly seized the marchers, allegedly forcing Yoani into a waiting car, pummeling her body and grabbing fistfuls of her hair. She fought back, clawing at their arms and grabbing one man's genitals. But Yoani was quickly overpowered and shoved face-first into the back seat, where she was restrained and briefly detained.

When Yoani returned home, the story circulated like wildfire among the island's small foreign press corps as the news wires quickly picked up the story.

I had to go interview her.

"Where does Yoani live?" I asked our office manager, Dagmara, who breathed a deep sigh before handing me the address scrawled on a piece of paper. Dagmara, per usual, knew far more than I did. This wouldn't end well. She knew that, but handed me the paper anyway. And the next morning I headed out to meet Yoani, arriving at her small Havana apartment just after breakfast time. There, I trudged up a series of concrete steps until an older man, with a pomp of salt and pepper hair, named Reinaldo Escobar—Yoani's husband—greeted me at the door.

"Hello, David," he said, welcoming me inside their apartment. The sun's morning light had already flooded their small living room, and cast a warm glow over Yoani, who was seated at the kitchen table. When she saw me, she strained to stand, leaning on a single crutch.

"*Quieres café?*" she asked, embracing my hand and offering me coffee.

She looked tired. Slight swelling had puffed up under her left eye, and a few bruises had surfaced along her foot and legs. We chatted a bit off camera as she told me her story. But as I adjusted the tripod and focused my lens, Reinaldo, also a dissident blogger, slid a collection of Yoani's painkillers into the camera's frame.

"Can you see this?" he asked me, before the interview started, pushing the stack of the bottles closer to Yoani, who was leaning forward on her crutch as we spoke. I ignored him and zoomed in closer to her face, largely erasing all but his wife's portrait from the camera's viewfinder. Yet Reinaldo was undeterred and slid the pills closer still, seemingly intent on ensuring his wife's suffering was evident for viewers. Neither was a media novice, and after a few more to-and-fros of this sort, I began to feel like I was being managed. Reinaldo adjusted her crutch. Suddenly aware of it, she shooed him away.

Only then did the small talk end and our interview commence. She leaned forward and recalled the men, their car, and her own sense of panic.

"'Yoani,'" she quoted one of her assailants. "'This is it.' And in that moment, I thought I was going to die."

There was a subtle resignation to her words, soft and deliberate as they were. And I listened intently. While the Castro-led government often viewed its opponents as mercenaries in America's employ, imprisoning dissidents and intimidating sympathizers, overt killings had not been in its playbook, at least not in recent years. What's more, Raul had announced a year earlier in 2008 that virtually all prisoner death sentences were to be commuted to lengthy prison terms.

Still, Yoani had expressed mortal fear. And I would include her words in my report. Only later, after the segment had aired, did I more carefully assess their gravity. At the time, however, there were precious few perspectives. Cuban authorities had refused to comment on the story, or even discuss the matter—a recurring frustration for anyone intent on sussing out a more complete version of events. And so I was left with just the account of a few dissidents, marks on Yoani's body, and the history of heavy-handed tactics by the island's state security. Still, the incident's aftermath indeed had felt a bit staged: the stack of pills, the crutch neatly placed in camera's view, and her insistence that her more profound bruises were in private places that she could not show me. That, of course, didn't mean it didn't happen.

So I went with it. Adding caveats where I thought appropriate, that CNN story was the first airing of Yoani's account to a global audience. It was my first big story in Cuba, airing on CNN en Español early that Monday morning, which is what may have finally provoked a Cuban response, and my first scolding from a man named Raulito Hernandez, overseer of foreign journalists at Cuba's International Press Center.

The ring of his phone call cut through the island's soupy air.

"David, why did you talk with her?" Raulito asked me, his tone a touch deeper than was his custom.

"It was news," I replied simply, and settled in for what was an inevitable, perhaps predictable, lecture on why Cuba's dissidents could not be trusted.

The conversation was short, terse, and to the point: he didn't like my report, which meant he had either seen it and called me, or someone had urged him to do so. The CNN bureau would field more of these calls during our subsequent coverage of other dissident marches. And our journalist visa approvals, which required state renewals every few months, would be delayed again and again. The message was clear: there were consequences for this sort of coverage.

Two years earlier, in 2007, Cuba had effectively expelled Havana-based correspondents Gary Marx of the *Chicago Tribune,* Stephen Gibbs of the BBC, and César González-Calero of the Mexican daily newspaper *El Universal* by not renewing their press credentials.[5] Marx had chronicled Cuba's black market and its dissidents. Gibbs had written about Cuba's response to the AIDS crisis. And González-Calero had detailed chronic shortages and currency devaluations. After their expulsion, the government issued a document that explained its right to revoke credentials when a journalist conducted "improper actions or actions not within his profile and work content."[6] Journalist visas, in other words, were leverage.

During that last night at La Fontana, Alejandro hadn't said whether he had seen my report on Sanchez, but his government clearly had and was all too familiar with the Cuban blogger. Fidel Castro had in fact criticized Yoani in the prologue of his 2008 book *Fidel, Bolivia and Something More,* deriding her as among those beholden to "imperialism's mass media."[7] The internet, which housed the island's growing blogosphere, was clearly something authorities were concerned about. It was "the wild colt of new technologies" that "can and must be controlled," Ramiro Valdes, Cuba's minister of communications and information, proclaimed in 2007.[8] And it had been. Cuba bore the lowest internet penetration in the Western Hemisphere, despite tens of millions spent under Presidents Obama and Bush to expand internet access across the island—part of a U.S. "democracy building" initiative designed to support activist bloggers like Yoani. The Americans saw new media as the lance with which they could finally skewer Castro's Communism, and quickly denounced Yoani's assault, while the U.S. State Department expressed "deep concern" to Cuban authorities.[9] Then, President Obama shocked virtually everyone by praising Yoani directly, saying—in a carefully choreographed statement—that he looked forward to the day "all Cubans can freely express themselves."[10] That sort of change, of course, required broader political will bubbling up from within the island. And it just wasn't clear that that existed. At least not yet. U.S. Interests Section Chief Jonathan Farrar acknowledged as much in a classified diplomatic cable, dated April 15, 2009, in which he described dissidents as lacking homegrown support. Be that as it may, tensions between Washington and Havana ratcheted higher.[11] And by early December, Cuba's state security agents were again on the move, this time entering Havana's Hotel Presidente and arresting a white-haired American contractor named Alan Gross who had covertly smuggled satellite internet technologies onto the island. America and her private contractors' emerging strategy of employing the internet, and its potentially galvanizing powers, against the Castro government appeared to be taking shape. And Gross had been snared as a somewhat unwitting pawn.

From atop his vaulted post within the Interior Ministry, which oversaw Cuban security and its intelligence services, few were better positioned to know this than Alejandro, who had just ordered another beer.

But Raul's only son wasn't why I was there. I was thirsty, and perhaps wanted to nurse these last hours with familiar faces I had assumed I'd never see again. Cuba, I thought, was soon to be but a memory. Of course, as it turned out, none of that was true. Yet in the moment, as I sat there and embraced the warm glow of just the right amount of rum wrapping its familiar cloak, I was for the first time starting to have second thoughts about leaving. What's more, I wondered what would become of this Castro upstart at the end of the bar. What would Alejandro's role be as his aging relatives died out and the fate of his island government, born of revolution, was thrust into uncertainty?

He wasn't Fidel. He wasn't even another Raul, who later seemed to go out of his way to elevate a bureaucrat and party faithful named Miguel Díaz-Canel as his successor. Yet Alejandro was at the helm of what had been perhaps Cuba's most powerful institution: its spies.

For generations, the island had influenced American politics and punched above its weight on the international stage, in no small part because of a remarkable intelligence-gathering apparatus that had once directly reported to Fidel. Alejandro now seemed its logical standard-bearer. Of course, without Fidel, would anyone beyond an aging group of Cubaphiles and Miami exiles really care? To most news executives I met, it all seemed like the distant inside baseball of Caribbean politics. To them, Cuba—an island of 11.5 million people with an economy slightly larger than that of Delaware—warranted a news bureau for just one reason: nostalgia.

Clichés here had been repeated a thousand times over by journeymen journalists who all seemed to have picked up the same phrasebook: "a time capsule" place that was "frozen in history." Americans who were "dying to see it before it all changes" could go and ogle the old cars, salsa, and cigars by virtue of our reports, and perhaps harken back to their own rose-tinted memories. I was no different. Though to be fair, Cuba's banalities were impossible to ignore. As the late photographer David Gilkey once recalled after attempting to photograph anything other than those vintage Plymouths and Fords that belched and grumbled their way through Old Havana, it was like "seeing a celebrity and trying not to stare."[12] The island's retro appeal was indeed its siren song; a gypsy seductress, whose wanderlust charms dutifully masked an identity many foreigners never really cared to know about. Best keep it simple, lest it spoil the fantasy. But those who lived here had little choice but to begin to wipe their eyes clear—the old cars, salsa, and cigars no longer sating their curiosities as the island's more unsavory underbelly became exposed. Authorities knew that. As such, journalists were to be monitored. I expected I was no different. And yet this particular moment in history was. Though I didn't know it at the time, a crisis was brewing—a watershed moment had coincided with the beginnings of a blossoming internet, a stumbling economy, and questions of confidence bubbling up amongst those jockeying for power. The old Communist guard had receded. And their country had embarked upon its biggest transition in more than half a century. Cuba's next revolution was at hand.

And the man who sat across from me, slowly sipping his beer in that windowless tavern, would be at the very heart of it.

2

THE SPIES AMONG US

It was around lunchtime when I got the call in my office. A woman's voice I didn't recognize purred through the receiver.

"David?"

"Yes?" I said.

"Hi, I'm Dalia." As in much of Havana, the air-conditioning in the Hotel Habana Libre—where CNN's bureau was located—had given out as the weather grew hotter. It was June 2009, and there was nothing to combat an encroaching lethargy spawned by Havana's swampy air. The days grew long and languorous. But Dalia's voice snapped me back to the present, her coquettish tone cut through the Libre's malaise like a knife. "You interviewed my cousin the other day and he thought we should meet." A distinct roll of the tongue flowed into her words. I had no idea who she was or about whom she was talking. Still, I had met with a variety of people after moving to Havana from Atlanta, just the week prior. So, it was entirely possible.

"I'm sorry," I said. "Can you repeat that?"

"My cousin," she said. "You interviewed my cousin."

In reality, the move to Cuba had left me a bit out of sorts and I was still trying to get my bearings. Havana, as I saw it, was the chance of a lifetime for a young American photojournalist who then boasted only pidgin Spanish. For news executives who regarded the island's best days as long gone, sending me wasn't much of a gamble. Fidel Castro had already stepped down from power. His younger, far less charismatic brother, Raul, had taken the reins. And a Havana assignment was considered little more than being on "Castro death watch." The biggest news about the island didn't even seem to come from the island. In fact, rumors of the elder Castro's death sprang up most Fridays and were usually traced back to Miami. Ironically, years later, on November 25, 2016, Cuban state television followed through on that very tradition. Raul, somber and clad in military fatigues, announced the death of the ninety-year-old leader that Friday evening, prompting both tears and cheers, which often depended on which side of the Florida Strait you sat. Of course, America's then president-elect handled the news with the kind of finely crafted statesmanship one might expect of the office. "Fidel Castro is dead!" Donald Trump tweeted, calling Castro a "brutal dictator" and casting fresh doubts on Obama's recent thaw with America's old foe.[1] Although, in 2009, all of that was yet to be. And what would begin to frame my grasp of those subsequent years and Cuba's transition started with a simple phone call from a mysterious woman on that June day in Havana.

"*Oye, chico.* Did you hear me?"

I eased back in my chair and gazed out the office window.

"Who's this cousin of yours?"

"Miguel."

"Miguel who?"

"He's my cousin."

"Yes, I know, but who is your cousin?"

"Miguel."

This wasn't going to be easy.

"Listen," Dalia said. "I know this might sound little strange to a *yuma*. But this is Cuba."

With one word—*"yuma"*—she had made it clear she knew exactly who I was. *"Yuma"* is street slang for "gringo" or really any foreigner from a non-Spanish-speaking country. It may have been derived from the thick Cuban pronunciation of "United States," or "YOOH-NUH-dead-states." Others point to the classic American western *3:10 to Yuma*, released in 1957 and shown in Havana theaters. Maybe Americans were considered cowboys and therefore *yumas*. It didn't really matter. Whatever the origin, I was a *yuma*. And as much as I wanted to think I was somehow different from those pink-faced tourists who now mingled about the island, I knew I wasn't. Instead, I was just another privileged outsider with a foreigner's salary and a forbidden island to explore. Somehow I thought if I didn't act like a *yuma,* then I wasn't one. But Dalia knew better.

She was also a welcome distraction, and she knew it.

"OK. Sure. Let's meet," I said. "Wait, who is this again?"

"Dalia," she replied, this time more forcefully. "Anyway, do you like pizza?"

"Of course," I said.

"OK, *chico,* I'll text you where," she replied, quickly hanging up without so much as a *ciao.* No one likes long phone conversations in a country where cell phones work on a pay-per-use basis and credit runs out fast. Moments later, my mobile phone vibrated with the coordinates. She had picked a pizzeria close to Havana's Central Park. It was hardly the shady, back-alley rendezvous of my Graham Greene fantasies, but the place had its quirks.

Leaving work, I made my way through the park and past a group of old men who were listening to a small transistor radio spew out commentary by a quick-speaking sports announcer. They were a fixture in a still baseball-crazed Cuba, and the usual suspects were again ranting about their favorite teams despite (or maybe because of) the diminished quality of the island's league. Often, I'd sit down for a bit. But not today. I had a date, and walked into the adjacent pizzeria, easing onto a wooden chair at a table in back. Dalia was late.

So I waited, ordered a Corona—one of the few imported beers available on the island—and reflected on who I was actually about to meet. When we spoke, her voice had offered only a slight Cuban lilt, rising and falling like waves against the Malecon. Now, as I waited, my thoughts were adrift with a flitter of excitement bubbling up alongside my still sudsy beer. Who was she? Where was she? And who was this Miguel she had mentioned? I wracked my brain, rattling off stories that might have included that name. None came to mind. But that didn't really mean much. Interviews were often left on the cutting-room floor. Miguel may never have actually appeared in a story. And yet he had apparently set in motion a chain of events that would soon personify that breathy female voice that drew me to this low-lit pizzeria at the edge of the park. Having grown a bit lonely in Havana, it was a welcome reprieve. And as the evening cooled and restaurant lights dimmed, the anticipation was building.

Of course, this is Cuba. Here, there was always more to consider. Months earlier, at my perch at CNN headquarters in Atlanta, a news executive asked me into her office and offered her reflections on my pending assignment. "Be discerning about who you meet and talk to down there," said Parisa Khosravi, then senior vice president for international newsgathering.[2] "Not everyone is who they say they are." Now as I waited, Parisa's words came flooding back. In 1997, when the United States removed restrictions barring American journalists from Cuba and granted licenses to ten news organizations, CNN opened a news bureau in Havana. It was the first U.S. news outlet in twenty-seven years to have a presence on the island, and Miami opposition groups wasted little time in dubbing CNN the "Castro News Network."[3] Khosravi was part of the team that named Lucia Newman "Our Woman in Havana," the first journalist from an American news organization based in Cuba since Castro expelled reporters from the Associated Press in 1969.[4] Newman set up the bureau on the twentieth floor of the Hotel Habana Libre, just three floors below where it was rumored that Fidel, Ernesto "Che" Guevara, and the rest of the island's bearded revolutionaries had planned their new Communist government after toppling Fulgencio Batista half a century earlier. It was a historic place.

When I got there, CNN had occupied an office at the Libre for twelve years, which was ample time for drama. In just my first week, I heard stories of past CNNers falling in love with Cubans and being quickly discarded by their would-be Cuban life mates shortly after they arrived in the States. With an average state salary of around $24 per month, getting off the island was often a top priority for Cuban women and men alike, and a brief courtship with a naïve foreigner was often an endurable price to pay for those anxious to leave. Was that the kind of woman I was about to meet? I took another sip of beer.

"Uno más," I said to the waiter shuffling past my table, and ordered a second Corona.

The heat had not relented, and I craved another drink. Caribbean summers soak the clothes and dampen the spirits of even the most ambitious travelers, making the prospect of doing anything other than lounging a laborious task.

In midafternoons, bare-chested boys can be seen splashing and diving off rocky enclaves in search of a brief reprieve from rising temperatures. Women strut through the old city in *chancletas,* or flip-flop-style sandals, beating the air with paper fans. A near-constant sheen of sweat gives virtually everyone a faint glisten. But temperature is only part of the lazy vibe that permeates the city. Havana also has a sultry character. Crackling old radios and the brassy tunes of street musicians seep through courtyards and down cobblestone alleyways in a way that gives the island its own peppery soundtrack. Music from trumpets or guitars ricochet against crumbling art deco buildings before mixing with the mechanical growl of a '57 Chevy Bel Air or '48 Studebaker. Beside me, a group of musicians had started playing. Their music was light and rhythmic and infused with that all-important "key" or clave—a classic five-stroke percussion pattern considered a core facet of many Afro-Cuban rhythms. Every Cuban who ever tried to explain it to me started by saying, *"Es fácil."* It's easy. They would then take their hands and slam them down against the table five times: twice fast, three times slow, mouthing a sound each time their hands struck.

"Bah, bah . . . Bah . . . Bah . . . Bah."

Though there are different varieties of the clave, this version is a baseline for much of Cuban music. And Habaneros often can't help but swing their hips when they hear it. As I sipped my Corona, three women dancing near my table were no different; the bright pastel colors of their flowy orange and red dresses making for stark contrast against their olive skin. As their hips rocked from side to side, their arms raised and bent at the elbow every other time the clave struck. It was in that moment when Dalia strode in. Her thin-sheathed yellow dress both billowed around her legs and clung to her chest amid that rising June humidity.

"Oye, mamita," grumbled one middle-aged patron as she walked in, his eyes surveying her jutting contours, which pushed and swayed as she strode up to my table.

"Hi, David," Dalia said, with subtle confidence. I stumbled to my feet. Her eyes sized me up as I asked her to sit down. In a single motion, Dalia slid back her wooden chair from the table and eased into her seat, crossing her legs and tossing a thick chestnut-colored braid over one shoulder. *So this is Cuba?* I thought, my mind wandering.

"Que bola, chico?" she said with a second greeting, switching into that familiar roll-of-tongue Cuban. *"Es un placer,"* she said, extending her hand as she leaned in for a peck on either cheek. She had swagger yet also the persona of a woman who had likely seen my type before.

"It's nice to meet you," I replied.

By then, only a handful of American journalists were still living on the island. Many had left a rather unsavory reputation. And it seemed that Dalia knew it. When American news organizations had been permitted back in Cuba, reporters boasting envious salaries descended just as the island grappled with economic disaster. After the collapse of the Soviet Union, Cuba's sugar and fuel subsidies had all but dried up. Capital vanished from the island and access to food waned, with many Cubans surviving on a diet of sugar water and rice. As the United States tightened the embargo's screws, the average Cuban shed up to 25 percent of their body weight, leaving the country on the brink of famine.[5] Desperation set in. Accordingly, Cuba's sex industry exploded as the country pressed its tourism sectors in a fraught attempt to attract foreign currency. Many grew accustomed to the sight of wide-eyed *yumas* wielding broken Spanish and pockets brimming with cash, scouring the streets for an adolescent girl to take home for the night. Later, in 2011, a Royal Canadian Mounted Police report determined that Cuba had become among the primary Latin American destinations for Canadian sexual predators.[6] But the problem was far more widespread.

Enough of these travelers had come to Cuba enticed by the prospect of sex, rum, and cheap cigars to earn foreigners a sleazy reputation. Relationships forged between poor Cubans and rich expats, including American journalists, were uneven at best and criminal at worst.

Was that how Dalia viewed me?

By 2009, the U.S. State Department had ranked Cuba a Tier 3 country in its *Trafficking in Persons Report,* labeling it a "source and destination country for adults and children subjected to sex trafficking," where "Cuban children are reportedly pushed into prostitution by their families, exchanging sex for money, food, or gifts."[7] Rather than targeting foreigners, who were rarely prosecuted for child exploitation, the Cuban government focused on prostitutes, who could be sent to detention centers if arrested. That seemed the backstory here, or at least part of it.

I refocused. Or rather, Dalia's questions compelled me to: "How long have you been here?" she asked.

"Just a few minutes."

"No, how long here in Cuba?"

Her tone restless, Dalia's eyes skipped about the room, alternating between mine, the bar, and a Bucanero our waiter had just served her.

"Almost two weeks," I replied. "Oh, and by the way," I added, "who was this cousin of yours? The one you said I interviewed." A smile crept up one side of her mouth as she affixed her eyes back toward her beer, her fingers toying with a moistened napkin wrapped around its base. "I have a confession to make," she cooed, leaning across the table as her cleavage plumed above a plunging neckline. "I don't have a cousin."

"Then how'd you get my number?"

She smiled again. The urgency had left her face, and she leaned back in her chair and took another slow sip of beer. "This is Cuba," she said coolly.

"Okaaay. What does that mean?"

"It means everybody knows somebody, who knows somebody," she said.

Maybe she expected me to understand. I didn't, my thoughts slackened by the beer. Instead of the phrase "everybody knows somebody," did she mean "somebody was always watching somebody"? Like most interactions in Cuba, it was almost impossible to know for sure. For years, an insidious inform-on-your-neighbor policy spread paranoia across the island. Informants could come from anywhere, and trust was at a premium. In some cases, dissidents—long ostracized by family and community—were later revealed to be double agents in Castro's employ. It was Cuba's proverbial rabbit hole. And no one seemed to know how far down it went. Sometimes just the expectation that someone might be listening, watching, recording could be enough to keep mouths shut and opinions withheld. Cubans I interviewed would often clam up, particularly in public spaces where closed-circuit cameras seemed ubiquitous. For a country with few resources, Castro's debt-ridden island could deliver world-class espionage. And many who lived here acted accordingly. Most had never experienced anything else; informants were a part of everyday life. And Castro's neighborhood watch committees, called Committees for the Defense of the Revolution, were widely credited as among his most effective tools, paralyzing opposition forces in those first years after the Revolution. Today, though they are more oriented toward community organizing and hurricane preparedness, Cuban authorities still call on local block leaders for information about their neighbors.

Murals still depict those CDR leaders with multiple eyes scouring their neighborhoods for dissent—reminders of a system that not only breeds distrust and surveillance, but weaves them both into the very fabric of society. At the time of my drink with Dalia, however, I didn't know any of this.

Her hair caught the light as she once again leaned across the table. A loose strand fell across her face. "What do you really think about this place? The politics, I mean."

I had a sense that question was coming. Our conversation had thrust and parried throughout the night, flirting and pulling back only to engage again about the elephant in the room. It had been almost two hours since Dalia sat down, and empty bottles of Corona and Bucanero now cluttered our table. The conversation had danced around politics, but never dug into it. Like most Cubans, she avoided discussing it directly. But as the alcohol set in, she started to press.

"So what's your story?" Dalia asked again, narrowing her gaze in an attempt to focus. Something was becoming clear. This mystery woman seemed less interested in sharing her thoughts than sorting out where this American newcomer was coming from. Dalia was talking, but she wasn't offering so much as digging.

"What do you think of Fidel?" she prodded again.

"Why?" I asked.

"You're in Cuba," she said with a laugh.

She was right, but I felt sluggish, and evaded. "Fidel is Fidel," I countered, resting my beer directly in front of her. The alcohol was having even more of an effect than I realized. Maybe she was just who she said she was—a Cuban woman wanting simply to get to know this single American man who had just stumbled onto her island. *Go with it,* I thought. It was easy to let a little knowledge add paranoia to an otherwise normal night out. And yet I was beginning to have my doubts. Dalia's leg brushed against mine under the table; the thin fabric of her dress pulled away against the denim of my jeans and exposed a hint more of her skin. It was still hot. She wiped her brow and smiled, but her eyes remained ardent, like the sea before a storm. As the sun receded behind the Capitolio, the dome-shaped building once the seat of government, temperatures inside our pizzeria had not abated. "You *yumas* are so crazy," she giggled. One thing, however, was starting to seem out of place—Dalia's laugh. It broke the heaviness of the thick Caribbean air and grew more noticeable as we chatted. Once seemingly light and flirtatious, it now appeared almost forced and unnatural. I can be funny. But not that funny.

Cuba's Interior Ministry often assigned minders to keep tabs on those living on the island. The so-called honeypot trap was hardly uncommon. Dalia seemed to have all of its makings, but I couldn't be sure.

In the murky world of intelligence, in which Cuba had excelled, the art of *kompromat,* a Russian word meaning the acquiring of compromising material, is a game played in months and years, not hours. Seduction and allure were only the beginning. The trust born of intimate relationships was forged over time, often gained by a femme fatale with a keen ear and an eye for detail. "We have many women who work for us," a former senior Cuban intelligence officer would later tell me. The amorous arts were well trodden, and hardly unique to Cuba. In fact, British intelligence was so concerned about it that in 2009 MI5 issued a fourteen-page document cautioning

Western financial institutions about Chinese spies seeking "long-term relationships" with the purpose of "exploit[ing] vulnerabilities such as sexual relationships."[8] Despite the warnings, honeypot traps remained effective. Yet as the sun set and alcohol flowed, Dalia may have overplayed her charms.

"La cuenta, por favor." I turned and motioned to our waiter for the bill. The haze was wearing off as the stale scent of cigar smoke wafted over our table. It was time to go. She sensed it too. I reached into my pocket and tossed a handful of moistened Cuban bills onto the table. But before I could get up, Dalia reached across the table and wrapped her fingers around my wrist. She held it for a moment before leaning in one last time. "It was a pleasure, David," she said, pressing her lips against my cheek in a way that lingered a bit longer than before. *"Bienvenido a Cuba."* With that, she slipped out the front door, leaving as suddenly as she had arrived. Dalia never looked back. "Welcome to Cuba," I mouthed.

3

MEN FROM STATE

My forehead throbbed, stinging evidence of that beer-soaked night with Dalia, as I fumbled for the precious few Advil, manna from heaven, left on my nightstand. Wiping my eyes, groggy from another sleepless night on sheets dampened by the island's humidity, the image of Dalia lingered. Whoever she was and whatever last night had been, I was a bit too hungover to give it much thought. Still, something about the exchange seemed a bit off.

This is Cuba.

I made my way to the window to give my mind a rest. Shards of Caribbean sun were already slipping past the translucent, cream-colored curtains that gently swayed in front of my new home. Havana's tired beauty stokes a potent brew of nostalgia and romance, real or imagined. And for a moment I was lost in both. Gazing through salt-stained windowpanes, I could almost make out what I had seen so many times on my walk to work: the faded wash of pastel homes and buildings that abut a long gray seawall outlining the city's northern edge. At dusk, on calmer nights, young lovers prop their feet atop this four-mile stretch of concrete, where a blood orange sun disappears beneath inky seas and offers the distraction young men need to make their move. At sunrise, lovers are replaced by white buckets nestled beside sunbaked legs and filled with needlefish and snapper as fishermen cast lines with both makeshift and carbon alloy poles. The great sofa, as it's occasionally called, is the Malecon seawall, which dates back more than a century to 1901, three years after the start of the Spanish-American War, or what then U.S. diplomat John Hay referred to as that "splendid little war."[1] "It has been a splendid little war, begun with the highest motives, carried on with magnificent intelligence and spirit, favored by that Fortune which loves the brave," Hay wrote in a July 27, 1898, letter to Theodore Roosevelt.[2]

Though American army engineers began its construction, the Malecon could not be more Cuban. It bookends a six-lane thoroughfare where classic Fords and Russian Ladas spew blackened exhaust that gives the air a bitter tinge. Sea birds dive-bomb fish near its wave breaks. And musicians with trombones and guitars walk its promenade, serenading tourists and Cubans alike. These four miles of concrete and coral are among the world's best taxi rides, nestled at the very crossroads of Cuban nostalgia.

And the Hotel Nacional offers a bird's-eye view of it all. The history felt thick here. Winston Churchill and Marlon Brando once strolled its promenade. Frank Sinatra and Rita Hayworth sipped at its bars, and the building's twin art deco spires and long columns reflect a Hispano-Moorish architecture that harkens back to a very different time, when commerce thrived and organized crime ran rampant across the island. In 1946, at the urging of New York gangster Charles "Lucky" Luciano, American mob bosses and Sicily's Cosa Nostra convened at the Nacional for what became known as the Havana Conference, a meeting of top capos meant to carve up mafia territory in the United States. The building was later commandeered by Fidel's revolutionaries, who excavated trenches and placed antiaircraft batteries atop its courtyard in preparation for an American invasion that never came (at least not there).[3] But by the time I arrived, all of that seemed like sepia-toned pages for the archives. Fidel was no longer president. The threat of invasion seemed absurd. The Nacional had essentially been transformed into a museum hotel, where gold-framed photos of celebrities and former Cuban leaders lined its hallways. Still, it was a popular meeting spot. More importantly, it was my home for my first month in Havana. Plus, it boasted among the best mojitos in town.

Too early for that minted rum drink, I left my room to track down the island's other famous pick-me-up: coffee.

First, however, I needed cash, and headed for the hotel's money exchange. As I approached, the loud, rum-soaked slur of an unmistakable American accent diverted my attention.

"C'mon, *señor*," the man barked, motioning to his luggage. "Let's go."

Two glassy-eyed Americans stepped forward and shuffled beside me. Each had a mojito. And though the sun was hours from its noon crest, they were already sweating. Jose, the Nacional's portly baldheaded hotel clerk, rolled his eyes and audibly exhaled—all too familiar with this sort of guest.

"*Momentito,*" Jose responded, unimpressed, and checked his watch, making it clear that he was no in hurry to be ordered around by a couple of *yumas*.

"Damn it, man," one of the Americans muttered.

Frustrated, both men's gaze darted across the lobby, alternating between the hotel's short-skirted clerks in their standard-issue fishnet stockings and back to their orphaned luggage. Their linen shirts were still creased with folding lines—likely just purchased from the hotel gift shop—and yet already showed sweat stains below the collar. Condensation seeped down their narrow drink glasses as perspiration poured through the speckled crevices of their thinning hair. I didn't want to talk. Not to them. It was one of those humid, still-hungover mornings in the Cuban capital, and all I really wanted was caffeine.

"You American?" one of the men grumbled, pointing his half-filled mix of rum and mint in my direction. *Ugh. Here we go,* I thought.

"I am."

"What the hell you doing here?" he said, slurring again and a bit aggressive for a still coffeeless morning.

"I'm a journalist."

For generations, Americans had been barred from working in Cuba, but there were exceptions. Church groups, university exchanges, and journalists were officially allowed in, provided they could garner both a Cuban work visa and permission from U.S. Treasury. That usually meant Americans just weren't that abundant.

"What are you doing?" I fired back.

"Oh, we're from State," one muttered, meaning the U.S. State Department. "Just checking to see how everything is here." (Every American spook I ever met outside the United States seemed to first say that they were "from State.")

"How everything is?" I asked.

"Yeah, you know. With Honduras," he replied. "Just seeing what might be happening here."

If they were in Havana on U.S. business, their early haze made it seem like it wasn't serious. Of course, in Cuba, there was often at least a little rum in the system. No matter what the situation, a mojito here, a Cuba Libre there was normal, especially on slow days. And it was usually slow. But not today. A week into my deployment a military coup had swept over nearby Honduras. The Honduran army had ousted its president, Manuel Zelaya, on June 28, 2009, on Supreme Court orders. And though the Obama administration insisted it was surprised, officials later acknowledged that American agents had worked behind the scenes to remedy a growing political

crisis, and seemed to favor the replacement of the country's democratically elected president. In her book *Hard Choices*, Hillary Clinton alluded to using her office as secretary of state to make sure
Zelaya, a leftist who had recently signed a trade deal with Venezuela
and Cuba that sought to challenge American hegemony in the region, would not return.

"In the subsequent days [following the coup] I spoke with my
counterparts around the hemisphere, including Secretary [Patricia]
Espinosa in Mexico," she wrote. "We strategized on a plan to restore
order in Honduras and ensure that free and fair elections could be
held quickly and legitimately, which would render the question of
Zelaya moot."[4]

Now, with Zelaya removed, speculation of U.S. involvement ran
rampant along classic Cold War lines. And Havana was ground zero
for the rumor mill. If you listened to conspiracy mongers, something
bigger was afoot. With scant evidence to back the claim, leaders like
Venezuelan president Hugo Chavez accused the United States of or-
chestrating the Honduran coup and fueling innuendo as to whether
it was an isolated case or if the Americans were considering other
Socialist countries like Cuba ripe for revolt. Could these men be the
tip of an American spear? It would be hard to prove. And yet, these
alleged U.S. officials were in Cuba, standing beside me in the lobby
of the Nacional, during the very week of Zelaya's takedown. It was
hard to see how the average Cuban wouldn't suspect conspiracy by
the very presence of these men "from State."

The prospect of America's hidden hand at work was hardly a
stretch. In 2009, congressional researchers warned in a report that
the United States Agency for International Development (USAID)
engaged in secret work that "often lends itself to political entanglements that may have diplomatic entanglements," and it wasn't always clear what the agency's contractors were involved in.[5] Fulton
Armstrong, a political-economic officer at the U.S. Interests Section
in Havana turned senior intelligence analyst who later worked for

the Senate Foreign Relations Committee, recalled over a beer how sensitive information was often flat-out withheld. "We were told we couldn't even be told in broad terms what was happening because 'people will die,'" he later told me. "I had the highest security clearance there was, and yet they wouldn't tell me what they were doing," he added. "There was no paper trail."[6]

Contractors were given tacit license to operate well beyond the parameters of the State Department's seventh floor, the agency's version of a C-suite, essentially placing large swaths of American foreign policy into the hands of an opaque mesh of third-party privateers with little oversight. And at least according to Clinton's accounts, America was no passive observer. Bona fide or illusory, as the crisis in Honduras unfolded, Cuba once again seemed to occupy the spotlight. Back in Havana, as I stood there fielding questions from those men from State in the storied lobby of the Nacional, Cuba suddenly no longer seemed like the editorial backwater that news executives back home had considered it.

"Jesus, Jose . . . the luggage, c'mon!"

The man's impatience snapped me back to the present. I had been staring, daydreaming in my still coffeeless haze, and my mind was wandering. The island could have that effect, especially with its mix of innuendo and few facts. Everything was a conspiracy; everything was part of a grander scheme. If you believed in coincidence, you were either naïve or stupid—or both. Of course, sometimes a drunk American was just that. Sometimes a random phone call from a beautiful woman was nothing more than a lucky break. And yet on an island decorated with Communist propaganda, it was easy to let a little paranoia seep into otherwise pedestrian thinking. Someone had forgotten to tell everyone here that the Cold War had ended. Maybe it hadn't. Either way, the humidity had a way of shuffling priorities. That warm wet blanket of air was all I kept thinking about. An energy-sapping languor had taken hold and coated Cuba with its sweat-stained patina, and stripped all manner of ambition and capacity for contemplative thought. Without coffee, I didn't stand a chance.

I rubbed my eyes again and ascended back to the hotel's second floor, where a small team of vested waitresses hurried about. Plopping down on a chair next to a table near the window, I didn't even have to ask. The waitress took one look and knew to offer up some steamy salvation: *cafecito,* an espresso-like rocket fuel that masquerades as coffee. Slugging back a first taste from its porcelain cup, a sugary coffee trail smeared along its side and then vanished as she poured me a second. All was right again. Beside me, foreign businessmen gobbled up buffet-style breakfasts as waiters darted in and out of the kitchen, their bright uniforms in stark contrast to the hotel's drab, aging carpet. But I felt alone. The reality of this assignment was setting in. I'd have to get used to that.

Back in Atlanta, before grabbing beers with colleagues or shooting hoops after work, I had usually called family in New Jersey. But in Cuba, U.S.-bound calls were outrageously expensive, even by international standards, and monthly bills could easily run into the thousands of dollars, routed through circuits in Mexico or Europe before returning across the Atlantic to U.S. lines. It wouldn't be until 2015—when ETECSA, Cuba's state-run telecommunications company, inked a deal with a New Jersey–based firm—that callers would be able to dial direct. So, in that drab hotel café, it was just me: no phone, no internet, and barely enough Spanish to strike up a conversation. Instead, I read. With my addiction quenched, I picked up *Granma,* Cuba's state-run newspaper, and scanned for a headline that might loosely be considered news. Beside predictable anti-U.S. rhetoric, Fidel Castro kept a regular column. Updates on the latest sugar harvest or ministerial shake-ups could also offer clues as to what was going on behind the scenes, even if it was through the filter of government censors. Morsels of information were there for the taking if you were lucky and paid attention. And every once in a while, there was something big. When Fidel Castro underwent intestinal surgery in 2006, the world would learn about it not from leaks or investigative journalists, but rather from Cuba itself. Officials simply published the news, later reading on state television a letter allegedly written by Fidel. The only leader most Cubans had ever known had for the first time in nearly half a century relinquished power to his younger brother and vanished for four days. And yet Cuba's leakless government had the discipline to let everyone know when it was good and ready.

Today, however, there wasn't much to report. Just a few headlines about the Honduran coup and unfounded allegations of America's secret hand at work. I made my way back downstairs. The lobby was now buzzing with a fresh tour group that added a pungent scent of suntan lotion to the air.

"What do you mean you don't take Visa here?" snarled a pale-faced tourist now arguing with the hotel clerk. Credit cards are one of those luxuries Cuba for years had little reason to afford. Cut off from American financial institutions for half a century, the island was slow to develop an infrastructure for it. The few locales that did accept them were usually tied to European banks. What this woman was about to realize was that not only were her credit cards not going to work, but also that she wouldn't be able to withdraw money . . . anywhere. Come to Havana without cash and pay the price.

"Oh for God's sake," she said. "Let me speak to your manager."

Meanwhile, the two men from State had nestled into plush leather chairs in the corner, pressing their phones to their ears while scribbling on yellow legal pads. Their demeanor had changed, drinks down and posture straightened. It was all business, as tourists sporting ill-fitting *guayaberas* and straw hats clamored about. The latter were now stealing the show.

"Did you see that old red Chevy outside?" one asked, clearly enamored by the fleet of classic car taxis parked outside.

"See this right here," another said, pointing to an oversized map. "This is where Hemingway lived." They were the same conversations

Cubans had likely heard for generations. Though few residents I met cared anything about the Nobel Prize–winning author, unless it was about how to swindle a few extra bucks from wide-eyed *yumas*.

Still, Hemingway-esque lures were part of a charm that filled state coffers and padded residents' pockets, and many Cubans often seemed only too happy to play along. Having moved to the island in the twilight of his life, the man many called Papa became a fixture on the island, puffing cigars with Fidel, fishing aboard his boat, and writing and drinking in the capital's bars. Whether Hemingway really downed his daiquiris at the Floridita cocktail bar in Old Havana or penned his famous Spanish Civil War novel *For Whom the Bell Tolls* in Room 511 at the marbled Hotel Ambos Mundos was up for debate.

But it almost didn't matter. Half a dozen tour groups were capitalizing either way, promising to take travelers on a journey "following the footsteps of one of the world's greatest writers." And in a country where the average salary could hardly pay for a single dinner in most any Western restaurant, those were extra pesos to be had. This was survival. Foreigners came to Cuba in search of nostalgia. Fulfilling it was an easy sell. That wasn't me, of course. I was convinced I was somehow above the fray. And yet deep down I knew it was actually only me that I was trying to convince.

"Oye, Jose, cómo estás?" I greeted the clerk, making my way to the money exchange, though really just trying to rekindle a rusty Spanish tongue. Part of me felt obliged to make an effort as sort of a *yuma* counterweight to those tourists and men from State. *We aren't all blind,* I thought, steeped as I was with a certain self-righteousness.

"Hola, señor." He smiled one of those half smiles waiters often throw their customers just before collecting their tip. And he knew the score. I was full of shit. So was he, but at least Jose had a reason to be.

"How do you like Cuba?" he asked.

How do I like Cuba? Wasn't that one of those throwaway questions for tourists? The kind who descend for their brief excursions so that they can later harken back during cocktail parties and use phrases like "it's another world" and "you really should go before it all changes." Didn't he know I was different? I was a journalist and I was now living here. Surely by now he knew who I was. My job was to peel back the layers and get past the fantasies.

But if that's what Jose thought of me at first, he probably wasn't too far off.

Yumas all seemed to have at least one thing in common: we didn't know a damn thing about Cuba. There was a chasm between us and the Cubans who actually lived here. I was blind as to how wide it was. Plunging a hand into my pocket, I fingered a wad of greenbacks, moistened by the island's humidity, and began counting my cash at the exchange.

"Twenty, forty, sixty, eighty . . ."

Just one of those bills roughly equaled Jose's monthly salary. And here I casually flipped through a fold of Andrew Jacksons in front of him. On his paycheck, it would take him nearly two years to afford a room for just one night at the Nacional, where I was holed up for a month. But it wasn't just the money that separated us. Up until 2008, Jose and other Cubans had been barred from even entering the Nacional. A decades-old ban prevented them from visiting their own hotels and tourist sites as a way, the government argued, to reinforce the nation's egalitarian structure. "Cubans who have dollars cannot go to the hotels because not all [Cubans] can go," Minister of Tourism Ibrahim Ferradaz told reporters.[7] "We defend equality." In his own way, Ferradaz had a point. Hotels were now charging their room rates in the so-called convertible peso, worth twenty-four times the normal pesos earned by state employees. It just wasn't realistic for the vast majority of Cubans to check in. Tourism apartheid, as critics often put it, reserved the best of Cuba for foreigners, while the markets geared toward foreigners, *diplotiendas,* kept the island's pricier imported goods for visiting businessmen and tourists. The law had changed, but the lingering vestiges of otherness remained, especially in hotels.

Hotels, of course, were not just hotels. They were places to mingle with foreigners and thus incubators of ideas and portals to the outside world. At the time, they were also virtually the only places with internet. Though social media sites like Twitter remained blocked, intrepid Cubans, like Yoani, could covertly check email and read uncensored news sites inside hotel internet cafés. For a country with the lowest internet penetration in the Western Hemisphere, hotels were information beacons and a potential threat to the status quo. But they were also black-market depots. Out of toilet paper? Ask a hotel housekeeper. Need a few extra cans of milk? Go see the kitchen staff. When belts tightened, consumer goods were skimmed off hotel inventories and sold in underground markets that more closely adhered to the principles of supply and demand. Cuba, it seemed, wasn't all Communist after all. And as such, those who didn't work in hotels had been largely kept out. The hotel ban was abolished in 2008 as Raul Castro formally assumed the presidency, but its legacy still largely kept Cubans separate from foreigners. Locals like Jose could help me with my bag, but strategically placed security guards often made sure he didn't come back and linger in the lobby or by the pool on his days off. The finest of Cuba was off-limits to Cubans. And to many foreigners, Cuba was just sex and cigars. It was a country of rhythm and rum; an island of the past. Best not get bogged down in details of the present. Cuba was a place to be used. And it had been.

That night, when I returned to my room after a day spent trying to decipher the island's jumbled accent, the hotel was again abuzz with talk of the region. Following the startling move by Honduran Special Forces and their removal of leftist president Manuel Zelaya at gunpoint, protesters had gathered in the streets of Tegucigalpa in a show of solidarity for their deposed leader. The coup's aftershocks rattled the region. Presidents from across Latin America condemned it as concerns mounted that support for a right-leaning takeover in Honduras could be the first domino to fall in an effort to counter the wave of leftist electoral wins that had swept the region. Though the Berlin Wall had longed since crumbled, the Cold War's domino theory still appeared alive and well, especially within the confines of the Nacional.

Though the men from State were gone, the hotel's outdoor courtyard hummed with talk of a quiet American hand at work. And coming revelations would begin to support that narrative. President Obama at first condemned the coup, calling it a "terrible precedent" that harkened back to a "dark past," but his administration ultimately threw its weight behind Zelaya's replacement, interim president Roberto Micheletti, and later a wealthy, center-right conservative named Porfirio Lobo Sosa, considered favorable to American interests. And new evidence would soon surface that America's elite were ignoring their own advice from the ground. A WikiLeaked cable from July 2009 showed that U.S. ambassador to Honduras Hugo Llorens said: "There is no doubt that the military, Supreme Court and National Congress conspired on June 28 in what constituted an illegal and unconstitutional coup."[8]

And yet Secretary of State Clinton avoided phrasing it that way and later contradicted her own ambassador's analysis, telling the *New York Daily News* that the Honduran legislature and judiciary "actually followed the law in removing President Zelaya."[9] America was backing a man it could likely control. It is limiting, however, to consider foreign policy in a vacuum. Though the United States had jettisoned support for Honduras's democratically elected leader, who leaned toward Cuba, the move also helped quiet Obama critics in South Florida, notably a powerful Cuban American congresswoman named Ileana Ros-Lehtinen, on the House Foreign Affairs Subcommittee, who had been particularly vocal on Honduras.

Ros-Lehtinen represented downtown Miami and Little Havana and had burnished hard-line anti-Castro credentials by working to isolate Cuba from other leftist governments in the region. Yet on October 9, 2008, much to her chagrin, the opposite had happened. The Honduran Congress had ratified its country's membership in a regional economic pact encouraged by Cuba and Venezuela. Honduras was moving closer to Castro's leftist orbit. And Ros-Lehtinen was intent on stopping it. At her urging, that relationship would be short-lived, as in 2010 the new, right-leaning Honduran administration dissolved the deal.

Yet the Honduran coup had far wider implications: despite the new American president's pledge of engagement, U.S. foreign policy in Latin America was nonetheless still being guided by a powerful, albeit shrinking, constituency in South Florida, whose leaders viewed Castro's containment as priority number one.

Cuba, meanwhile, was taking notes.

I listened for a bit. But really, I was just craving a mojito. A trio of white-vested musicians was playing yet another selection from Buena Vista Social Club. It was always Buena Vista, always "Chan Chan." I once enjoyed their music, even knockoffs, but as I encamped on one of the hotel's wicker chairs, my brain secretly plotted ways to inspire the men to leave. That's all they played. Every. Single. Night. I pictured each musician in bed at their homes, after finishing an hours-long set, waking up in a cold sweat to another "Chan Chan"–themed nightmare. "Make it stop!"

The Nacional could easily feel like Disney's version of Havana, where straw-hatted men with floral shirts and fanny packs sat down for an "authentic Cuban experience."

I had to get out. Surely the city must be brimming with clubs, restaurants, and music halls. But it was Monday, not exactly a big night in Cuba. Still, I had to find out. Jose was still there, his shoulders now fatigue-worn and stooped. But he nonetheless flagged me down another cab. This time a royal blue Studebaker pulled up in

front of the hotel roundabout. Its driver sported a faded Yankees cap
and a toothy smile. *"Adonde vas?"* The metal beast looked like it had
just rolled out of a blacksmith. That it was still functional at all
seemed a minor miracle.

"Someplace with live music," I said, my imagination awash with
images of smoky taverns and brass bands. I had already been to a
few expat-type dinners but still hadn't seen the Cuba that America's
silver screen had promised.

"OK . . . La Casa de la Musica it is," the cabbie said, and dropped
the stick shift back as we thundered forward. The blue behemoth
growled and sputtered before settling into gear as Havana's commercial Vedado district faded behind us. The city's surrounding incan-
descence dimmed. And as I peered out the window, streetlamps
painted silhouettes and offered neighbors just enough light for their
evening rum and dominoes. Old men smoked on crumbling stoops.
Old women looked out from behind their windows' rusted iron bars.
And baseball-obsessed boys were everywhere, still wielding stick
bats and squinting in the dying light to make out each incoming
pitch. My cab rounded the bend.

As we approached the club, a gaggle of youngish-looking women
huddled around the car, their makeup and lipstick caked on and their
hair greasy and pulled back. Each sported a different version of the
same fluorescent dress, which cinched at the waist and rode high up
the thigh.

"Where you fraam?"

"Hello?"

"Oye, chico. Where you fraam?"

That was their broken-English mantra. As I left the cab, they
tugged and pulled at my shirt, even as I pushed past them and entered
the club. Inside, a mix of Europeans in cheap suits filled a scattering
of high-top metal tables. They fixated on the same kinds of women
I had seen outside, pulling them by the waist as a frizzy-haired DJ
blared reggaeton over an aging sound system.

"Who here is from Italy?" he bellowed into the microphone. "How about Spain?"

The DJ's list of countries wore on until there was no one left to offer an even half-hearted clap. It all felt cheap and inauthentic. I had come to Cuba with blurry-eyed longing for a slice of the old world. But what I found instead was a stale scene of thin-suited sex clients, pawing underage prostitutes who feigned painted smiles. This is the kind of place Dalia would have assumed I'd go, because it's where all foreign men eventually seemed to end up. The snarly, cragged, aging expats with these striking women, who pretended to be enjoying the *yuma* company, created a disjointed mix. But there were moments of honesty. Brief but unmistakable ones. In between clients and among themselves, the faces of these women—known as *jineteras,* or jockeys—would betray their party-girl personas. Boredom, fatigue, and an inevitable reveal of disgust crept across their faces: a whisper, the subtle raise of nostrils, then a look away. And yet they'd quickly refocus, recross their legs, and flash smiles at these men who were paying their tabs. I ordered a Bucanero at the bar and sat down. As I did, a teenage-looking girl slid onto the stool next to mine. "Hola, papi. Buy me a drink?"

This isn't the real Cuba, I thought. But I worried that maybe it was.

4

THE MISSING SINK

My sink was gone.

Standing in the landing of my stairwell, I stared down into my bathroom at the hole in the ground that a porcelain basin and iron pipe once occupied.

Am I crazy? I thought. There was definitely a sink here this morning.

After a month of living out of a hotel room at the Hotel Nacional, I had finally moved into a house in a leafy Havana suburb known as Miramar, once home to many of the capital's wealthy residents. Upscale homes and mansions line the district's broad avenues, the alter ego of Old Havana's narrow and bustling cobblestone streets. Jagüey trees with their drooping branches and cascading roots dot a landscape greener and browner than much of the capital's. And yet bizarre events like disappearing sinks offered a stark reminder that Miramar was still very much Cuba.

When foreigners moved out of these comparably lavish homes, it wasn't uncommon for them to be gutted. Everything from curtain rods to light fixtures to sinks were up for the taking, often reused or resold on a black market that helped fill consumer gaps for residents contending with U.S. sanctions and a centralized Cuban economy that could make the Department of Motor Vehicles seem like a paragon of efficiency. In a system in which shortages and delays plague virtually every aspect of the supply chain, the human spirit inevitably devises ways to get what it needs. So by the time I lugged my suitcases across the threshold, every light bulb in the place had been snatched. From conversations with neighbors once familiar with the home's inner sanctum, I deduced that the house had been rendered but a shell of its former self. Still, I had assumed that would stop once the new tenant moved in.

Wrong.

Not only had the place been stripped bare, but less than a week after I moved in, a major bathroom fixture was already missing. I had never lost a sink before. The rust-lined hole in the linoleum floor where iron and porcelain once met mocked me from the adjacent toilet.

Nothing quite replicates the look of those who spot you emerging from the bathroom knowing you haven't yet washed. Will Weissert, a reporter for the Associated Press, would later move in with me and split the rent. And our sink-that-was quickly became a recurring joke.

Still, there had to be an explanation for the crime.

I phoned Raulito, our press liaison at Cuba's Foreign Ministry. A middle-aged bureaucrat with a penchant for afternoon mojitos and making journalists pay for them, Raulito Gonzalez Hernandez didn't often make things happen for you, but he could easily make things *not* happen—which made the occasional mojito splurge well worth it.

"Hola, Raulito," I said as he answered his phone with a customarily staccato, *"Oigo?"*

My ensuing question seemed ridiculous. But there are only so many ways one can bring up a sink theft. So I just came out with it. "I feel strange for even asking this," I said. "But did someone take my sink?" I didn't really have any idea of who else to ask. And I expected him to brush me off for wasting his time.

Instead, he let out an audible sigh and replied, "Yes. It was broken."

And there you have it. It wasn't vandals or local thieves who crawled in through the window, wrenching the bloody thing off its mount before speeding away. No. It was the government. Some official work order had been issued, I assumed, to be served likely when authorities knew I was at work. And the workers simply let themselves in, presumably with a key. They just took it. What's more, Raulito was somehow in on it. He acknowledged as much in a "what are you going to do about it?" sort of tone over the phone.

Rendered momentarily speechless, I regained composure. "Raulito, it was not broken. I used it this morning."

"Well, I understand it was broken," he replied.

To his credit, the man didn't mince words. I had asked, and he had answered. And for a moment I just let that hang between us, coming to grips with this bizarre new world I had stumbled into where uninvited sink removal by government officials was a thing.

"Okaaaay," I said. "Am I going to get it back?"

"Well, you know, Ariosto," he said. "This is Cuba."

"What does that actually mean?" I asked.

Ariosto. Unless it's Fidel or Raul, Cubans tended to call people by their last names. I waited, expecting some sort of explanation beyond the bald-faced lie that it had been removed because it was broken.

"Ariosto . . . Is there anything else?"

Then, nothing. He stopped talking. That was it. With the empathy of an impound attendant, Raulito was among the first to use the three words that I'd hear again and again.

"This . . . is . . . Cuba."

Like that was some sort of code to mean things here were not only a little bit screwy, but that even those who had grown up here— who had few sources for comparison—knew it.

My sense of American entitlement didn't mean much. And Raulito didn't need to say anything else because I didn't deserve anything more.

The hole in my bathroom floor, where I had washed my hands earlier that day, would *remain* a hole until I could find its replacement. And in an economy plagued by chronic shortages, that could take a while.

"There probably was some higher-up in the government who just needed a sink," theorized a fellow cameraman, when I relayed the story. I had no idea whether that was true and certainly couldn't prove it. Even if I could, there was no recourse to be had. Someone wanted it. And so someone had no qualms about letting themselves into my home while I was at work and just taking it.

What course of action does one have when the people to whom one would report a theft are the very people who allowed it to happen? In a country where private property is the prerogative of the state, it wasn't mine to keep. I was on their turf. And that was becoming clear: even something like a sink can have the feel of a broader politic. Cuba was not just a story to be covered. It was to be lived. As it turns out, the porcelain basin of the sink actually wasn't gone. It was discovered weeks later, tucked into an upstairs closet. It was the sink's iron pipe, valuable in that it could be used for a variety of purposes, which had been snatched. Whoever took it actually had the courtesy of carrying the unused basin upstairs and putting it away in the closet. They were thieves, but at least they had manners. It was a not-so-subtle reminder that material belongings ultimately were not your own.

It was violation without recourse. Then again, it was just a sink. Soon after Castro's revolution in 1959, authorities nationalized private property, including homes. Sinks were just the tip of the iceberg.

I wondered about those thousands who had lost everything when Castro's government seized family homes, small businesses, sugar mills, and oil refineries. The deeds they clung to all of a sudden worthless as they fled north with the underlying hope that Castro's reign would be short-lived and that their jaunt to Miami would be but a brief one. But as faces wrinkled and black hairs turned gray, these exiles eventually raised families in the States, many of whom viewed Cuba less as a paradise lost than as a distant ancestral land: a reminder of a Grandpa familiar only in stories and grainy photographs. A tangled history had seeped into every crevice of this Havana assignment, and my eyes were still quite wide and green.

When I first moved into my Spanish colonial home on Twenty-Eighth Street and First Avenue at the edge of the sea, I couldn't help but wonder who had lived there before. What had life been like before the Revolution? In Miami, this would have been a multimillion-dollar listing, and I pictured a well-to-do Cuban family who might have spent lazy afternoons by the ocean and evenings at restaurants or taking in a show at the Tropicana. Before the Revolution, this upscale neighborhood—and indeed Cuba—was a much different place and boasted a growing upper-middle class with deep ties to the United States. American corporate interests commanded 90 percent of its mines, 80 percent of its public utilities, and 40 percent of its sugar production, which at one point was so large that it provided nearly a third of the world's supply.[1]

U.S. culture and luxury, meanwhile, found its way in. Cubans played baseball, sported American fashions, and drove Chevy Bel Airs and Cadillacs built in Detroit factories. Cuban president Fulgencio Batista, in his second term after leading a military coup in 1952 that preempted elections, had cultivated close relationships with America's budding business tycoons. But as income disparities swelled and Batista cracked down on dissent, the seeds of a nascent, homegrown opposition germinated. American historian Arthur M. Schlesinger, who worked as a speechwriter and later special assistant to President John F. Kennedy, offered this analysis: "The corruption of the Government, the brutality of the police, the government's indifference to the needs of the people for education, medical care, housing, for social justice and economic justice . . . is an open invitation to revolution."[2]

That powder keg set the stage for a young Fidel Castro, scion of a wealthy landowner, who would soon rally supporters. And on July 26, 1953, he launched an attack on the Moncada Barracks in the eastern city of Santiago de Cuba in a bid to kick-start a revolution. The move would prove a spectacular failure that left him imprisoned and the majority of his troops dead or in jail. And yet the young Fidel was later pardoned by Batista, who had worked to consolidate power. That decision would prove disastrous. Six years later, Fidel, with a reconstituted force following a guerilla campaign in the Sierra Maestra, would oust Batista and reach Havana in triumph, to the cheers of revelers who poured out onto the streets. The honeymoon, however, ended quickly as the young lawyer and his bearded revolutionaries set about remaking Cuba's government along Socialist lines. At the urging of those like Che Guevara and Fidel's brother, Raul, who had over the years been drawn closer into the Soviet orbit, he laid plans for an increasingly Communist regime. But what would spawn a more than half-century-long embargo and estrangement with the United States was Castro's decision to nationalize private property.

In 1960, when Soviet oil tankers arrived in Cuba to deliver crude oil that Esso- and Texaco-owned refineries, at the urging of U.S. diplomats, refused to refine, Cuban authorities decided they no longer had use for those American companies and simply seized their facilities. In response, the Eisenhower administration drastically cut sugar imports and slapped Cuba with trade sanctions, which strengthened under the Kennedy administration. Not to be outdone, the

Castro-led government, intent on breaking corporate influence over its economy, would then pass legislation that allowed for the expropriation of all foreign holdings.

The die of the Caribbean Cold War had been cast. And those exiles and these new neighbors of mine had borne the brunt of it. We journalists, by comparison, had it easy, and could leave the island to restock—or simply leave. Still, when in Cuba, there were rules to follow. Foreign press was only permitted to live in designated areas, and we tended to be grouped together, presumably making surveillance easier.

"Will!" I shouted. "Do you want to call Enrique or should I?"

Will Weissert had already been working on the island for the Associated Press for more than a year, and he had just moved into my spare bedroom so that we could split the rent and save a little cash.

The benefit of having Will there was not only his living room set and stash of Oreo cookies and Twizzlers—worth their weight in gold amid a barren marketscape—but the guy had also been in Cuba long enough to learn how to get around a few things. There were little luxuries. Our smuggled-in DIRECTV satellite dish, which allowed us to beam down American baseball games, was among them.

"I'll call him," Will said, and picked up his phone.

Per usual, the satellite signal had just dropped, so we called Enrique, a DIRECTV technician who lived somewhere in South Florida. Enrique worked off the books for clients across Cuba who couldn't call DIRECTV's standard customer service number. The operators, we all figured, would probably take issue with servicing one of their dishes covertly smuggled into Havana.

Though the dish was registered near the Florida Keys, Havana was apparently close enough to register a signal—which would frequently drop out. All Enrique needed was to be alerted and provided the account number and a few extra numbers on-screen to resolve it.

Indeed, when the signal inevitably dropped, a three-digit number usually appeared on the bottom of the television screen: a service provider number DIRECTV used to identify the type of outage. But it wasn't that simple to relay that kind of information over the phone—it was generally assumed there were no private phone calls among the foreign press corps. The state-owned provider maintained a monopoly over communications on the island and offered a listening platform to Cuba's Interior Ministry, which seemed to view tapping phones, internet censorship, commandeering illegal satellite dishes, and monitoring conversations as a part of its broader purview. One couldn't simply say over the phone: "Please fix the signal on my smuggled-in satellite dish. Here's code 023." Instead, Will had devised what we presumed was an ingenious way of casually working the number into conversation. All Enrique had to do was wait for it.

"I'm thinking of throwing a party this weekend," Will might say. "It should be a lot of fun. Lots of friends and family."

"How many people are coming?" Enrique would reply.

"About twenty-three."

A few days later, the signal issue would be miraculously resolved. In retrospect, our little ploy wasn't exactly the stuff of Navajo code talkers. It likely didn't fool anyone, especially those listening at Alejandro's old haunt, Cuba's Ministry of the Interior, should they have even cared to eavesdrop. But unlike many Cubans who erected these illicit dishes in a desperate bid for entertainment and information about the world outside their own, our dish was never confiscated. Perhaps there were just too many. At one point in 2007, prior to a series of crackdowns in which operators and owners were jailed and fined, Ministry of the Interior official Mauricio Barroso estimated that more than one-third of all Havana residents enjoyed the benefits of a satellite connection. Many presumed the number was far higher. But satellite dishes and their operators weren't the only goods and services being traded on Cuba's black market.

Batteries. Clothing. Fish. Even sugar. All seemed available with
the right connections. Everybody skimmed off the top. Fishermen
always seemed to have an extra stash of their catch to be sold privately for a higher price. Thirty pounds of snapper could fetch up to
$25 on the street—more than a month's salary.[3] And when some-
thing around the house broke or simply stopped functioning, which
happened often, it quickly became apparent just how reliant one
could become on "a friend" who knew how to get things.

The reasons why my sink and light bulbs had been removed were
becoming much clearer. In a state-controlled economy, warehouses,
restaurants, gas stations, and even empty homes are places where residents can even out what they don't earn or can't buy through official channels. Theft is a relative concept. And virtually everyone takes
part in the black market it supplies. In a 2005 study, economist Archibald Ritter estimated that approximately 95 percent of the country participated in this "shadow economy," in large part because
"many economic activities that are normally permitted elsewhere are
either prohibited entirely or else are limited directly through the
refusal to grant licenses to applicants who then must remain clandestine if they are to exist at all."[4]

"Everything is purchased on the black market," Cuban economist
and dissident Oscar Espinosa Chepe told me. "It's where you go to
buy your eggs and your milk."

Yuma or not, if you live in Cuba, the shadow economy is where
you go. And in the summer months, the pickings were often slim.

"It's broiling in here," Will said, breaking the momentary silence
that had fallen over the house after calling Enrique. His dog, Gallo,
a personable, coffee-colored cocker spaniel, had chosen a cooler spot
on our kitchen linoleum, spreading his belly across the floor in a
fraught attempt to offset the afternoon's rising temperatures. Summer had just ended. But it was still brutally hot. And our air-
conditioning was hardly functioning. Meanwhile, the house's thick

concrete walls blocked the ocean's breeze, trapping the hot air inside. All we could really do was wait for both Enrique and the evening's cooler air.

"We've got to sort that out," I said, referring to our broken air conditioner. But after calling in a friend of a coworker who doubled as a repairman, it became clear that the machine would need parts that were unavailable through official channels.

"Why didn't you come to me before?" asked Tony Ossorio, who worked in the CNN office in an inherently Cuban job known as a "resolver." In a country where improvisation and repurposing in the face of adversity were all but a national pastime, men like Ossorio—known as much for their ingenuity as they were for their network—would prove invaluable. "I know someone."

Within two days, I had a visit from a man who would, allegedly, bring me my air conditioner fan in exchange for cash. When he showed up that Sunday, Fernando—as I'd learn his name to be—didn't arrive by car or get dropped off by a friend. He simply walked around the corner and up onto my front porch, empty-handed.

"David?"

"Yes," I said.

"It's a pleasure," he replied. "Fernando." The sunbaked lines of his face creased as he spoke and folded at the edges of azure-colored eyes that seemed to furrow and squint even in the shade. "Show me this air conditioner," he said, brushing back the gray wisps that jutted from beneath his olive-green cap. Rail thin yet spry, Fernando had to be in his late seventies.

I guided him inside the house and toward the foyer, where the metal beast hung above a thick wooden table. He inspected the machine and seemed to recognize it immediately. Of course there just weren't *that* many varieties of Chinese-made air conditioners available on the island, so it likely wasn't all that difficult.

Fernando then a pulled out a small notebook and pencil tucked inside the front pocket of his overalls, scribbled down a few notes, and turned to me.

"I'll be back Tuesday," he said, sucking back the glass of water I had offered him before making his way to the door.

"Tuesday, huh?" I repeated for emphasis. He nodded before turning to the street, picking up his small gray satchel, and walking off.

And that was it. In the United States, I would have made quick work of the exchange after a Google search, a cross-check on Yelp, and a seamless booking through an app like Handy or TaskRabbit. Pure transaction. But here, that sort of thing wasn't possible. There was no app to guide me. No preset price. Fernando's appearance on my doorstep was the product of a guy who knew a guy, whom I ultimately had to trust. His small business, like most, would rely on that: an interdependent community of resolvers and tradesmen and neighbors turned clients who made Fernando and Ossorio indispensable. Cut off from the rest of the world, business remained personal and relied on personal networks because it had to. It was neither efficient nor the most lucrative approach, but there was a certain authenticity to the social fabric it engendered and preserved. Forget the old cars; maybe this was the old world that Cuba-bound travelers had craved.

"It's complicated," Ossorio once told me when I asked about it. In a country where news is censored and information restricted, human networks often also carried greater influence, contributing to a rumor mill chock-full of half facts, anecdotes, and innuendo. Though the internet had only begun to ooze onto the island, fake news was already alive and well. Perhaps Ossorio's response was just his polite way of saying: "Only you *yumas* would see a lack of technology and progress as an attractive novelty."

Either way, I was assured that on Tuesday my air conditioner would be fixed, hopefully cooling my hotbox of a home. Much like waiting on Enrique to fix the satellite dish, I just needed a little patience. Of course, since the market was hardly saturated with suppliers, there wasn't much incentive for Fernando to rush things. Predictably, when Tuesday rolled around, there was no sign of him. Fernando didn't own a cell phone. So I just sat there, waiting on my front porch for his wiry frame to appear from around the corner. An hour ticked by. Then two. I phoned the bureau to let everyone know I would be late. Reporter Shasta Darlington picked up.

"Not much going on here today," she said. "Take your time."

Those Havana days in 2009 indeed felt uneventful for a place with a permanent news bureau, and lethargy could creep in if you weren't paying attention. That happened easily, especially given the pace of people like Fernando. In fact, he never showed that day. It would be another two weeks before I'd see him saunter around the corner again, this time with the metal part he needed.

The air conditioner would get fixed. The hole in my bathroom would be repaired, too, but not for months.

5

HEARTS, WE DO NOT KNOW

Caras vemos, corazones no sabemos."

It was fall 2009. A few months of work in Havana had elapsed, and that old Spanish proverb seemed to best describe many of the people I had met in the Cuban capital.

"Faces we see," the saying went. "Hearts, we do not know."

None of the Cuban employees at our bureau worked directly for CNN. Like any international organization operating on the island, CNN had to contract with a government agency, which in turn hired local professionals and paid their state-controlled wages. As such, they were expected to submit reports on what Shasta Darlington and I—the only two American CNN journalists in the office—were up to. They were part of a state surveillance effort, which meant conversations at work had to be somewhat censored, sometimes for no other reason than to protect our colleagues from themselves. Warm and helpful, they were my friends. But they were also part of Cuba's eyes and ears, whether they wanted to be or not.

Though I saw their faces, I wondered what was in their hearts. Was I just another privileged outsider, the latest in a long line of foreign journalists to funnel through the bureau, or rather a colleague and friend? Did it matter? Monse, our office accountant, had a way of making me feel I was the latter.

"Daviiiiiiiid!" I'd hear most mornings when I walked into the CNN offices, a usual precursor to a barrage of questions about a cell phone bill or some other expense likely to become a battle with the bean counters in Atlanta. With a gray-and-blond bob of hair and oval-shaped glasses framing a wrinkled face, Monse had the look of someone on the brink of a smile. Her warm demeanor cushioned the impacts of the outrageous cell phone bills that she'd hand me most months.

Then there was Dagmara, our office manager. A hard-boiled Cuban who had reason to be, she navigated the byzantine permissions and credentials process required by the island's Ministry of Foreign Relations. Tough and street-smart, Dagmara was a crucial intermediary with the government, and sometimes the only sentry standing between us journos and an hours-long interrogation in a gray-walled bureaucrat's office. She was also connected. The paper Rolodex on her desk, jam-packed with pen-scrawled names and numbers, was pure gold.

"David!" she'd yell, akin to Monse.

The manner by which they both called out my name had all the charm and sweetness of a line-order cook. But there was also genuine fondness there, and we eventually grew close.

"*Quieres café?*" Dagmara asked.

A steady stream of Cuban coffee circulated through the office, offered up in small, espresso-sized cups balanced on tiny white saucers. The wafting aroma of roasted beans and the bitter sting of that first sip were all that were needed. Bleary-eyed fiends beforehand. Sated addicts afterward.

Dagmara knew its importance.

"*Oh, por Dios, sí!*" I said, grabbing a cup from its tray.

Of course, there was also Tony Ossorio—the guy to call when

you needed something, or rather when something broke. Blessed with the ingenuity of a Cuban mechanic, Ossorio was often fixing the bureau's aging wiring, nestled behind tape decks and computers, and enmeshed in a proverbial rat's nest of cables that dated back to the late 1990s. It seemed a daily miracle that any of it functioned at all. On an island plagued by shortages and often devoid of connectivity, Ossorio was invaluable.

They were all a part of the daily tapestry of life at CNN Havana, the people with whom I'd spent the most time and on whom I most often relied. Yet in some ways there was also distance between us. When I arrived in Havana, in addition to being an outsider, my Spanish was only mediocre, so it was no surprise our relationships only went so deep. But over time, I also suspected that gap was intentional: few benefits could be gleaned from too close an association with an American journalist. Keeping a bit of distance was likely a smart decision for them. The exception, of course, was Rafa, CNN's driver, who kept the office Mitsubishi Jeep in working order.

"Compay!" he'd begin each morning, kicking back in the supply room while sipping his coffee next to a pile of plastic pelican cases. Rafa was a particularly emotive fellow, and we'd chat in the morning hours before the day's work—though never about politics. Fishing was his preferred topic. He described hooks and lures in great detail, along with the finer points of swordfishing, offering tips for piercing the snout of a sardine, which he used as bait, without killing it.

"You have to be very careful," he'd say, using his index finger and thumb to mimic the act in the air. An angler by trade, Rafa knew where and when to catch the freshest marlin and swordfish. He had one of the city's relatively few licenses, which granted him permission to own a small fishing boat. Authorities kept a scrutinizing eye on their coastal waters, and unlicensed fishermen could be fined up to 1,500 pesos ($70) and have their boats and gear impounded if they were caught. So Rafa guarded his permit fiercely.

I often thought that's all he really wanted: to be at sea and to fish. His eyes, kind and weathered, reminded me of my grandfather's.

Before dawn, when Havana's coastal seas are calm and inky blue, Rafa would set out in search of fish, stringing dozens of hooked sardines on a line that stretched across the water to a neighboring vessel. If the sardines were still alive, they'd wriggle and dance on the line, enticing the swordfish to bite. As the sun peeked from beneath the horizon and threw millions of sparkles across the sapphire sea, Rafa kept watch on his boat. Slugging back coffee and beers and wiping the cake of salt spray from the gunnels, he'd wait for that familiar pull and tension on the line, a cap pulled low over squinting eyes as he scanned the water. If he was lucky and snared one, he'd have to act quickly and pull the swordfish up onto the boat, lest lurking sharks or barracuda steal bites of their own. He would then puttputt his way to shore and fillet his catch on the hot concrete slab of the Malecon beside other fortunate fishermen.

When he came into the office, Rafa's eyes often seemed like they were still out at sea, gleaming with the predawn sparkle of azurecolored waters. But it was usually short-lived. By late afternoon, a grayer patina swept over him, especially when an old back injury flared up. I'd often hear about it.

"I can't go out today, David," he'd say, clutching his back with a grimace.

As a younger man, when Fidel's Cuba was still relatively new, Rafa had been sent to the war in Angola and sustained injuries. He was among the tens of thousands of Cuban soldiers and aid workers deployed and often injured (or killed) in proxy moves, often in close coordination with Soviet forces. Fidel had been eager to export revolution, deploying his Cold Warriors across Africa and Latin America in support of leftist Marxist movements. Rafa was among those who went, helping to cement his country's place on the world's stage and earning the gratitude of leftist leaders. Upon news of Fidel's death years later, Angolan vice president Manuel Vicente was quick to offer his condolences, calling Fidel a friend and a comrade who was "an unforgettable figure to us."[1] But for those like Rafa, Angola had meant hardship. Thousands of his countrymen had died there. Thousands more had deserted. And many who stayed and fought would later openly wonder why they had been sent at all. Another veteran of Angola, a former army pilot named Senen, wondered whether "we forgot to continue developing this country" while fighting foreign wars.

"We don't live," he added, referencing their $13-a-month equivalent pension. "Cubans survive."[2]

As part of the older generation, Rafa and Senen's futures were among the most uncertain. Unlike Cuba's youth, they could remember leaner times. And a gap between the two generations was growing. Cuba's young people, who enjoyed free health care and education, worried about being left behind, while older veterans often fretted about the future of a revolution they had fought for and the subsidies upon which they had long relied. Yet when I first arrived in Cuba, the transition seemed relatively stable. And the people who filled CNN's office at Habana Libre knew the game they had to play.

But that office also felt confining. And so the Malecon became my daily escape. Walking home to the lapping sounds of waves as the sun began its western retreat over the Florida Strait was almost meditative. After work, I'd linger along its promenade, taking in its gold and orange hue, in no rush to get anywhere.

Yet, one evening after returning home, something outside the house caught my eye: a folded piece of notebook paper impaled on the fence that surrounded my house, tips fluttering in the evening breeze. I walked over, slipped it off its metal rung, and unfolded it. There, scrawled in pencil across the inside of the paper, was a message:

I'd like to get to know you better—Yuneisi

There was a number written just below her name.

I didn't recognize it, but frankly I didn't care. The thought of

getting to know anyone better perked my interest. The island's crumb-
ing elegance could stoke a romance, or just a dalliance, but it could
also feel oppressively isolating.

I dialed the number, half expecting another Dalia. No answer. I
tried again. Still nothing but that empty tonal ring. So I walked
toward the trash bin and was just about to throw the crumpled paper away when my old Nokia vibrated. I pulled the phone from my
pocket again.

It was a text.

"Quien es?" scrolled across the screen from the same number I
had just dialed. Like I previously mentioned, virtually no one wants
to talk on the phone. It's just too costly.

"This is David. You left this number on my fence?" I typed.

Moments later another text: "Siiiii. I'm your neighbor. Yuneisi."

While a sort of low-grade suspicion had seeped into most aspects
of my life in Cuba, this was probably just a new neighbor being
friendly. Besides, I was craving interaction.

The Nokia vibrated again.

"I live in the yellow house across the street," she texted. "Look at
the window."

As I looked over, a light flicked on. The shadow of a young woman
crossed behind a thin curtain of the once-darkened second-floor
window. A hand reached around its far edge and pulled, revealing a
slender shape that was still mostly silhouette. It was difficult to see
a face in the dying light, and yet I could see that she was smiling.
The distance between us was too far to speak. Yuneisi stood there a
moment, looking down before resuming her typing.

The Nokia vibrated a third time.

"I'll come by tomorrow? 4 p.m.?"

"OK," I replied.

And with that, the curtain again drew closed.

Tomorrow then.

My blood churned as I thought about it. Her slender silhouette.

Her smile. The fact that since I'd arrived I had socialized with few Cubans outside of work, save for Dalia. But when I walked back inside, it dawned on me that I had virtually nothing to offer. One look at my pantry, and it was clear that I was a Havana novice. Unlike other journos who prepared for the shortages that inevitably swept the island, I was lacking provisions. In fact, most foreigners boasted an impressive stockpile of items like canned milk, toilet paper, cereal, diapers, and a variety of nonperishables.

"Don't get too attached to any brand," Will, who was working late that particular evening, had warned. "Because that may have been the last shipment for a while." I'd find out what he meant soon enough.

I needed to go to the market.

So the following morning I walked to the end of the driveway, where I kept a cheap Chinese version of a Vespa against the fence. Having purchased the bike from a departing Mexican diplomat, I already regretted it. Its bald tires and rusty frame had left me stranded on more than one occasion. But it did have a detachable seat with a small storage space underneath that could hold a few precious groceries. It wasn't much, but I didn't need a lot. And when it did function, it was a good way to zip around the city.

Pulling a small metal key from my pocket, I slipped it into the ignition. And . . . nothing.

"C'mon!" I muttered, twisting the switch a bit harder.

The bike gave a few half-hearted sputters before slipping back into its coma. I tried again. A trail of steam curled from the engine. This wasn't going to work. The yellow scooter just sat there, refusing to budge. Why did I buy this damn thing? It had been unreliable since I got it, a bundle of cannibalized parts of unknown origin and age. When it did start, it had often gasped and putt-puttered itself to near death on a roadside somewhere far from home. But in Cuba there aren't many options. And pushing a broken-down car, truck, or scooter down the road is practically a rite of passage.

For anyone either foolish enough or compelled to actually want to buy one of these three, the process got even more convoluted.

For starters, despite popular *yuma* misconceptions, not everyone drives a classic. There are, in fact, new-car dealerships in Havana. The thing is, buying a new car could mean taking out a house-sized loan. A new Peugeot, for example, listed at $262,000, roughly five times its U.S. asking price. That had to be a mistake, I thought, or at least some sort of currency conversion snafu. How could a French sedan in Cuba cost the same as a Rolls-Royce in the States? For a country where the average state salary hovered around $24 a month, the math just didn't add up.

The answers could be found in a well-mixed island favorite: one part embargo, one part Castro.

Soon after he took power, Fidel banned the import of American automobiles and their parts. Then U.S. lawmakers doubled down, banning virtually all U.S. exports to the island. Once enacted, the import supply of new American cars and car parts dried up. Today, most of the old ironclad beasts that still rumble across Cuba were imported before the Revolution and are often ripped up and refurbished with Chinese carburetors and Russian engines. American-made? Kind of. But back then, Fidel saw new cars as public expressions of wealth and an affront to the nation's more egalitarian endeavors. To fathom why the island would have luxury car dealerships now, one had to start by understanding the island's money.

There are two currencies in Cuba: the peso, generally meant to be used by Cubans, and the convertible peso (CUC), meant for tourists, foreign companies, entrepreneurs, and a scattering of state-run businesses. Pegged to the U.S. dollar, the CUC had been created as a temporary solution to stem inflationary pressures after Cuba's economy plunged into free fall following the Soviet collapse. It was worth about twenty-five times that of the peso. Both were legal tender, and often used in parallel ways. Of course, if you're now wondering how anyone can run an economy with two currencies that maintain two wildly different values, you wouldn't be alone. Even Raul Castro called the system a "headache," and sought to replace it.[3] In fact, government officials had been talking about scrapping the two-tiered scheme for years. And they had indeed been preparing for that day for as long as I could remember—an unknown date to which Cubans ominously refer to as "Día Cero" (Day Zero). To most economists I spoke with, currency unification was long overdue, if for no other reason than to make doing business on the island easier and more transparent. But unraveling it wasn't that simple. On a Communist island where state enterprises had for decades been propped up by artificial exchange rates, and where most Cubans usually kept both kinds of bills tucked into their wallets, fears of rampant inflation (and subsequent shortages) were quite real. Markets here already routinely ran out of milk as it was. Though officials seemed committed to getting rid of the CUC by virtue of a bevy of public statements they had made over the years, their efforts would be delayed again and again. Perhaps it was best not to make dramatic currency changes at a time when the economy was only just holding on. Though most Cubans were paid in pesos, the CUC was still widely used to purchase all sorts of consumer goods, such as televisions, refrigerators, and, indeed, cars.

But here's the problem. Neither currency is exchangeable in foreign markets. That means when the government imports luxury items, it has to pay in a hard currency like dollars. But when local state-run dealerships sell cars, they're paid in a currency that has no foreign exchange value. So Cuba actually can't afford to sell the cars it imports. If it did, its chronically low supplies of foreign reserves would further drop as dealerships replenished their fleets.

So why does Cuba have dealerships at all? It's a question perhaps best answered by the island's anglers, who affix their hooks with so many worms and sardines.

In other words, it's bait. Dealerships look good to potential foreign investors. "It's all part of the marketing strategy," John

Kavulich, president of the U.S.-Cuba Trade and Economic Council, said during one of many interviews I'd conduct with him over the years.[4] "When a company representative comes in from China or from Russia or from France . . . and then they see 'oh wow, Peugeot is here,' everybody thinks there must be a lot of money to be made here." Dealerships are also often placed conveniently close to popular hotels, where traveling businessmen could more easily see them. But doing actual business in Cuba is a different story. Several European investors I spoke with, who declined to be named due to concerns of spoiling their relations with Havana, complained of the "glacial pace" of investment negotiations, Cuba's insistence on keeping majority share on larger projects, and a sheer lack of the kind of financial information normally required in investment decisions. Of course, if foreign investors *were* interested in Cuba there was a bigger elephant in the room: U.S. sanctions.

The trade embargo not only restricted U.S. businesses and its subsidiaries from engaging with Cuba, but it also barred any ship that docked in a Cuban port from docking in an American one for at least six months—unless it had a U.S. waiver. Forged amid pressure from right-wing Cuban exiles, it was a product of the 1992 Cuban Democracy Act and intended to disrupt shipping routes and penalize foreign companies that continued to do business with the island.

I figured this out pretty quickly after my furniture failed to show up until several months after I did. In fact, it would take nearly seven months for the container carrying my dresser, couch, table, chairs, and bed to arrive in port. In the meantime, I slept on an air mattress and lived in a near-empty house for months until Will moved in.

"Why don't you just go buy a couch?" my sister, Elizabeth, once asked over the phone.

That seemed logical. The thing is, like car costs, furniture costs were exorbitant. With prices better suited for Manhattan showrooms than the retreaded 1970s knockoffs they resembled, couches sold through official channels could run into the thousands—the product of sanctions, a liquidity crisis, and Soviet-style central planning that reduced inventory and drove up prices. So instead, I settled for a leaky air mattress and a busted scooter. Those Graham Greene fantasies were quickly fading.

Then there was the paperwork.

"You have to apply for one," Dagmara informed me, referring to the scooter. Virtually every country requires some form of documentation to operate a motor vehicle, but Cuba seemed to especially love its licenses. Everything from hair salons to street vendors required some form of documentation and regulation. To critics, it was yet another lever of control in the island's control economy.

"They need your press credential," Dagmara chimed in.

That still didn't sound too bad; it was akin to most DMV experiences in the States. But Dagmara wasn't finished. It turned out that the type of license plate the state assigns actually determined which vehicle a foreigner was permitted to buy. Foreigners were barred from buying vehicles directly from Cubans. It would be another two years, in 2011, before Cubans could legally buy and sell their cars. The color-coded license-plate scheme would also be phased out as the state loosened rules on private ownership. But for now, car *swaps* were the most one could hope for. And because Cubans couldn't sell to me, that seller had to be another foreigner, which of course reduced the pool of choices. But at least the foreigners were easy to spot, courtesy of a nation that always seemed to have surveillance on its mind.

Here, license plates told the tale.

The system mirrored an old Soviet coding scheme designed to quickly decipher who was on the road. Cuba government workers got blue plates. Diplomats got black plates. Journalists and religious leaders bore bright orange plates. Green was for the Ministry of Interior. Light green was for the military. The first letter of the plate also indicated in which of the sixteen provinces the vehicle was registered. And the last three numbers denoted professional rank, making it easier for inspectors and police to make way for government big shots.

I was looking for orange, and in my case a departing Mexican diplomat who seemed overly happy to get rid of the bloody thing. Back in my driveway where I had plucked the note from Yuneisi, I figured out why. In addition to bald tires, the rusty contraption needed a new spark plug: the proverbial needle in a haystack of the island's shortage-wracked markets. Finding a new plug would take weeks, which I didn't have.

I had company coming over.

6

POR BOTELLA

It was ten o'clock on Saturday morning. Six hours seemed like plenty of time to find groceries before Yuneisi arrived. My scooter sat idle against the fence at the far end of the driveway, practically chiding me as I pushed open the metal gate. *Serves you right,* I thought, walking past it toward Third Avenue, one of Miramar's few thoroughfares, in search of a ride. It was the first leg of an all-day trip to the market. A mix of Russian Ladas, Chinese motorbikes, and old American Studebakers had already rattled by. It was the latter sort I was looking for.

Hitchhiking was a normal way of getting around in Cuba. Not all drivers were open to picking up foreigners, but if you hung out long enough and didn't seem too eager, eventually you'd get lucky. The mode of transport even has its own expression—traveling *por botella,* "in a bottle," since the outstretched thumb resembles the motion for taking a drink. Attractive women never seem to wait long and can be seen most mornings with their thumbs out on main street corners, flagging down oncoming traffic with practiced smiles.

Though there are also public (Chinese-made) buses known as

guaguas, many commuters are also "bused" in pre-1959-era cars. And just like their larger Chinese counterparts, these so-called *colectivos* run fixed routes through the city, packing as many as five to a car. It was this kind of ride that I was looking for. If the driver had room, he or she would usually stop. The cost for Cubans is about 50 cents; for *yumas,* it's about 1 CUC (one convertible peso), the equivalent of an American dollar—though it's not a fixed price. It varies depending on whom you ask.

Then, a glimmer emerged on the horizon.

There it is, I thought.

An old Cadillac was approaching. It was fire-engine red and packed to the hilt. So it continued on, belching a sooty exhaust cloud in its wake. A few others followed suit. With more than sixty thousand classic cars—the largest collection of vintage American cars outside the United States—there had to be one that would stop for a *yuma.*

Then it happened.

Amid heat waves that blurred distant views, a Plymouth Belvedere came into focus and began to slow. Its sky-blue frame was so rusted and full of holes that the front bumper looked as if it might detach at any moment. But the metal beast was pulling over. The driver, a portly man whose stomach rested against the steering wheel, eased his hulking colossus to the shoulder. And its brake plates squealed as it came to a halt.

"To the circle?" I asked, referencing a traffic circle a few miles east, which I knew he'd pass. The trick was to keep it simple. Those willing to pick up *yumas* usually would do so as long as they didn't ask for anything more than a Cuban might. The traffic circle was somewhat close to Supermercado 70, situated on Third Avenue and Seventieth Street, which by Cuban standards was better stocked. From the circle, I could walk.

The driver grumbled something inaudible and motioned with his hand for me to climb in. *"Gracias, caballero."* Inside was another world.

The vehicle's interior seemed a microcosm of the island itself. Once-shiny chrome that lined its windows now flaked with speckled rust. The tin sound of reggaeton blared over Chinese-made speakers while a pair of fuzzy dice danced from the rearview mirror. I squeezed into the back onto bench seats encased in cracked brown leather beside a woman who had a young girl, presumably her daughter, propped on her lap. To the woman's left sat a sun-cragged man clad in the greasy denim of a mechanic's overalls. In front, two teenage boys sporting barbershop-fresh coiffures fixated on their black-plastic Nokia phones. The Belvedere then lurched forward as our driver pushed into gear, its coughing muffler adding a diesel stench to the surrounding air until the old car could get up to speed. The ride was hot and cramped and only brought me somewhat close to where I needed to go.

But it felt real.

In the back seat of that old Plymouth, the other passengers barely noticed me. The woman beside me was tending to her daughter, who bounced playfully on her legs. The mechanic swung his arm out the window, lost in thought. And the two teenage boys were doing what most young boys do: snickering and spiritedly punching each other's arms. As the Plymouth clanked its way eastward, I began to relax. Despite the radio's high-pitch throb of reggaeton, this seemed a better way to get around. Forget the scooter.

"*Aquí, caballero,*" I said, as we approached the traffic circle. The driver pulled off to the shoulder and I handed him a coin before hoisting myself out.

"*Suave, suave,*" he said, motioning with his hand, instructing me to shut the door gently. *Yumas* had a penchant for slamming doors. But in Cuba, where metal leviathans from the 1940s and '50s thunder through town, if and when something broke, it could be months before the right parts were located. The parts—everything from car windows to carburetors—would then have to be neatly wrapped up (usually in blue plastic) and squeezed into the luggage of travelers from places like Miami. A single visitor could haul in more than a hundred parts, selling to the highest bidder, all a part of a thriving black market government officials tacitly accepted. But the process took time and remained expensive, especially for those state salaries. With few original parts available, mechanics often cannibalized the guts of Russian Ladas and Volga sedans to keep these American beasts running. A bit of baling wire here. A Russian spark plug there. And soon the aging Frankenstein would roar back to life. But it took work, time, and money. In short, it was generally understood that doors should not be taken for granted.

"*Suave!*" the driver barked.

I lightly pushed the door shut until it clicked, signaling that it was safe for him to putter off.

About ten minutes later, I was making my way to a market situated close to the Russian embassy, among the tallest buildings in Havana, shrouded in a tangle of razor wire and a hulk of concrete. It's sort of a Communist thing. Government buildings. Hotels. Hospitals. All built of massive concrete slabs. While the old city boasts an array of architectural styles, from colonial to art deco to neoclassical and baroque, much of the post-Revolution construction was decidedly Soviet. Featureless gray monoliths peppered the landscape, including the market where I was headed. Supermercado 70 sported a pale white coat of primer on the square concrete slabs that encased its spartan persona. And yet this was one of the better ones. Locals called it *diplomercado*—taken from a time when only diplomats shopped here due to its size and selection, albeit with higher prices.

But by the time I arrived, at around 1:00 p.m. on a Saturday, the market had been picked clean. Just a scattering of lonely packaged foods sat in row after row of empty shelves. What remained of the bread looked stale and crumby. The meats resembled Spam. Plastic-wrapped snacks and cereals I didn't recognize were tucked below the registers. There were, however, plenty of sugar-saturated juice boxes—I'd soon grow addicted to the mango version—and red cans of condensed milk. Walking up and down each aisle, I floated by in a bit of a haze, pushing an empty shopping cart around each bend in search of something, anything, familiar.

"Excuse me," I said to a clerk in a dark green smock. "Where is the chicken?"

She smiled. "No chicken here today."

"Cheese?"

She almost laughed.

Shortages were so constant they had become fodder for jokes, the dark psychology of good comedy. Great jokes often seem to borrow from something tragic. And in Cuba, if you listened close enough, there was often a touch of subversion. On one otherwise routine day at the market, I overheard this one from a store clerk who didn't quite seem to realize how loudly he was talking:

"A man walked into a store, walking up and down the aisles," the man explained. "Eventually, he turned to the shopkeeper and in frustration proclaimed, 'Sir, you have no fish!' The shopkeeper, unfazed, looked up from his register and replied, 'No, sir, you are wrong. My store is the one that has no meat. The store across the street is the one that has no fish!'"

The clerk clutched his belly and roared with laughter at his own joke. But his message was clear: get accustomed to having less. Sometimes "having less" for Cubans, however, meant living under graver than normal conditions. In 2009, food scarcities gripped the island after a cash shortage forced Cuba to reduce imports by almost a third. Up to 80 percent of what made it to Cuban dinner tables each night was imported, with an annual price tag that fluctuated around $2 billion per year.[1]

The thing is, it didn't have to be that way. Cuba is the largest island in the Caribbean, with millions of acres of fertile farmland. The raw materials were there. Scarcity was another example of economic dysfunction. Most of the food that's grown on the island (about

70 percent) is produced by semiprivate farms, even though they only control about 40 percent of the farmland. And getting what they did grow to market was often its own challenge. Farmers, who were commonly obliged to send up to 90 percent of their harvest to the state, had come to expect that part of that harvest would be lost due to slow distribution systems and a lack of refrigerated trucks, which would have prevented their fruits and vegetables from spoiling under the hot Caribbean sun. That meant during sweltering summer months produce was often scarce, contributing to the shortages and empty shelves. Thinking ahead, and wary of suffering big losses, farmers often grew fewer crops during summer months, further contributing to the shortages and spiking prices.

But the problems would start much earlier, as mismanagement and graft (hallmarks of Communist centralized planning) left farmers waiting.[2] During a trip out to Pinar del Rio Province, I spoke to a farmer named Jesus Rodriguez, who bemoaned the fact that his seeds "just wouldn't get here in time." With seeds rotting in warehouses before delivery, Rodriguez and other farmers would often miss the planting season entirely. So when imports dropped, domestic agriculture and industry weren't enough to make up the difference. And so Cuban shelves lay bare, which was just what I was experiencing at the Supermercado 70 that morning.

"You have to come early," the store clerk told me, almost scolding. "The line starts at eight a.m."

Because the stock ran out so quickly, most weekend shoppers knew that by midday there wasn't much to be had. The queue would start to wrap around the front of the store long before the sun had risen. When the doors opened at 9:00 a.m., customers poured in, rushing up and down the aisles to secure the precious few items left.

I grabbed a few cans of condensed milk, toilet paper, a packet of coffee, two boxes of cereal, and a handful of cookies that bore a label I had never seen before. That would have to suffice for now. And that was lucky. Milk is often first to run out. In the coming months, I'd learn to stock up, piling dozens of cans in the pantry. For fruits and vegetables, I'd have to head across town to a state-run open-air market in Vedado, one of the few places *yumas* could buy products using the cheaper Cuban pesos. When I got there, I couldn't believe how much food I could get for so little.

"How much for rice?"

"Ten cents per kilogram," said the vendor. She stood behind a wooden crate with a sweat-stained red bandana wrapped around her forehead.

"Ten cents, huh?"

Of course, those were pesos. So that meant the rice actually cost less than the equivalent of a penny, a product of Cuban price controls. Piles of potatoes, yucca, and lettuce still sat in front of her. I unfurled a small plastic bag and gathered a couple of onions, at 25 cents each, and a few stalks of yucca at a similar price.

"Gracias," I said, wandering farther into the market. Though it was late afternoon, crowds still swarmed. And I noticed something. While some shoppers swapped a few cheap-looking bills for handfuls of rice, onions, and yucca, others wielded a small, tan-colored booklet. These were called *libretas,* or ration books. Inside, a grid of blue-and-black-colored ink separated categories that were labeled "rice," "meat," "eggs," "sugar," and other basic household items. Each family registered for a *libreta* with a local supply shop, which then entitled them to a basic ration of groceries, which could be purchased at state-run markets.

The coupon book, created near the end of 1962 by then economy minister Ernesto "Che" Guevara, was one of Cuba's most recognizable food welfare systems. State salaries were rarely enough to buy food at market prices, even when those prices remained artificially low. And yet with each passing year, the amount of food the booklet provided residents was diminishing. When I arrived in 2009, peas and potatoes had been stripped. In August 2010, President Raul Castro called the state sector—where up to 90 percent of all Cubans worked—"bloated" and in need of market reforms. One in five government employees was considered redundant, or roughly 1 million Cubans.[3] By October 2010, the state media went further, publishing an editorial in the government-run newspaper *Granma* that called for an end to ration books altogether.

Cuba had been subsidy rich and cash poor, but now even senior Communist leadership quietly acknowledged a need for market-based reforms. In August 2010, Raul vowed to scrap "various existing prohibitions for the granting of new licenses and the commercialization of some production, giving flexibility to the hiring of labor."[4] For Cubans, that meant stripping the social programs that many had relied on.

But half a century of state-provided food subsidies was not easily undone. And here in central Vedado, residents still mingled about the market with their *libretas*. I checked my watch. It was almost 4:00 p.m. My neighbor Yuneisi would be arriving soon.

What had started out as a quick jaunt to a local market had evolved into a day long endeavor. And in the end I had still come up short. Beer, toilet paper, milk, cookies, and a few vegetables were all I had to show for an entire afternoon of shopping. My housemate, Will, had warned me about this. "What takes thirty minutes in the States will take all day here. Sometimes more." For the trip back to my house I flagged down a regular yellow cab this time and stared out the window as it chugged eastward and toward home. When I arrived, Yuneisi was already waiting.

With one leg propped up against the fence, her head slowly turned with my cab as it pulled up to her. Like Dalia, she exuded confidence and looked up at me with eyes accented by dark eye shadow, her hands shoved into the front pockets of a pair of tight-fitting, low-slung jeans.

"Hola, David."

"Yuneisi?" I asked.

"*Sí.*"

"It's a pleasure," I said, exchanging a kiss on both cheeks and inviting her onto my porch. We walked back and I offered her a seat. She took it, swung one leg over the other, and leaned back against the metal patio bench, resting her weight on her palms, while I pulled a chair beside her.

"Are you thirsty?" I asked.

"Very."

Cuba offered essentially two basic varieties of beer. One was Bucanero, the darkish brew in the red-and-black can. Its lighter cousin, Cristal, came in a green can with red letters. If either was out of stock, it was a sign—indeed a bellwether—for more difficult times ahead. I had a few cans of each tucked in the back of my fridge.

I pulled two Cristals from the shelf, cracked them open, and offered her one. She accepted it, taking a slow sip. "Gracias, David."

I did the same, savoring the beer's icy sting against the balmy summer air.

"So," she began, delicately wiping the corner of her mouth, careful not to smudge her rose-colored lipstick. It looked freshly applied. "Welcome to Cuba." Yuneisi seemed to already know who I was. I wasn't just her new neighbor. I was a foreigner. And she knew it. In one sentence, she made that clear. Her house across the street was obscured by an iron-wire and corrugated-tin fence, cinder blocks comprising its walls. The outlines of the blocks were visible despite a thin layer of yellow paint that coated its street-facing façade. The windows had no glass: instead, iron bars were affixed behind wooden shutters that pulled shut when the rain came. A red-and-chrome motorbike sat in the driveway. At dawn, the piercing crow of a rooster, which I'd grow to hate, seemed to emanate from somewhere in the grassy, dirt patch of her backyard. Like many Cubans, Yuneisi didn't seem to have much material wealth. Yet she had an ease about her.

"So, what do you do?" I asked, quickly realizing how very American—or very New York—the question was.

She said she had briefly worked at the Karl Marx Theatre on

First Avenue. Formerly known as both the White Theatre and the Charlie Chaplin prior to Cuba's 1959 revolution, behind the aging blue-and-tan-colored façade lay Havana's largest indoor venue. In 1979, record executives Bruce Lundvall and Jerry Masucci convinced Billy Joel, Stephen Stills, and Kris Kristofferson to take part in a groundbreaking three-day music festival there. Known as Havana Jam, it featured both American and Cuban artists. In 2001, the Marx was also home to the performance of a Welsh rock group called the Manic Street Preachers, who warned then president Fidel Castro about how loudly they planned to play. Castro, rarely one to be up-staged, responding simply by saying, "You cannot be louder than war!"[5] Local stars such as Carlos Varela, Silvio Rodriguez, and Pablo Milanes would later perform there in front of close to 5,000 screaming Cubans. Yuneisi had likely seen more than a few bands pass through. Despite the embargo, Cuban and American musicians had traveled to each other's cities for generations. Varela even visited Washington, D.C., in 2009, urging lawmakers to normalize relations with his country, and breaking out his guitar in a House Budget Committee meeting room. "Music is not going to move governments. But it might move people. And people can move governments," he told the *New York Times* in December. Music was not only a diplomatic tool, but also an indication of popular sentiment. Those whose lyrics pushed too far, such as Cuban hip-hop artists Los Aldeanos and rocker Gorki Águila, were often censored and detained. Working at the Marx offered a front-row seat to the push and pull of what authorities would tolerate. She likely had a good sense of what the state would allow.

But by now Yuneisi was looking up. For a moment, I seemed to have lost her attention as she cocked her head and affixed her eyes on my roof.

"You have a satellite dish," she said, returning her gaze to me. It was less question than statement.

I just looked at her. How did she know that? It was hidden from

street view, tucked behind the water tank, and obscured from nearly
every line of sight. But somehow, she knew it was there.

"Yes," I said.

She flashed a mischievous smile.

"How did you know?"

Then I looked down. While one of Yuneisi's hands still clutched
that green-and-red beer can, the other held a cell phone. It wasn't
the cheap black-plastic kind where one would have to press the 2
button three times just to start a text that begins with the letter c.
It was an iPhone. And it looked new. Just a year earlier, in March,
authorities had for the first time allowed Cubans to own cell
phones—a luxury once reserved only for those in top government
posts or with connections to foreign firms. Priced in convertible pesos, the cost was well out of reach for most Cubans using only their
government salaries, but those with family abroad often brought
them in.

"Nice phone," I said. Unlocked, it could home in on a mobile signal broadcast by the island's state-owned provider. But in this case,
it could also lock on to a wireless internet signal, like the one being
pumped out over the router that was connected to my satellite dish.
By connecting to that small Apple router, I had unwittingly fired a
flare over an internet-barren landscape for all to see. Yuneisi knew
there was a dish up there without even seeing it. Her iPhone told her
so. Now she just needed the password. That's why she was here.

"*Oye, papi,*" she cooed. "I just want to check my email."

She was no Dalia. Yuneisi didn't seem to care much about politics. And she certainly didn't seem to care what I thought either. She
just wanted to get online.

"Just write it down here," she said, crisscrossing her legs while
retrieving a small notebook from her back pocket. She then took a
slow sip of beer, batted her eyelashes, and awaited my response.

I could have easily given her the code. She was my neighbor, after
all. What harm could it do? But I didn't.

"Sorry, Yuneisi," I said. "Just can't do it." With that, she finished her beer, wiping the corner of her lip with her finger, again careful not to smudge her lipstick, and abruptly excused herself. Like Dalia, she disappeared as suddenly as she arrived.

At the time, I didn't quite know why I had turned her down. Maybe it was the desire to avoid converting my house into a neighborhood hot spot. Perhaps it was out of fear of having our smuggled-in dish revealed to authorities.

But what I eventually realized is that I simply didn't trust her. I had been living in Cuba just a few months. And after apparent phone taps, missing sinks, and would-be informants, I didn't see any value in giving anything to anyone I didn't know. It was me who was now keeping my distance. The fantasies were fading. And I was the one calling myself *yuma*. That was my word now. And I didn't trust anyone.

7

LOS YANKEES

Fantasy has a way of fading when it has the misfortune of coming true. Like so many outsiders, I had envisioned a crumbling darling of an island, manufactured by American pop culture. Cuba's outsized place in history only added to its lore. Indeed, the Revolution had been captured on 35 mm film, recut and recast on newsreels over the generations. Castro. Kennedy. Soviet missiles. And yes, of course, the old cars were all elements from a bygone era that were somehow trapped in the present—red meat to anyone with a penchant for the past. Yet here in the present, there was so much more to discover. Surely a *yuma,* equipped as I was with a somewhat ungainly Spanish tongue, would find no real barriers to those hidden treasures. All I needed was time. I had been sure of it. Meanwhile, Havana still masqueraded as a "dream assignment." I had never quite understood why CNN offered an extra monthly hardship stipend to the journalists who took it. Only the network's Baghdad bureau staff had that comparable benefit, and the two places had virtually nothing in common. But after a few months, a different island was emerging. Shortages and the near-constant specter of surveillance mingled with red-tape frustrations; not to mention, it was turning out to be terribly isolating. Up until recently, I had still enjoyed the Buena Vista Social Club, its bygone feel and brassy sensibility all part of a neatly wrapped Cuban identity that *yumas* like me had so often conjured. But now, in my adopted city, the pendulum was swinging back, and I instinctively left the room whenever musicians played yet another "Chan Chan."

"It's the 'Cuba creep,'" Will told me. "Every few months, you've got to get out. Otherwise, you start to think this is normal."

"Right," I said. "I'll just go for a run."

Running was my escape. Though the first few miles were always a bit trying in that Caribbean heat, by mile three or four, my body had a way of settling into stasis and getting acclimated.

I laced up a pair of old sneakers and headed out the door for my customary jog along the Malecon's seawall, where a mix of teenagers had already congregated. It was another blistering summer day, and I soon was in my trance, listening to the hypnotic rhythm of waves crashing and the salty feel of the ocean spray. In the distance, two sun gazers perched on the wall with a flask of rum between them listening to a small transistor radio. They were straining to hear. One had picked it up, and both were leaning in, stretching their necks and angling their heads. As I got closer, I began to hear the commentary of a quick-speaking sports announcer. The signal, obscured by static, faded in and out. Each time it cleared, the pair seemed to relax. But that reprieve was usually fleeting, and they'd squint their eyes and again stretch their necks when the signal inevitably scrambled, as if their physical gestures could somehow clarify the distant broadcast.

"What station is that?" I asked, stopping mid-gait. They each looked up for a moment. One grumbled something inaudible and refocused his attention on the radio. By this point, I had walked over and was standing just a few feet from their perch. So I asked again.

"What are you listening to?"

The older of the two tipped his cap and took a healthy swig of rum before answering. Both donned brimmed caps, and had to be at least in their midfifties, with deep creases reflective of both sun and time.

"*Pelota*," the older said. "Baseball."

"Really?" I replied. "American?"

He nodded, then added, "not well," denoting the quality of the transmission. "But if you twist it just right," he said, mimicking in the air a motion that resembled giving the knobs a slight turn with his thumb and index finger. His rust-covered radio—corroded by the sea's salty mist—looked better suited for the Smithsonian than daily use. It was astonishing that the little thing could get any signal at all.

"Mind if I sit with you?" I asked, easing onto the wall as the two shifted across the concrete promenade to make room. The radio announcer's voice was mostly lost in a sea of pops and crackles, and they stared toward Florida—just over ninety miles north, yet a world away. The radio offered them a window to America, albeit an imperfect one. Through that rusted box of wood, metal, and wire spouted bits of information about a country that so many Cubans had risked everything to reach, pitching makeshift rafts in a fraught attempt to cross shark-infested waters.

In 1994, as the island flirted with collapse and Fidel announced that "whoever wanted to leave, could," more than thirty-five thousand men, women, and children took him up on it, piling into small, crudely fashioned boats to make the long, perilous journey north. They had started with a very similar view to the one I had right then: a shimmering sea of untold danger and near-infinite possibility. Some would drown. Others would reach the new world and find it unforgiving. Still others would thrive, developing businesses, organizing and contributing to the thriving Cuban American community in South Florida. But for now, on the Malecon, it was baseball that occupied us.

"Bottom of the fifth," the announcer bellowed before cutting out, his voice disappearing in a sea of static. The break provided the men a chance for their own commentary and debate until the signal could lock on again and their awareness of the game could continue.

"All of our best guys go there," one said to me, motioning across the water and referring to Major League Baseball. There was a sort of quiet resignation in the way he said it.

"Ramírez rounds first!" the announcer shouted as the signal cleared.

"*Oye!*" the men bellowed along with him, their excitement palpable as that old radio offered a welcome distraction from the searing heat.

"*Ciao, caballeros,*" I said, thanking them. Baseball was one of the few topics that I could engage in, at least for now.

It made me think of New York, and the Yankees. It was August 2009, and the Bombers boasted the league's best record following a four-game sweep of their Boston rivals. I was following every pitch, albeit from a spotty satellite connection made possible by our not-so-clandestine DIRECTV. My father and I had been Skyping about the season most days in preparation for an upcoming trip we had planned to Seattle, where the Yanks were poised for a four-game stretch against the Mariners.

"So the plan is to fly to Chicago first," my father, Rob, explained over a garbled Skype phone call. "Then, we'll hop a westbound overnight train to Seattle."

"I know," I said. "We've talked about this half a dozen times."

"Just making sure," he replied. A Staten Island native and New Jersey resident, he had grown up in the Yankees orbit, and his love of the pinstripes dated back to the days of Joe DiMaggio, even though the Yankee Clipper had retired when my father was barely two years old.

"He was my favorite player, whom I never saw," he told me.

Thrice voted in as the Major League's Most Valuable Player, with a record fifty-six-game hitting streak, DiMaggio was an unquestioned

star. But it was the fact that he was Italian that may have most en-
deared him to my father.

"There weren't many Italians who played [major-league] baseball
back then," he recalled. "And my father reminded me of him." His
father, Savino, who later changed his name to Sam because "it was
easier to find work with an American name," was the product of a
different era. It was the Depression, and work was scarce. He eventually landed a job on a Ford assembly line in Mahwah, New Jersey,
after returning from war and staving off frostbite and German
bullets in the winter of 1944 on the Allies' European front. As an
adolescent, I would pepper him with questions, which he'd deflect,
or oblige with only abbreviated answers.

"Did you ever have to kill anyone?" I said with all the tact my
youth could afford.

He looked away. My grandfather had a way of slowing things
down to a pace that suited him. The lines on his forehead furrowed
and curved, like rings on a tree, before he drew a breath and turned
back in my direction.

"Yes," he answered, exhaling, though never quite looking me in
the eye. The weight of my question had caused his body to sink. The
air felt heavy. I felt heavy. And all of a sudden I wished I hadn't asked.
He looked away again and paused. As he did, I observed the pockmarks etched in the back of his head: the battle scars of skin cancer.
He was tough, having twice beaten back leukemia, and it showed in
the simplest of things, like the way he dunked a biscotti into his
coffee each morning. His fingers wrapped around the mug, lifting
the almond biscuit, while also revealing the hardened calluses of a
life spent in toil. Hardness was survival, and yet there remained a
glimmer of softness in the way he looked at us.

"Yes," he said again, this time looking me square in my eye. And
that was it. He never uttered another word about it. And I never
again asked. I had inadvertently tapped into the dark recesses of a
mind that had been tested and, indeed, damaged. It wasn't weakness

but rather the conscience of a gentleman who might endure war but was never meant for it. He had killed and he had watched friends die. When he looked at you, you could see he wanted to forget all that, but struggled to. The severity of life had obscured his softer edges. My father shared that trait. Both were imposing men, hovering just around six feet tall. For all their civility and restraint, the eyes of each would narrow and gleam during fits of anger, as if freshly removed from a furnace. But those moments were usually short-lived as they cooled and rounded again, while the corners of their mouths edged upward in a smirk, and eventually grew into a half smile. They were different. But their similarities were unmistakable. Among those was a love of baseball, practically passed down through genetics. Though my grandfather could hardly bring himself to root for the Yankees after his beloved Brooklyn Dodgers uprooted and left for California—he later adopted the Mets when they came to New York in 1962—my father had inexplicably grown up a Yankees fan. I did the same. And in Cuba, that was a stroke of good fortune.

"Oh, Los Yankees," I'd hear time and again after naming my choice team.

Though soccer was gradually making inroads across Cuba, as residents increasingly sported the jerseys of the Spanish clubs Real Madrid and Barcelona, talk of baseball was usually a safe conversation starter, especially among the older generation. It was one of the few times I didn't feel a divide between us. Baseball was an equalizer, and their skeptical faces would soften and smile when I'd mention hard-throwing pitchers like Aroldis Chapman and Orlando "El Duque" Hernandez—both had defected and found their way to major-league stardom with the Yanks. Chapman, considered among the best left-handers in the game, simply walked out of his Rotterdam hotel in the Netherlands, where Cuba's national team had been playing in a tournament. But Hernandez in 1998 was obliged to take a more perilous route. Secretly boarding a twenty-foot boat the morning after Christmas, he, his girlfriend, and at least six other Cubans reportedly employed the vessel to traverse the Florida Strait. Disaster struck, however, and the refugees were thrown off course, landing on a reef off the Bahamas ten hours later.[1] After three days of surviving on bottled water and Spam, they were eventually rescued by the U.S. Coast Guard and given visas on humanitarian grounds. The Yankees pounced, and signed Hernandez to a $6.6 million contract, making him a part of a World Series–winning run against the San Diego Padres in his first year. Two decades later, they shattered that deal with a record $86 million, five-year contract inked with Chapman, then the highest-ever Major League Baseball payout for a closer. The Yankees had occupied a special place in the hearts of Cubans. El Duque even claimed to have worn a New York Yankees T-shirt under his Cuban uniform while pitching in Havana. The promise of local stardom and American riches likely played no small part. Even Fidel, a baseball fanatic, had been mythologized in its lure, rumored to having tried out with the Yanks before assuming power in 1959. It was a tale largely debunked by baseball historians who say Castro's prowess on the field was greatly exaggerated, but it had nonetheless been repeated enough times over the generations to reinforce a Yankees mystique on the island. Cubans, like New Yorkers, needed their heroes. I've yet to meet anyone who doesn't like an underdog.

The sun had peaked, and now started its western retreat. But it still scorched uncovered skin, and the men pulled down their caps, casting deeper shadows across their eyes, which remained fixed on that rusty radio.

"*Oye, chico,*" a man yelled as I walked beyond them. "*Bicitaxi?*"

He was rail thin and sported a blue flip cap that covered his curly black hair. His bicycle had a seated carriage attached to its rear, and he was offering me a ride. It was sort of a modified rickshaw used to cart tourists mostly around the older, colonial sections of the city. More importantly, it was a wake-up call. For all my baseball connections, I still stood out as a foreigner. I was still *a yuma*. And that wasn't going to change.

"No, *gracias, caballero*," I said, refusing the ride and heading south toward Centro Habana. But baseball was never that far out of mind. The game as we know it today is said to have germinated in New York City just before the American Civil War, organized by bank clerks whose shifts finished early enough to play under the early evening sun. It came to Cuba just a few years later in the late 1860s while the game was still young. And to many, it was as much Cuba's pastime as it was America's.

"Nobody gave a thought to baseball being American or Cuban," wrote Cuban-born historian Roberto González Echevarría, a professor at Yale University. "We revered the great players we heard about and whose pictures we saw in newspapers and magazines, no matter what their nationality or race."[2]

A professional league cropped up in 1878, soon after its introduction, and—like many things Cuban—politics never trailed far behind. League officials on the island were soon channeling profits to rebel groups battling for independence from Spain. And that passion had been a source of diplomatic back channeling over the decades. In 1974, baseball commissioner Bowie Kuhn broached the idea of "baseball diplomacy" with Henry Kissinger, then U.S. secretary of state, akin to the sort of "Ping-Pong" diplomacy that paved the way for President Richard Nixon's visit to Beijing.[3] It wouldn't actually happen for another two decades, when Bill Clinton became president and sanctioned a trip to Havana for the Baltimore Orioles. It would take nearly another three decades—until 2016—for President Barack Obama to go further, joining President Raul Castro in the stands for a game between Cuba's national team and the Tampa Bay Rays. Politics, it seemed, had always been wrapped up in *pelota*. (The Rays won 4-1.)

Someone was fighting. I could hear it. I made my way through Centro Habana, strolling through the city's Central Park, adjacent to its Grand Theatre and Capitolio building, where a crop of stone benches offered a perch to a regular gaggle of verbal jousters. Baseball was the usual topic. That particular spot was called Esquina Caliente, or Hot Corner, even though the shady grove offered a respite from the searing heat. In fact, the term was slang for "third base" and hot because right-handed hitters tend to hit the ball hard and fast in that direction. But in Cuba, it was hot for other reasons. Here, baseball fans argued all day, virtually every day, hands often flailing to help make their case. But it wasn't just baseball. Listen long enough and something else happened—the subtle, unmistakable whisper of politics. In a country that restricts free speech, Cubans who gathered here spoke their minds. Bits of honesty, complaints about the state, and even dissent could and often would escape in short bursts and hushed tones, bookended and obscured by talk of *pelota*. I walked over.

"*Oye!*" barked one man as I approached.

He was wearing a royal-blue T-shirt emblazoned with the city's signature cursive *I,* the logo for the Industriales, one of two baseball teams based in Havana. "*Los Industriales son el mejor equipo del mundo,*" he bellowed, professing an allegiance to the capital city's team and his belief that Havana's Industrials were indeed baseball's greatest. "*Mentira!*" screamed another man, his hands waving emphatically to punctuate the fact he felt he was being lied to, while professing an affection for the rival squad in Camagüey. It was an in-your-face, full-throated spar that looked as if at any moment it might escalate into a brawl. I sifted through the crowd, made small talk with those willing to engage with a *yuma,* and waited. I was often on the prowl for an interview.

It was a place I would return to often. The cast of characters largely remained the same, and it was always a good place for a quote. But years later, as I slipped through the crowd, a man I didn't recognize with a shorn head and a purple cutoff T-shirt approached. He'd tell me his name was Jose, though he withheld the rest, knowing I was a journalist and likely fearing the consequences of his coming frankness. Then he mumbled something I couldn't quite make out.

He repeated it, lowering his head and looking away.

"The king needs to go." Jose almost whispered it, leaning in and speaking under his breath. "Castro. He's our king. And he needs to go," he said a third time. The words felt heavy. This sort of criticism in public was usually off-limits—just the sort of thing CDRs and undercover agents tracked. But times were changing. Most Cubans I met expressed concerns about politics only as it pertained to them. Most had never known a leader other than Fidel or Raul. But now, many seemed to be speaking more openly. Unlike others I spoke with, Jose didn't seem to give a damn. "No more Castros," he added, though he suddenly appeared worried and scurried away. A conditioned response; Big Brother was always watching. And I was a creature of habit, especially in the evenings, which likely made for an easy target.

At night, La Roca, a cheap state-run restaurant, was a common dinner go-to. Vested waiters hustled about, and a grand piano kept things loud. My usual: Espresso. Roast chicken. Rice and beans. Followed by flan. It was when the flan came that she walked in. Form-fitting floral; a dress that cinched more than it billowed. Our eyes met as she walked by. *"Discúlpeme, señor,"* I asked a waiter as she sat down. "Do you have a pen?" He produced one, and I scribbled down my number. As if by instinct, the woman excused herself, briefly passed my table, and scooped it up. A week later, I received a text. "Hi. This is Yisette," was all it read. That was enough. Her family were Castro stalwarts, so she had to keep her dalliances with an American journo secret. Or so she told me. It wouldn't be until years later that I began to doubt her story, and wonder who Yisette really was.

8

BLUE SHRINK-WRAP

Toilet paper. Soy sauce. Flak jacket. I wrote down those three items on a small yellow notepad, usually holstered in my back pocket. Its blue-lined pages were filled with a chicken-scratch collection of notes, quotes, and unfinished to-do lists. And that incongruous trio was what I was obliged to pick up in the States on the way back from the baseball trip with my father. It was August 2009. And I was in need of resupply. When I first bounded off that Cuban jet nearly three months earlier, ready to start my new life in Havana, I had little concept of what basic items were essentially unobtainable. So, this trip north was an opportunity to stock up on necessities as much as it was a family visit. Supermercado 70 *had* been noticeably bare in recent weeks, and my stash of Charmin was running low. Soy sauce was a luxury that just didn't seem to exist here. And the flak jacket—which I'd pick up at CNN headquarters in Atlanta—wasn't really for Cuba. On occasion, the network would deploy its journalists to hot spots around the globe where a bullet-resistant vest was a precaution. I'd eventually need mine, but never for Cuba.

"Dagmara!" I yelled out from my office, packing up as I readied to head out the door.

"Tell me!" she replied.

"Anything you need from the States?"

"Chocolates," she said. "*Godiva* chocolates."

"OK."

"Don't forget," she insisted, walking in and dipping the lenses of her glasses, emphasizing her seriousness about the matter.

"I won't," I said, popping my eyebrows as if to say "OK, OK, I got it."

Dagmara wasn't asking. The chocolates were a demand.

"Monse, how about you?"

"Batteries. Make sure you get double A's, triple A's, and D's," she added, emphasizing her pronunciation of *Deeees,* which powered the bureau's lapel mics. We burned through D's like nowhere I'd ever seen. And here, they were all but unattainable, at least through official channels.

"OK. Fine. Rafa? Need anything?"

"Fishhooks," he replied.

They were all modest, though necessary requests. None of this stuff was here. It all had to come from the States. Razors. Q-tips. Nail clippers. They all had to be carried in.

"Make sure you get condoms!" yelled Ossorio.

I smiled. "Ossorio, they sell condoms in the pharmacies here," I said. "I've seen them."

"Yes," he replied. "But they're Chinese made. And you know there are a lot of people in China!" he roared, clutching his belly and shaking with laughter.

"Fine," I said with a smirk, pulling my pack over my shoulder and rechecking my list. Chocolate. Batteries. Fishhooks. Condoms. It seemed like the ingredients for some sort of bizarre sexual escapade. But each request spoke volumes about the person behind it and what he or she considered prized in a land of scarcity.

"I'll see you all next week."

And with that I was off to catch a connecting flight through Miami International Airport, my restocking station of sorts—except for the fishhooks. That would require a special trip to a marine and fishing supplies store on the outskirts of Miami.

When I landed the airport's flashing neon advertisements and billboards were rough on the eyes after the comparatively drab fade of Jose Marti International. After living in Cuba, it took a few moments to adjust. Meanwhile, hundreds of Havana-bound travelers filled the airport atrium, carting coffee makers, microwaves, children's playpens, and wide-screen televisions, all wrapped in shiny blue shrink-wrap, presumably to thwart the sticky fingers of Cuban customs agents. With an uncle, a mother, a grandma, or some friend waiting for those glossy packages, goods and remittances had quickly become a cornerstone of the Cuban economy, funneling more than $3 billion to the island a year, roughly twice the value of the island's top importer, China.

In fact, about one-third of Cubans received some form of financial help from abroad. Buoyed by a relaxation in regulations under the Obama administration, the money ballooned by 116 percent between 2008 and 2014. Cuba had become Latin America's fastest-growing remittance market. And Miami was the funnel. It seemed like something to explore.

I had a few hours between flights and figured I'd waste some time in the city, wandering down Eighth Street in Little Havana for a *cafecito* at Café Versailles and a stroll through Maximo Gomez Park, where an indefatigable smattering of old-timers still donned *guayaberas* and tipped their fedoras when they shook hands. Pedro Real was among them. An eighty-seven-year-old exile who was more interested in his game of dominoes than he was in talking with me, he had fled Cuba aboard a makeshift raft sometime in the 1960s. Traversing the straits before settling in South Florida, Real—and many like him—had been convinced he wouldn't stay long.

"No, I won't go back," he told me, as long as a Castro remained in power. As I strolled farther down Eighth Street and in and out of its cigar shops, a store owner in his early forties named Ricardo Vasquez greeted me and offered a different perspective.

"I'm a Marlins fan," he said when asked of his connection to the island. "Cuba might be where my parents are from, but Miami is my home."

Today, at least four generations of Cubans and Cuban Americans fill Miami and its outskirts, composing approximately one-third of the entire city, a fact that helped garner sizeable political influence in the perennial swing state of Florida. And the anti-Castros in Florida wielded outsized influence in Washington. "Cuba is not a foreign policy question," said Brent Scowcroft, national security adviser to President George H. W. Bush. "Cuba is a domestic issue. In foreign policy, the embargo makes no sense. It doesn't do anything. It's quite clear we cannot starve Cuba to death. We learned that when the Soviet stopped subsidizing Cuba and they didn't collapse. It's a domestic issue."[1]

Over the decades, Miami's anti-Castro political guard had stopped ten previous presidential administrations from extending the olive branch, and had actually tightened sanctions and ceded to Congress what had once been the president's prerogative in lifting the trade embargo.[2] Those measures drew support from those like Jorge Mas Canosa, a Cuban exile turned construction tycoon and an influential campaign donor, who founded the Cuban American National Foundation (CANF), which poured money into the campaign coffers of politicians who rallied against Castro, and eventually extended its reach well beyond Florida politics. In 1988, CANF's support helped underdog Connecticut attorney general Joe Lieberman unseat three-term incumbent senator Lowell P. Weicker Jr., who had advocated a warming of relations. It also enabled Bill Clinton to carry Florida in the 1996 U.S. presidential elections, helping him become the first Democrat to take the Sunshine State since Jimmy Carter.

But over time, as exiles aged and Canosa died of lung cancer, groups like CANF, which had once advocated the violent overthrow of the Castro government, would adopt more moderate positions. By the time I was walking through Little Havana in the summer of 2009, the city was in the midst of transition. Its traditionally Cuban enclaves were being redefined by growing numbers of Colombians, Brazilians, and Venezuelans, whose Miami-Dade population had soared by 117 percent over the past decade. Years later, when Charlie Crist announced his Democratic bid for the state's governorship in the 2014 elections, he named a Colombian American woman (not a Cuban) as his running mate. Little Havana had also diversified as new groups of Salvadorians and Nicaraguans moved in. By 2017, Cubans would make up less than a third of that neighborhood, compared to 85 percent just two decades earlier.

But, Miami still remained home to the world's largest diaspora of Cuban exiles. And many remained sympathetic to the anti-Castro cause—forcing the aging leader from power, restoring democracy, and returning property rights of those whose land, homes, and businesses had been seized in the Revolution. Florida Republicans like Senator Marco Rubio and Congresswoman Ileana Ros-Lehtinen were among its standard-bearers, supporting a loose association of lobby groups, media groups, and nongovernmental organizations that continued to draw millions in taxpayer dollars.

The money, however, was hardly well spent. In 2006, federal auditors discovered that almost all of the $74 million that USAID had doled out in prodemocracy Cuba funding between 1996 and 2005 had been given without a competitive bidding process. At least one Miami-based company also used the funds to purchase Sony PlayStations, cashmere sweaters, and Godiva chocolates.[3] And yet the spigot never turned off. Another $26 million per year went to the Office of Cuba Broadcasting (OCB), which continued to beam anti-Castro news programming to the island. Though it faced allegations of serving as a U.S. propaganda tool and was cited in

2014 by a U.S. oversight committee that recommended it "improve its adherence to certain aspects of journalistic standards," Congress continued to reauthorize OCB funding.[4] All in all, U.S. taxpayers have spent roughly three-quarters of a billion dollars on the project since the Reagan administration created it in 1983.

"I'm not going to say that's a small amount of money," Carlos Garcia-Perez, director of the OCB, later told me during an interview in 2015. "But democracy doesn't come cheap."[5]

Yet twenty-six years after its creation, there were few signs of success. The OCB's radio station consistently failed to penetrate Cuba's frequency jamming, and only an estimated 3 percent of Cubans polled paid attention to the tens of thousands of DVDs and flash drives that were delivered to the island. Cuba also seemed light-years away from adopting a multiparty system.

But America's secret effort would nevertheless continue, much of it under the guise of "democracy building," despite amateurish tactics and repeated public failures. Among them was a botched Twitter-like social media network aimed at organizing street protests, as well as a covert attempt to infiltrate Cuba's hip-hop scene; both uncovered by Associated Press investigations.[6] Both projects were also orchestrated by Creative Associates International, a Washington-based company that scored a multimillion-dollar USAID contract to co-opt Cuban rappers and provoke dissent. The company hired a Serbian music promoter named Rajko Bozic, who established a front company in Panama and began helping a Cuban rapper named Aldo Rodriguez promote his music. What Rodriguez didn't know was that Bozic was supported by the U.S. government. His group, Los Aldeanos, rapped about the hardships of the Cuban people and criticized government censorship, and so it seemed a natural fit.

"Go and tell the captain this ship's sinking rapidly," Rodriguez spat in one such lyric, with the words *"El Rap Es Guerra,"* or "rap is war," tattooed across his forearm.

Cuban authorities had an official state-run Cuban Rap Agency to handle these sorts of rebellious freestylers, yet signs of discontent and protest nonetheless began to creep through. Bozic noticed and convinced Rodriguez to allow his team to promote him, though reportedly left out the fact that USAID would be footing the bill.

A month later, in September 2009, I was in Havana, and a major concert was approaching. Musicians from across Latin America were descending on the Cuban capital to perform on Cuba's biggest stage: Revolution Plaza, where hundreds of thousands were expected to gather. Sensing an opportunity, the scruffy Serb sought to convince Colombian singer Juanes, a seventeen-time Latin Grammy winner, to put Los Aldeanos on the ticket. The upcoming Peace Without Borders was a major opportunity to reach a huge Cuban audience. On the afternoon of the concert, hundreds of thousands of concertgoers packed the plaza as Juanes took the stage amid soaring temperatures. I loaded a few extra batteries into my camera pack and dipped into the crowd. Fans were collapsing due to the heat and excitement. Medical teams carrying stretchers whisked away the afflicted, while state security looked on. But, the energy was palpable amongst so many Cubans, who were unaccustomed to such a massive music show.

Clad in white, the Latin stars strode onstage. Olga Tanon of Puerto Rico, Miguel Bosé of Spain, and Cucu Diamantes of Cuba jammed alongside Juanes to a sea of concertgoers who bayed and clapped beneath the gaze of Revolution Plaza's massive steel mural of Che Guevara. In the end, Los Aldeanos weren't invited to perform, but Juanes publicly thanked them afterward and the men posed together in a photograph.

It wasn't perfect, but Bozic's plan had worked, garnering Los Aldeanos new public exposure that he hoped might insulate them. And yet his team had been sloppy. Cuban intelligence was monitoring Rodriguez, and he faced continued harassment from police, who routinely detained members of the group and those affiliated with it. Only this time authorities also uncovered a smoking gun: documents that tied Los Aldeanos to Bozic and USAID. The young rappers were in Uncle Sam's pocket. The revelation damaged the group's reputation among Cubans, and compromised an authentic protest voice that had been gaining ground in Cuba. Rodriguez eventually left the island.

And Creative Associates International was behind it. Yet funds from Washington kept coming. Between 1996 and 2011, Congress appropriated $205 million to these "democracy assistance" programs in Cuba run by Creative Associates and other companies, peaking in 2008 with total combined appropriations of about $44 million.[7] For those interested in a lucrative government contract with little oversight and few expectations of results, democracy building in Cuba seemed like a golden opportunity. And it was just around this time that a white-haired Marylander named Alan Gross would start making trips to the island. It was a name I had first heard on December 3, 2009, when I learned that an American subcontractor had been detained. Gross had been covertly smuggling in advanced satellite communications gear at USAID's behest in an effort to set up illegal internet hot spots in Cuba. He was eventually charged with plotting against the state and would languish as a Cuban prisoner for the next five years, chilling what had been a warming of relations between the two nations. After he was freed, I was eager to interview him. But that would take some time, so I'll get to that later. As for me, I would eventually obtain my soy sauce, flak jacket, and fishhooks, along with two economy-size packs of Charmin Ultra. The good stuff. I'd also make sure not to forget Dagmara's Godiva chocolates, lest I hear about it.

My father and I had reconnected, pounding coffees and pancakes in a Seattle diner. It was Cuba's polar opposite. Though the Emerald City boasted the sort of earthy, crunchy merriment often ascribed to Pacific Northwesterners, the rain had a way of dampening those fleeced spirits. We watched the Yanks take three of four games in that drizzle before I headed back and restocked for my return to Cuba.

9

RUMBLE TO THE EAST

A rooster's crow broke the morning stillness. That was how I usually awoke: a screech that pierced an otherwise quiet and sleepy morning. It didn't matter that I lived nowhere near a farm. Wherever I went, there always seemed to be a rooster nearby, its dawn caw beckoning the start of another day—my morning alarm cock.

Havana's early hours are often cool and quiet, especially in winter. It was January 2010, a time of year when cold fronts cast fishermen ashore as massive waves crash over the Malecon. Breakers explode against concrete and spray up from underneath. Larger swells crest over the wall, spawning seawater archways pierced by passing cars and the occasional Chinese-made bus. It was an inauspicious time for fishermen and lovers alike, and so the Malecon was often empty, jellyfish and seaweed strewn across its six-lane boulevard. When the winds really picked up, residents often waded through flooding that seemed all but inevitable. It was usually worse in the fall months, when tropical storms from the Atlantic swept through the Caribbean and morphed into hurricanes, barreling west then north and cutting over the island. Streets became canals and rolling blackouts left many in the dark. And yet Cubans had gone through this routine often enough to be practiced at disaster response, conducting annual drills and marshaling resources in a way few Caribbean nations could. For now, however, the city was quiet. Few could predict that a different sort of disaster was looming.

It was January 12.

By now, I had been in Cuba just seven months, and my furniture was due to arrive from the States any day. Work had been slow, so I left early. The weather in Havana was uncharacteristically hot and I had just finished fixing myself an icy infusion of sugary mango concentrate, mixed with a splash of Habana Club, when the ring of my cell phone cut through the hot, stagnant air.

Some sixty miles off Cuba's eastern shores, many Haitians had also just finished work, commuting home after what had been a scorching January day. Within the hour, the ground would open up beneath them.

At its narrowest point, just sixty miles of sea separate Cuba from Haiti. As I sipped my rum drink in Havana, two great slabs of the earth's crust were about to move in a sudden eruption of energy. Six miles, beneath the small Haitian town of Léogâne, just sixteen miles west of Port-au-Prince, tension had been building between two major tectonic plates: the North American plate and the Caribbean plate, which had been moving upward at a rate of roughly a quarter inch per year.

At 4:53 p.m., the slip finally happened.

More than two centuries of latent energy released in a sudden shock wave as these massive plates lurched back like a rubber band, delivering an enormous ripple through rock and sand just outside the capital—a city of more than 2 million people, many of whom lived in hillside homes constructed of nothing more than tin and wood.

The quake registered a magnitude 7.0, and its shallow depth allowed much of its power to wave across Haiti's surface, like a stone cast into a still lake.

I turned on the television and CNN's Wolf Blitzer was already on-screen, standing in front of a map of Haiti—a pulsating red dot to indicate Port-au-Prince—while conversing with aid group director Frank Williams on scene. He seemed shaken.

"People are screaming all around," Williams said into the staticky phone line.

CNN had no staff journalists in Haiti at the time. And communications lines were down, rendering much of the world blind to the ensuing trauma. Meanwhile, my phone was ringing. Transfixed by the television, I snapped out of my stare and rushed over to answer. When I did, the breathless Irish accent of a woman shouted through the receiver.

"Where are you?" yelled Emer Sutin, CNN's senior planning editor. Hardly waiting for a response, she continued, speaking fast and deliberate. "We're sending teams to Port-au-Prince. How fast can you get there?"

"Emer?" I replied.

"Haiti!" she yelled back. "How fast can you get to Haiti?"

News teams from New York, Miami, Atlanta, and New Orleans were all gearing up to fly south. The Western Hemisphere's poorest country had just been hit with its worst natural disaster in modern history. And at that particular moment, few knew how bad it had gotten. But news networks were mobilizing.

Houses had shaken in eastern Cuba without major damage. But Haiti was more vulnerable. Beneath the island of Hispaniola, which Haiti and the Dominican Republic share, the Enriquillo-Plantain Garden fault system hadn't experienced a major seismic event in nearly two centuries. A sudden burst of energy along what geologists refer to as the strike-slip, where horizontal compression eventually ruptures, was all but inevitable. Though there had been warnings. Less than two years earlier, in March 2008, a group of five scientists presented a report at the Eighteenth Caribbean Geological Conference in Santo Domingo, which was meant to alert governments in the region to a "major seismic hazard." The last major quake to strike the area dated back to 1770 according to historical records, and the tension was reaching critical mass.[1]

All that was needed was a slip.

Few of Haiti's buildings had been constructed to withstand that kind of shaking, and most had crumbled almost instantly. Even the presidential palace was reduced to rubble. The overall picture would never be fully clear, but some 3 million people were affected, with death toll estimates as high as 230,000 people.[2] More than 300,000 others were injured and 1.5 million rendered homeless. It seemed that almost in an instant, Port-au-Prince had fallen, and trapped thousands beneath it.

"How long will it take you?" Emer shouted, knowing that our Havana office was on Cuba's northernmost coast and still some seven hundred miles away. Nonetheless, we were the closest CNN journalists to its epicenter. Of course, being geographically close to anything when you're in Cuba means relatively little in terms of travel time. It was about 5:45 p.m. The last flight out of Havana had left twenty minutes earlier. Jose Marti International wasn't exactly a hub. But Emer wasn't one to be deterred. "OK, well . . . see if you can find a boat."

"A boat?" I replied, wondering if her solution to all of this was really a seven-hundred-mile sea voyage to Haiti.

"Just ask a local fisherman if you can hitch a ride," she said.

I could hear her breathing, awaiting my response, waiting to know whether she could count on Shasta and me to sit in a trawler's hull as it puttered east.

"Uh, sure," I said. "I'll . . . look for a fisherman."

"OK, great," she replied and promptly hung up.

"Right," I said to an empty phone line, wondering if Emer had completely lost her mind.

There would be no Haiti-bound ride-along that evening. And by the next morning, our two-person crew was largely forgotten amid a deluge of Haiti coverage carried out by Anderson Cooper and Sanjay Gupta. As the first images of the devastation poured in, we all were only beginning to come to grips with what had actually happened.

It was indeed "a catastrophe of major proportions," to quote Haitian ambassador Raymond Alcide Joseph, who was already making his case for aid. Even the UN mission headquarters in Port-au-Prince, a central coordination point for its nine thousand peacekeepers, had collapsed. From Washington, President Barack Obama promised Haitians "would not be forsaken," announcing a $100 million aid package and relief effort, while instructing America's military to deploy rescue teams and begin preparing humanitarian aid.[3] But it was unclear where those teams would go. In Haiti, where a quarter of the people live on less than $1.25 per day, infrastructure and transport links reflected decades of underinvestment. Airports, bridges, and communications lines were down across much of the quake zone, making for a logistics nightmare. One day after the earthquake hit, a Lockheed P-3 Orion surveillance plane departed El Salvador and headed toward Port-au-Prince, banking over the capital and capturing images of what looked like a confetti-strewn landscape of a city on its knees. Roads had buckled, entire blocks were all but destroyed, and the dead and dying were everywhere. Even the control tower at Toussaint Louverture International Airport had partially collapsed, halting all civilian flights and hampering aid efforts right from the start.

On a training mission nearby, the USS *Carl Vinson,* one of the navy's Nimitz-class supercarriers, had been ordered to change course and head for the island. Its first order of business was assessment, explained the commander of U.S. Southern Command, General Douglas Fraser. But as the United States evaluated, thousands of Haitians who were trapped beneath shattered concrete and twisted rebar were in increasingly dire straits as they desperately waited for help.

The United Nations was the more logical first responder. But with its mission head and deputy head among the dead, the UN's response in those critical first seventy-two hours was maddeningly slow as the force focused on security and the prevention of looting rather than humanitarian relief, according to several witnesses and journalists on the island. "At the very beginning it was very difficult because the headquarters was completely destroyed, and all the leadership of the mission was killed," UN acting head Edmond Mulet later told the *Telegraph*.[4] And yet, as the UN regrouped, the Cubans were already at work. More than three hundred Cuban medical workers were already in Haiti. They were part of Castro's soft-power foreign policy, where some thirty-seven thousand medical professionals had deployed across some seventy-seven countries, generating an estimated $8 billion in revenue. Cuba's medical brigades had helped victims of the 2005 Pakistan earthquake, the 2004 Indian Ocean tsunami, and the 2006 Indonesian earthquake, and were even offered to the United States after Hurricane Katrina pummeled the Gulf Coast, having earned a reputation as being among the longest-remaining international medical teams following disasters.

Often touted as among the Revolution's greatest achievements, Cuba's medical expertise and health systems were both valuable exports and a cherished homegrown institution. Community-based clinics and a phalanx of family doctors and nurses were available to Cuban residents free of charge, with Cubans living as long as Americans, but at a tenth of the cost. With the focus on providing rather than purchasing primary care and the promotion of health rather than treatment of illness, the island ran a predominantly state-run health system, except for its black-market practices and medical tourism. The United States, by comparison, employed a hybrid model of public and private payers and providers with a fragmented insurance system of deductibles, cost sharing, and out-of-network charges that left more than one in four Americans with medical debt. Cuba's system, however, was hardly perfect, and the influences of diet and lifestyle invariably played into the wellness of its people, making it difficult to accurately assess the real impacts of its methods. In other words, reality was far more nuanced than the rosy portrait Michael Moore conveyed in his 2007 documentary *Sicko*, in which Cuba is the land of cheap drugs and free doctors. For instance, during the 1990s, when Soviet subsidies dried up and the U.S. embargo tightened with the Helms-Burton Act, restricting the import of pharmaceuticals and leaving the island near famine, Cubans experienced population-wide weight loss that researchers later correlated with falling rates of diabetes and heart disease.[5] Researchers from the United States, Cuba, and Spain determined that during the crisis the island's general mortality rates had also declined, along with the incidences of strokes, while type 2 diabetes dropped by more than a third. They found the "abrupt downward trend" closely linked to the twelve pounds the average Cuban shed during this so-called special period, as opposed to the level of care that they received, as residents biked to work and subsisted on meager diets.[6] But by 2010, during comparatively more abundant times in Cuba, obesity and cardiovascular mortality rates had rebounded, followed by a 116 percent rise in incidences of diabetes. With such revelations, the island's often-praised health care system would be hard-pressed to claim credit, especially since many of its doctors were abroad. In December 2010, for instance, Cuba's Ministry of Health announced a "personnel reduction in the already extremely stretched health care sector to export more doctors and earn hard currency." The report added that "our paid professionals would be increased in countries who[se] economies allow it, so they may contribute to the national health system."[7] Doctors, in other words, were a money maker.

That said, domestic health care in Cuba was made a priority in a way few countries could claim. The island had trained students from across the world in sixteen Cuban medical schools, which UN secretary-general Ban Ki-moon described as having produced "miracle workers."[8] Now, many of those doctors—the most highly trained of whom in Cuba could earn no more than $60 per month—were quietly spearheading a massive disaster relief effort in Haiti. Under the coordination of Dr. Carlos Alberto Garcia, a team of 344 Cuban health workers swelled to four medical brigades, operating five field hospitals and five diagnostic centers alongside nearly two dozen other care centers.[9] They worked day and night as the injured poured in at a seemingly unrelenting pace.

"We're going!" Shasta shouted. I was green. From my perch in Havana, a nasty stomach bug had taken hold four days after the quake and I was vomiting in the toilet just as she walked into my office. "They've got two seats for us!"

Raulito had secured us a spot on a Soviet-era An-26 cargo plane bound for Haiti with a group of Cuban doctors. The plane was already jam-packed with medical supplies, but authorities had offered space to a batch of Havana-based journalists, which included CNN.

"Great!" I yelled back, only half meaning it, and wiped my chin before packing: two cameras, microphones, laptops, food, satellite phones, transmission gear, batteries, and plenty of water. I stuffed it all into two soft-shell cases and slung them both over my shoulder as we headed out.

"Where are our seats?" I asked the pilot as we boarded the plane.

He looked at me with a kind of exasperated stare before replying. "No more seats. Just sit on the boxes."

The crates behind him, bound in rope and twine, were filled with various medical supplies that ranged from gauze and IV bags to needles and surgical gloves. I slid on top as we took off into the Cuban airspace that Havana agreed to share with the U.S. Air Force.

The gesture reduced U.S. flight times from the naval base at Guanta-namo Bay to southern Florida by some ninety minutes.

"Cuba is ready to cooperate with all the nations on the ground, including the US, to help the Haitian people and save more lives," explained Josefina Vidal, the Cuban diplomat in charge of U.S. affairs at its foreign ministry.[10]

Meanwhile, I was slumped over, dehydrated and nauseous as our old Soviet-era airliner rattled and rocked in descent, eventu-ally touching down in Port-au-Prince. We had landed in Toussaint Louverture International Airport, but it didn't seem like it. The control tower was badly damaged, and there was no terminal from which to unload. A distant metal gate, blurred by heat waves and manned by a handful of UN officers clutching their rifles, swung open and closed on a rusty hinge. And so we started to walk.

"Over here," yelled one of the men, motioning to a flatbed pickup truck. "We're going to Peace," he said, a reference to one of the field hospitals where the Cuban medical teams were operating. "Let's go! Let's go!"

Shasta climbed into the front passenger seat. I loaded the gear on the flatbed and hopped on as the truck drove off, bouncing around corners to an unfolding scene of near-apocalyptic proportion. The capital was in ruins: a crumbled mix of cinder blocks, wires, and metal piled high, which often hid the bodies. Their rotting stench, however, was unmistakable and made worse by the island's soaring temperatures. As we drove past block after block, it all seemed the same. Dust, debris, and bodies. Our truck rounded another bend and slowed to a walking pace as it navigated rebar and cinder blocks scat-tered in the road, offering a chance to get our first real glimpse of the people we were sent there to cover. Port-au-Prince had finally come into view.

I readied the camera. But much of what I'd shoot would not, could not, be used. Vacant stares and bloody entanglements would be captured on tape, only to be later erased, never having been broadcast due to their graphic nature.

Just then, I heard young voices.

"CNN! CNN!" yelled a group of boys, who had taken to running behind our vehicle, presumably spotting the CNN logo on one of our bags. The road ahead was still a mess, forcing the vehicle to move ever more slowly, which afforded the boys their chance to catch up. I spun around and pointed the camera at them. "Hey, CNN!" they now shouted with more enthusiasm, waving their hands and pointing.

No matter the circumstance, teenage boys all tend to act the same in front of a camera. And why not? The prospect of being on television seemed a welcome distraction from the surrounding misery. Estimates of the dead were still rising from thousands to hundreds of thousands. And yet these boys were smiling.

"Thank you," one said, still jogging alongside the truck.

"Hey! Thank you," another added.

Thank you? What did these boys expect? It was 2010. Perhaps CNN still seemed among the best ways to reach a global audience. A CNN sticker on a dusty camera bag signified that the world would be listening. And if the world was listening, so the logic goes, help couldn't be too far away.

Indeed it wasn't. Aid workers were descending en masse, and nations would eventually pledge billions in disaster relief. And these boys knew it. Despite a massive upheaval to the worlds they had known, they still appeared hopeful. They could not know then, however, that eight years after the quake, nearly a quarter million of them would still reside in tented slums and temporary housing, that a cholera epidemic the United Nations would bring to the island would infect some seven hundred thousand people and leave more than nine thousand of their countrymen dead, and that only about half of the $13.34 billion in total aid pledged would actually be delivered.

"Thank you," said another, repeating his friend's gesture for a third and final time. They still focused on that CNN logo, perhaps hoping they would not be forsaken.

I wanted to share the boys' enthusiasm. But I knew we wouldn't be staying long. Broadcast news organizations like CNN usually took their leads from the pictures they captured, especially when it came to international stories. As the drama diminished, so too did the coverage. A year later, CNN would win awards for its reporting in Haiti. Gold statues and glass frames would adorn journalists' desks. And yet we all seemed destined to let those boys down.

"We're almost there," shouted the driver as we rounded another bend. "This is it," he barked. And with that, we disembarked and made our way into the field hospital, where hundreds lay strewn on stretchers and on the ground, receiving or waiting to receive treatment. The stench was more powerful here and filled virtually every room with a sickening sweetness. And yet my own nausea had curiously dissipated, paling in comparison to the misery around us.

"CNN!" yelled a man sporting a buzz cut. "Over here!" Jorge Fran Martinez, a Cuban physician, had been among the first to greet us. Like a dozen other Cuban doctors at the hospital, he wore a white T-shirt with the word "Cuba" emblazoned on his chest in bright blue and red letters. The doctors were here not only to provide medical assistance but also to be seen, a not-so-subtle advertisement for the Revolution. Yet after five days, with staff treating an average of five hundred patients per day, Martinez's energy had been sapped, his movements rendered slow, deliberate, and methodical as the dead and dying continued to stream in.[11]

"Those rescued are usually already suffering from gangrene," Martinez explained, tending to a young woman whose leg had been crushed. It would have to be amputated. Too many to count had suffered similar fates. Walking through that narrow blue-flecked corridor, it became clear that dozens more were propped against walls or stretched out on hospital beds. Outside, blue tarps had been strung atop tent posts, offering the wounded a brief reprieve from the blistering sun and casting a pale blue light over patients who now lay on the ground. Doctors and nurses shuttled about, stitching wounds, refilling IV bags, and hauling in more of the injured.

They just kept coming.

Every few minutes, rescuers would show up with more. Meanwhile, blood pooled on the floors. In some rooms there was so much of it that it was difficult not to slip. I moved from room to room methodically filming the injured and dying and tried to stay focused.

Make sure you get the eyes, I remembered an old cameraman once telling me. The eyes would tell the story. I looked through my viewfinder and refocused. Dilated pupils moved across the whites. Some were panicked. Others resigned. Still others had their eyelids shut and dripped with tears. An intermittent scream or moan filled the air as the Cubans worked almost robotically. My lens captured the details. Each grimace and wince dutifully recorded. And I kept filming.

"Over here," Shasta called out.

We walked into another part of the hospital where a nun was kneeling beside a badly injured little girl no more than five years old. Her short black braids were still twisted and wrapped in red rubber bands, while the left side of her face was nearly concave, having been smashed and buried. For four days, she clung to life as maggots inched their way onto her face and bored holes into her cheeks. Crushed beneath the rocks, her face had become infected. When rescuers pulled her out, she was barely alive. Her left eye was shut and a translucent glaze covered the other, rendering the child nearly blind. She moved slowly, as an IV restricted her arm, and the tube tightened as she reached forward. When we arrived at her bedside, a nun sat beside her.

"It's in the Lord's hands," she said, smiling.

It was that smile that finally made me put the camera down. In the quake's aftermath, Christian missionaries had flocked to Haiti. Eager to help, they worked in tandem with aid groups, transporting the injured, tending to the sick, and digging wells. But they often lacked a basic understanding of Haitian Creole or local culture. And while many focused on aid, others viewed the disaster in Haiti more as an evangelist's battleground, an opportunity to spread the faith. An estimated 1,700 long-term missionaries were doing just that, though some had begun before the quake struck. Now, the island was awash in Christian aid and aid workers, often with little oversight or supervision. Though many would construct homes, care for the sick, and build sanitation systems, reports of sexual abuse by aid workers and UN peacekeepers were rife, particularly among Haiti's poorly regulated orphanages, where the ranks of children had swollen in the quake's aftermath. I knew all that. But it was her smile that got to me.

"It's part of God's plan," the nun repeated of the battered girl in front of her.

I just looked at her. The extent of her injuries and infections was beyond repair. She was going to die, the attending physician had explained. I felt numb.

The girl then stirred. And I suddenly remembered why I was there, raising the camera to capture her movements. "If your pictures aren't good enough," posited veteran war photographer Robert Capa, "you're not close enough." I rembered those words, and moved closer.

Focus on the eyes, I remembered. But where were they? One was shuttered, the other unrecognizable. Her cry, barely audible, came from a mouth slightly agape as she struggled to breathe.

"Right now," said an attending nurse who had slipped behind me to change her IV bag, "it's about making her comfortable." The woman moved with the clinical efficiency of someone who had made this same motion hundreds of times before. "There's just too much damage."

I lowered my camera.

Though rescuers and medical teams had raced to keep her alive, they were now effectively giving up, or rather, they were moving on. The girl seemed confused—frightened and in pain. And I was filming her death. Each draw of breath seemed to bring her closer to that eventuality. It was just a matter of time. And among her last moments would be an American journalist hovering by her bed and sticking a camera in her face. That is, of course, if she even knew I was there. She could scarcely see and was hardly responding. And there was no family in sight. No parents. No aunts. No siblings. Had they died in the quake? Were they out there somewhere trying to find her, calling her name atop the rubble? There was no way to know for sure. But the nun was beside her. She would see the girl through, I hoped. My own anger at her smile had subsided. I didn't care why she was there. I was just glad someone was. And I knew I had to leave soon.

"It's OK," I whispered, leaning in. She didn't seem to hear me or rather couldn't understand. It wasn't OK, but what else does one say to a dying five-year-old girl? It was empty and meaningless, the sort of disingenuous bullshit I had so desperately tried to avoid. Years later, I would remember that haunting face through the camera's lens: those cement-dusted braids, the way she'd tilt her head skyward and look down, as if trying to peer through a small slit in her one good eye.

"Let's go," I said, finally.

We had our story. And there was nothing more to do. These doctors who had tried to save her were the instruments of Cuba's PR machine. But at least they had tried to save her. Indeed, they had been saving lives all week and were doing it much quicker than most. Their role was clear. I was now less certain about mine.

10

RISING DISSENT

When our plane landed back in Havana, there was rumbling of a different sort. Some two dozen women, clad in white and wielding long-stemmed flowers, were marching through the capital. In a country that does not tolerate political protest, theirs was a direct affront to the Castro-led government. Known as the Ladies in White, they were protesting the imprisonment of their husbands, sons, and uncles who were swept up in a 2003 Castro-led crackdown on dissent, an action referred to in the dissident community as Cuba's Black Spring. Seventy-five dissidents had been jailed after demanding democratic reforms, many of them supporters of what was known as the Varela Project, a grassroots effort to bring about constitutional reforms and new protections for human rights. Some were handed decades-long prison sentences following convictions of "U.S.-inspired subversion." But the London-based rights group Amnesty International cast doubts on many of those accusations, claiming they were "politically motivated prosecutions" and that Cuba's laws governing public disorder, contempt, dangerousness, and aggression had been in place to reinforce a status quo.[1]

In 2010, nearly seven years after their arrests, the Black Spring anniversary was again approaching. But this time, opposition forces, who remained mostly in exile in places such as the United States and Spain, had a new cause. In February 2010, just one month earlier, a hunger striker named Orlando Zapata Tamayo had died in prison, galvanizing opposition just as the anniversary approached. A plumber and mason from Banes, in the eastern province of Holguin, Tamayo was not politically active until he moved to Havana. It was through dealings with a dissident named Enri Saumell Pena, dissident sources say, that Tamayo became involved in a fledgling grassroots effort that advocated for change. But Tamayo wasn't a hard-liner, at least not comparatively, nor did he seem particularly well connected. Tamayo had never been a political firebrand and therefore wasn't an obvious springboard for change. In 2003, he had been sentenced to thirty-six years in prison after being charged with contempt, public disorder, and acts of defiance.

But unlike many other political dissidents in Tamayo's position, he was never charged with using U.S. assistance to subvert the Cuban government. Subversion was a top Castro concern, and the Cuban leader remained wary of coordinated efforts by exile groups in South Florida. Since the early 1980s, they had benefited from more than $1 billion in U.S. taxpayer funding to unseat him. As such, dissidents were often accused of being American collaborators. And in some cases, the Cuban government had evidence to prove it. In 2011, two diplomatic cables disclosed by WikiLeaks showed that the chief of the U.S. Interests Section in Havana, Jonathan Farrar, had made a series of money requests for the Ladies in White. One of the documents, dated July 31, 2008, showed $5,000 intended for the group's leader, Laura Pollan, one of Cuba's most public dissidents.[2] Whether or not those like Pollan actually conspired with U.S. officials wasn't entirely clear, but Farrar would grow frustrated. In another secret cable he delivered to Washington less than a year later, he described many of the island's dissidents as "comparatively old," out of touch, and preoccupied with U.S. funding. Farrar advocated a change in approach, noting that dissidents lacked the sort of local buy-in an effective opposition would require. "Informal polls we have carried out among visa and refugee applicants have shown virtually no awareness of dissident personalities or agendas," he wrote.[3] Cuban authorities, of course, were taking no chances and prosecuted "subversion" claims liberally. And yet, curiously, they made no such accusations against Tamayo. Still, he sat in jail, the toll of his incarceration evident in both body and mind.

After six years, the skinny plumber from eastern Cuba was cracking. According to his mother, Tamayo's back was "tattooed with blows" at the hands of overzealous guards. He was losing weight and his health was deteriorating in a maximum-security complex called Prison Kilo 7, in Camagüey Province, that rights groups had denounced the complex for its poor treatment of inmates. Inside, cells were often "damp and caused respiratory problems."[4] The U.S. House and Senate report claimed that the head of Kilo 7 had once acknowledged that at least "60 percent of the prison population was infected with tuberculosis." Meanwhile, digestive ailments and other health problems were "repeatedly ignored" by prison staff. The veracity of such reports is difficult if not impossible to determine, though former political prisoners have expressed similar grievances. Whatever the conditions Tamayo faced, on December 3, 2009, he decided he had had enough and exercised the only control he had. Tamayo simply stopped eating. Even as guards approached with food, he turned it down or let it sit uneaten. As the days turned into weeks, his eyes sunk deep into their sockets and his body grew emaciated, according to photos and interviews with family members. He was just "skin and bones," said his mother, Reina Luisa Tamayo, who confirmed that her son had given up solid foods.

The weeks multiplied and his condition worsened. Authorities then transferred him to a hospital at Combinado del Este prison in Havana. By then, journalists had taken note of the move and started counting the days. Seventy. Seventy-five. Eighty. It wasn't clear how much longer his protest could go on, but it had an effect. The foreign press, and in some ways the world, was finally paying attention, and opposition groups grew emboldened as Cuba's record on human rights was thrust into the spotlight.

But Tamayo wouldn't last. On the eighty-fifth day of his strike, his body, frail and weakened, finally gave out as his last gasps of air exited his lungs. He died at the age of forty-two, becoming the first political activist to starve himself to death on the island in nearly four decades.

"I knew Zapata and I knew he wasn't going to give in," explained Belkis Balzac Lugo, a member of the Ladies in White. His body was flown back to Holguin for burial. Tamayo was dead, but new political energy had slipped back into Havana, prompting President Raul Castro to issue a rare statement of regret.

"We took him to Cuba's best hospitals, and he died," Castro said, refuting allegations that Tamayo had been tortured. "Tortured people do not exist."[5] But opposition forces had already been roused, stoking a firestorm of criticism that prompted additional hunger strikes and protests in the Cuban capital.

Was Tamayo's death the match to a Cuban powder keg the Castros had long feared? Many Cubans I spoke with seemed either unaware or uninterested. But Raul wasn't taking any chances. Some thirty dissidents were simultaneously arrested on the same day as Raul's comments, while dozens of others were barred from leaving their home. Chepe, the economist and dissident, claimed that Tamayo's death had spawned "unprecedented commotion." And the marches grew more frequent.

It was March 18, the anniversary of Cuba's Black Spring, and we had been expecting another march. The women were gathering at the Havana home of Berta Soler, the future leader of the group. Clad in white and wielding long-stem gladiolus, they seemed to be waiting for the press corps to arrive.

And we were late. A slew of familiar faces from the Associated Press, Reuters, BBC, and the Spanish newspaper *El Pais* had all gotten there ahead of us.

"Hey, *chico!*" bellowed a long-haired, mustached cameraman named Osvaldo Angulo, who proceeded to rest a hairy forearm on my shoulder. "Here's another one."

We had all done this before, were all there to cover the same story and get the same basic sound bite from women who wouldn't march until we were all in place. These were dissidents in a land where dissent was forbidden. But it also felt a bit staged for our benefit, not to mention that the number of journalists often rivaled the number of marchers. Filming a demonstrator that didn't also include another journalist in the shot would at times prove impossible.

When they were certain the cameras were rolling, the women marched down the street, chanting "liberty" and pressing forward with flowers raised.

"Here they go," said Osvaldo, and we started walking beside them, interviewing onlookers and demonstrators, who were now bellowing chants of *"Libertad! Libertad!"* (Freedom! Freedom!)

An eerie quiet had settled over the neighborhood, broken only by the women's voices. Centro Habana usually teemed with life. But this particular street had emptied out. Two Cuban officers sat inside their police car, parked less than a block from the staging point. And for the first time I noticed how many security cameras dotted the street.

While some neighbors looked on, others retreated inside their homes, perhaps sensing what was about to come.

"Libertad! Libertad!"

Their words echoed as they wound around corners in single-file succession. As they continued, more and more people looked on. A crowd was gathering.

"Did you see those buses?" asked Osvaldo, pointing to a small grouping of blue, Chinese-made tour buses parked in a clearing. "Just wait for it."

The crowd indeed seemed to be shifting. Expressionless men in red shirts, many sporting buzz cuts, were now walking beside us—heads on a swivel—speaking in short bursts into their cell phones. The surrounding crowd had grown larger, enveloping the marchers as they moved throughout the city. More gathered. Many wore red. They were counterprotesters.

"*Libertad!*" the women continued to chant, though they seemed a bit more anxious now, looking around at the gathering crowd. The circle was closing.

Then a voice screeched above the others, piercing the low hum of the marchers. "*Mercenarios!*" a counterprotester yelled.

Clad in a denim jacket with short brown hair pulled tight, she screamed again.

It was a battle cry.

"*Gusanos!*" (Worms!)

Soon more counterprotesters would join in, closing in on the Ladies in White.

"*Mercenarios!*"

Even more men and women began shouting, their demeanor ever more menacing. One emerged and shoved Pollan. Another pushed Berta. The pair stumbled, though they kept up their chants. The crowd intensified and grew more aggressive, and yet they too seemed to be part of a managed event. Authorities knew the Ladies had planned to march. If they had wanted to stop it, they could simply have detained them before they left. But instead they allowed the march to go on, chose to let it be overrun by counterdemonstrators, who had conveniently arrived on government-run buses.

"*Mercenarios!*"

Frenzied, these counterdemonstrators surrounded the women, who were still holding their flowers. But they were now vastly outnumbered. And it was becoming clear that the group was forming a human bubble around the women, intent on blocking our view and indeed my camera's lens.

"I told you," said Osvaldo, turning to me before plunging into the mass with his camera held high. I followed, but a man quickly grabbed my camera. I pushed him off. Another grabbed my arm. No sooner had I ventured into the crowd than a hand grabbed a fistful of my shirt as a punch landed squarely against my ribs. I winced and turned, but the culprit could have been any of dozens in the crowd. A second punch landed against my kidney as a separate, disembodied hand grabbed at the camera. I again pulled it back as another pulled at my shirt.

This wasn't going to work.

I took a few steps back to regroup but then tripped over something in the road. A piece of debris? A pothole? I couldn't be sure, but I nonetheless crashed onto my side just as the broadside of another disembodied foot delivered a swift kick. It was a glancing blow but reason enough not to stay down.

"Bastard!" I growled with a half smile. I often enjoyed a good scrap and pushed in again, this time elbows out and less concerned about the shot than pummeling my way through. It worked. The human bubble had been popped, albeit briefly. Once inside, I could see the women were being smacked and shoved by the crowd.

"Long live Fidel!" one man yelled. "Get out, worms!" another screamed.

But the women refused to back down.

"What do you want?" I asked one of the women during a momentary pause in the standoff.

"We want nothing from this government!" she screamed. "For seven years they have destroyed our families," a reference to the jailed dissidents.

This back-and-forth went on for several city blocks until we reached another group of buses. This time, Interior Ministry officials in their signature olive-green uniforms were waiting and hauled the women onto buses, which then carted them off to a holding facility.

Under Fidel, this type of protest might have been met with a lengthy prison sentence. But Raul, perhaps cognizant of growing world attention, had instead adopted a different approach: catch and release. The Ladies would be returned to their homes that night or usually within a few days. Their plan, however, seemed to have worked. Networks like CNN and the BBC would be broadcasting our footage that evening, and it made for popular headlines in Miami. But to me, the government's approach didn't make much sense. Images of flower-wielding women being shoved and dragged onto buses hardly seemed like the kind of message Cuba would want to send the world, especially one from which it was now trying to attract investment. Maybe it was just habit. This is just what Cuba did and had been doing for decades: overwhelming any signs of dissent. But times were changing. Raul was known as more of a pragmatist than his older brother. He at least seemed to be open to dialogue for potential solutions to Cuba's problems. And one would come from an unlikely source.

THE CHURCH BROKER

I was never one for church. There *was* one brief stretch when I tried it, as I assume many had when questions of life, death, and the world outside first come into focus. But as a young man, the only consistent time I'd really venture to Mass was with the grandparents, for whom the ceremony seemed important. But mostly it wasn't for me. And that was something I had in common with many Cubans. The Vatican claimed the island was majority Catholic, though many also adhered to West African religions, such as Yoruba. Recent polling suggested that the number of self-identified Catholics was a far lower figure than the Vatican had assumed: only an estimated 27 percent of the country, according to Miami-based polling.[1] Half a century earlier, the state essentially sought to stamp out religious influence, confiscating church property and expelling religious workers, particularly those who had supported anti-Castro forces. Few were spared. More than 130 religious workers were expelled, while hundreds of others were sentenced to forced labor camps beside homosexuals, vagrants, and others whom authorities deemed undesirable. Even the Jesuit high school the Castro brothers had attended as boys was one of four hundred shuttered across the island. Fidel would officially turn Cuba atheist.

It wasn't until 1992, when the constitution was amended and references to atheism were replaced with secularism, that Christmas was reinstated and Communist Party members again openly practiced their faith. But religious access to state television and the administering of religious schools remained tightly restricted. During one interview around Christmastime in 2009, a woman named Isabel Fuentes, who spoke to me after erecting a modest Christmas tree replete with twinkly lights in her Vedado apartment, put it succinctly.

"Are we Communists or are we Catholics?" she asked. "I guess it's possible to be both."[2] But most still didn't attend church. Perhaps after generations of Fidel's hours-long speeches, few Cubans were in the mood for another sermon. Neither was I. Here, Christmas seemed like just another day, overcome by the Marxist-Leninist tradition that had regarded religion as the "opium of the people."[3]

Still, Communism had made its exceptions. In twentieth-century Poland, where—like Cuba—much of the population was rooted in Catholicism, authorities knew better than to deprive residents of their holiday fish and meat. Families often still gathered around a tree. And in 1973, about half of adult-age Poles reported receiving a Christmas gift. In Cuba, celebrations were more muted. But churches and their clergy still led Mass. And a few like Isabel still put up their trees. But December 25 in Havana was hardly distinguishable.

I had a call scheduled with my family, who had gathered in New Jersey for their annual holiday reunion, and headed out for my office: the only location I knew of in Havana with a strong enough internet source to carry a Skype video call. Clicking that blue-and-white S icon on my desktop, I waited. Nothing. I tried again. It rang twice, then cut out. This went on for about twenty minutes before the signal could manage to lock on. Finally, it rang clear.

"Hello?" an indistinct voice responded through crackling audio.

"Merry Christmas," I replied, as a cacophony of other familial voices poured through the laptop's speakers. I could hear Christmas music and barking dogs in the background. Both were a bit grating, but it was good to hear them. Then, into the frame shuffled my grandmother, who sported fresh beauty parlor hair but a face of fatigue. At ninety-three years old, Mary Ariosto was tired. She had lost her husband of sixty-four years, Sam, nearly a decade earlier and had never quite recovered. In her younger years, she had a vise grip of a handshake, born perhaps of decades of stirring tomato sauce and scrubbing dishes. But Mary was no housefly. During World War II, as Sam deployed to a U.S. Army artillery brigade in Europe, Mary took a job at a bomber factory in northern New Jersey, installing rivets on a production line. Seventy years later, she was staring into what must have seemed like a modern marvel—a Dell laptop that offered a video portal to Cuba. We chatted a bit and confusion seemed to wash across her face as she stared back at me. I tried to wipe it clean with promises of visiting.

"Soon," I said. "I promise." She smiled again before the connection cut out.

It was a promise I wouldn't keep. Some five months later, on May 27, I sat down in my office and opened an email from my father. My grandmother had died. She had stopped breathing at around 3:00 a.m. that morning. Stark and to the point. I reread it a few times more, digesting each word as if by rereading it, I could delay the reality of its contents.

"I haven't made funeral arrangements yet," my father wrote. "That will depend on your ability to get here."

Ultimately I wouldn't go, a decision I'd long regret.

But for now, it was still Christmas. And she was slurping back a bit of holiday punch, having just peered through the small laptop camera before the signal cut out. I tried calling back. And . . . nothing.

"Damn it," I yelled into the empty halls of my office. There was no answer. I tried connecting again, but that dreaded Apple pinwheel had already started its perpetual spin. The app was frozen. And I was alone. I felt it more in that moment than I had in months. Connectivity in Cuba, or lack thereof, only added to a now palpable sense of isolation. But for whatever reason, I wouldn't try again, instead refocusing my efforts on new stories to pursue. Though more distraction than journalism, there was a new and emerging story to be told. And the church would be at the very center of it.

With Raul now firmly ensconced in power, the archdiocese of Havana had somehow also bolstered its bargaining power. Curiously, much of that course change seemed to trace back to just one man, Jaime Ortega, who in 1966 was sent as a young priest to a military-run agricultural work camp in east-central Cuba. After toiling in the fields and under a merciless Caribbean sun, Ortega nonetheless returned to the cloth as a pastor in the sugar mill town of Jaguey Grande, Matanzas Province, just east of Havana. But the young priest had grander visions, and in 1978 he rose through church ranks to be named bishop of the island's Pinar del Rio Province. In 1981, he was named Havana's archbishop and would eventually become just the second Cuban to wear the cardinal's frock. When Pope John Paul II accepted Fidel Castro's invitation to travel to Havana, it was Jaime Ortega who would be seen at the pontiff's side.

But helping with the pope's visit didn't come without risk. A revolutionary in his own right, Pope John Paul II had a penchant for politics, and his words packed a punch, carrying influence with millions of Catholics. His actions in Poland in support of an independent workers' union just before the fall of the Berlin Wall had proven that. An adept politico who engaged in and even helped define the civil discourses of the places he visited, this pontiff was a consumate player in world affairs. Few expected a mere photo op. Human rights, to this pope, were sacrosanct. In a 1985 speech at the General Assembly of the United Nations, the pontiff expressed his concerns that "some people currently deny the universality of human rights," a speech that might as well have been directed at Fidel himself.[4] By inviting the pope to the island, the Cuban leader risked being upstaged. And if that happened, Ortega would most certainly feel the heat.

But Fidel, a practiced reader of tea leaves, had developed a knack for co-opting movements, and then adjusting. He had demonstrated an uncanny ability to remain one step ahead of those who threatened him, and appeared to adopt a strategy of sanctioning behavior he could not control, folding those forces into his own public perception of power. Though church attendance was sparse and few Cubans openly practiced their faith, religion was slowly creeping back into daily life. And it was hard to believe that Fidel, who was once baptized as a Roman Catholic and taught by Jesuits, didn't know it. Sporting a salt-and-pepper beard and having discarded his signature olive-green fatigues for a double-breasted suit, the seventy-one-year-old Cuban leader greeted the pontiff warmly at Jose Marti International Airport, clasping John Paul's hands with both of his as the pope stepped off the plane.

It was a "happy and long-awaited day," John Paul II declared. But the pope would not be sidetracked, and almost immediately called for change. "May Cuba, with all its magnificent potential, open itself up to the world, and may the world open itself up to Cuba," he said, also calling for an end of U.S. sanctions.[5] This seemed the beginning of something bigger. For starters, Christmas was reinstated as a national holiday. What's more, the church was emboldened, eventually advocating for greater human rights, freedoms, and the release of political prisoners. Ortega himself was also reinforced. His influence was on the rise.

It was early spring 2010 and I was sitting alone in my office in the Hotel Habana Libre sorting coverage plans for the week ahead as rumors swirled that Ortega was again up to something. Small protests by the Ladies in White had continued throughout Havana, each time being met by raging counterdemonstrations. Then, all of a sudden, the counterdemonstrations stopped. The Ladies were allowed to march with their flowers—uninterrupted. Ortega, with his direct line to Raul, had somehow found common ground.

"The Cuban government does not respond to external pressure," Phil Peters, of the security-focused think tank the Lexington Institute, later explained during an interview. But "the church is a Cuban institution, and it seems to have found a way to work with the government in a way that outside pressures have not."

Then, on May 21, Ortega, clad in a black frock and red cardinal's cap, emerged from a rare four-hour meeting with Raul. The old cardinal had a smile on his face and told the island's press corps of a "magnificent start" to negotiations with the Castro government. They would include a range of topics, including the release of the island's dissidents. In June, exactly that happened. After several rounds of talks, authorities decided to release two prisoners, a small first step but nonetheless evidence that Raul was not beyond reproach on human rights. He seemed willing to negotiate.

The first prisoner was an ailing man named Ariel Sigler. The second was a dissident named Darsi Ferrer, a psychologist who had helped organize a small protest at the UNESCO headquarters in Havana. He, like Zapata Tamayo, had begun a hunger strike while in prison. Now that he was out, I had to go interview him.

"Rafa!" I yelled across the room from where I could see him sipping coffee from a tiny porcelain cup and saucer. He always seemed to have one in his hand or at least nearby. "Have any idea where Darsi lives?"

"Here in Havana, I think," he responded, pressing the cup's rim back to his lips. "Dagmara probably knows."

She was indeed our Cuba oracle of sorts, connected in a way few residents were.

"Dagmara!"

"*Siiii*," she replied from the other room.

"Darsi Ferrer," I yelled. "Do you know where he lives?"

"Let me see," she said, flipping through the paper Rolodex on her desk that always seemed to have contact details for just the right person. Within the hour, she had gotten Ferrer's coordinates and permission from his wife, Yusnaymy, for us to bring our cameras.

When I arrived later that afternoon, Yusnaymy was hanging laundry on her porch in the city's dusty Santos Suarez neighborhood. Her near-platinum hair was pulled tight into a ponytail, and she was affixing wooden clothespins to a line that hung loosely between two rusted metal poles.

Darsi was inside playing with his eight-year-old son, whom he hadn't seen in more than eleven months. The boy was shy, rail thin, and skittish, even around his father—likely still processing what it meant to have him back from prison.

"Come in, David," Darsi said to me as I walked inside, looking at me briefly before again gazing down toward his son, who was now clinging to his leg. The boy refused to let Darsi out of sight. "I'm so happy to see you," he said, turning to me and shaking my hand.

Darsi had been arrested in July 2009 for illegally purchasing black-market cement to make repairs on his home. He may have been a dissident. It was possible he had connections to the exile community in South Florida, which had long endeavored to oust the Castro-led government. But it seemed clear his jail sentence was based on a trumped-up charge.

By the letter of the law, he was guilty, having purchased the bags of cement illegally. He admitted as much. But an estimated 90 percent of the population also made use of the black market. "It's where you go to buy your eggs and your milk," Cuban economist and dissident Chepe explained during an interview.[6] It wasn't just a better option; it was often the only one. I had done the same thing countless times for my own home repairs: everyone at some point had to buy their equivalent of cement from a guy who knew a guy. That also meant most everyone, at some level, could be considered a criminal and thus vulnerable to arrest, which afforded authorities a certain discretion in whom they arrested.

"It means a lot to be back with my family and friends," Ferrer told me, still swarmed by his son. He then wrapped his arm around Yusnaymy, who had wandered into the home. By now, her eyes had welled up with tears.

"The sad thing is to know about the people I left behind," he told me. Little did either of us realize that Darsi's cell mates would also soon gain their freedom. Less than a month later, Cuba's Catholic Church, working in tandem with Spanish foreign minister Miguel Angel Moratinos, announced that fifty-two political prisoners were to be released. It was the largest emancipation on the island in a decade, and Raul wasn't finished. In coming months, that number swelled to 127 prisoners, with many seeking asylum in Spain. Though Raul's government would later snare and imprison a new crop of dissidents, for now he had essentially emptied the island's jails of nearly everyone Amnesty International had categorized as a prisoner of conscience. It seemed as if Raul might be open to warmer relations with his nation's old enemies. And the Catholic Church had solidified its place as an important broker. As for Darsi, he emigrated to the United States in 2012 and gave interviews to local Florida television stations about life in Castro's prisons. Five years later, police would find his dead body in West Palm Beach. The cause of death remains unknown.

12

"THE WILD COLT OF NEW TECHNOLOGIES"

O*ye, chico,* are you connected?" a young boy yelled as I walked past a seaside stretch of Vedado, a central business district in Havana. For generations, this roadway, situated just beneath the Hotel Nacional and locally known as La Rampa, had been illuminated by hotel lamps, streetlights, and the occasional glow of a cigar. But now on the corner of Twenty-Third Avenue and Malecon, a different sort of flicker cast a faint blue light across the faces of a gaggle of young teenagers, all perched together on a concrete ledge.

"*Sí!*" the boy exclaimed. "Finally!"

It was a cell phone. And incredibly, it was connected to the internet. The boys had logged on to a Wi-Fi hot spot and were looking down, their brains awaiting a fresh rush of dopamine as they scrolled.

To residents of almost anywhere but Cuba, this would seem quite unremarkable. But here, where information is tightly controlled and private media is all but banned, it felt groundbreaking. The boys had tapped into a once-rare portal linking Cuba to the outside world, scratching off a Wi-Fi card to reveal an impossibly long passcode before logging on to a signal that by most foreign standards would feel maddeningly slow.

"Give it to me!" yelled another boy, grabbing the phone from his outstretched hand. Once he had it, they gathered again, heads bowed, eyes fixed on the glossy screen. For years, La Rampa had been a place to stroll beyond the Malecon, where packs of teenagers congregated, often with a guitar and a bottle of rum between them. But the fingers that once picked and danced over nylon strings now binged over crystal displays and Gorilla Glass, faces aglow. Precious information from news sites, blogs, and social media slipped in through devices they could now stuff in their pockets. Though their phones were never there long. Click. Scroll. Refresh. A flood of neurotransmitters carried urgent messages to the brain, rewarding action and compelling more. Fresh hits for addicts in the making. Compared to much of the rest of the world, Cubans had some catching up to do. Of course, it wasn't just consumption. For those with an aunt in New Jersey or a brother in South Florida from whom remittances regularly flowed, this new connectedness also allowed for a Skype call or a WhatsApp text that could make those miles of separation disappear, if only for a moment.

But fiber-optic pipelines also brought much of the rest of the internet, despite the censors. Out there, cyberbullies and bots mixed with pictures of food and holiday travel, an algorithm-fueled dross that could polarize, amplify, and anesthetize. Cuba had been on a delay, largely insulated from the fire hose of the optimized addiction that allowed YouTube stars, cat videos, hate speech, and fake news to spread. And yet I wondered as I walked past those boys, with their heads bowed, if all that was coming to an end.

They didn't notice me, so absorbed were they in the screen's changing pages. Soon each boy would have his own phone, refreshing, clicking, and scrolling his way into retreat. Though sites like Twitter and Facebook remained restricted, the world from which Cuba had long been shielded had broken through. At first, it was agonizingly slow, a gradual dribble that began during the late 1990s. Officials said the internet was limited largely as a result of the U.S. trade embargo, which deprived the island's infrastructure of the cash and technology it needed. But that wasn't the only reason. Cuba also liked its control. Internet and mobile charges were also a source of revenue. And ETECSA—the island's telecommunications monopoly—wasn't about to let that go. But the internet was also a potentially galvanizing force. Dissident voices and calls for change could be amplified. It was uncharted territory. Yet that was also changing. The government had pledged to help connect half the country by 2020. And the island was already abuzz. In 2016, an estimated one in four Cubans could get online, while 37 percent were online weekly.[1] Only a few years earlier that figure hovered closer to 5 percent. But for many, it was still too expensive. More than a hundred Wi-Fi spots had been set up across the city, yet prices were exorbitant: an hour of service cost up to the equivalent of a third of a month's salary.

Still, a rising online tide had over time reached Cuban shores. All that was needed was a work-around. Through a patchwork of smuggled-in satellite dishes, a ramshackle network of homegrown, file-sharing entrepreneurs had emerged. Everything from HBO series to Mexican telenovelas to BBC documentaries, news magazines, apps, and music could be downloaded to hard drives and delivered to thousands of Cuban clients, often just a few days after they were released. The appetite was there. Clandestine networks were being forged in underground markets to satisfy it. And for those bold enough, there was money to be made.

It was against that backdrop that I met Dany Cabrera Garcia. A skinny twenty-six-year-old with a skater's demeanor, Dany looked far younger than his age and sported the kind of laid-back persona one might expect from a hipster clerk working at some East Village guitar shop—certainly not a top capo of a pirated media operation. But by many accounts, that's exactly who he was. Dany was a principal dealer in charge of Cuba's El Paquete Semenal, or the Weekly Package—a terabyte of bootlegged digital media distributed each week by a brazen group of internet pioneers who risked imprisonment by circumventing Cuba's media blockade. And they made a relative killing while doing it.

"It's our Netflix," young film school graduate Giselle García Castro told me. "Everyone gets the Weekly Package."

The film school was a place many of us looked to find local producers. And Giselle had grown accustomed to helping *yumas* capture the "Cuba story" for a week or two before they returned to their edit suites in Miami, Los Angeles, and New York, wielding the sort of cocktail banter that could impress the casually curious. She had seen more than a few of us wade through her country in a rum-soaked haze, happy in our ignorance, and sported the expression of a woman unimpressed. Though she seemed content to play the part of "resolver" to our stories—connecting journalists and filmmakers with those who might tell the tale—she also had her own ideas.

"Dany is a guy you should meet," she told me.

As the rest of the world dove into the information age, an alternative IT revolution had taken hold in Cuba. And Dany Cabrera Garcia, known by the moniker Dany Paquete, was at the center of it. Inside his Havana apartment, he collected and curated the world's latest media, downloaded from an illegal satellite dish or delivered to him on hard drives: one for movies, one for newscasts, and one for music. His network spiderwebbed across Cuba and into Miami. Once the material was collated, Dany sent his team into neighborhoods across the island, brokering deals in Havana and in the more distant Holguin, Camagüey, and Guantanamo Provinces, where it was sold and resold to smaller dealers and distributors. The way it was distributed was simple. Once a week, one of his couriers showed up at predetermined homes across the country, offering up a tray of illicit media options to customers at varying prices.

A terabyte of the latest media cost about $17 and was usually reserved for those interested in resale. Older media started at around $2 per package, depending on what was included. It essentially created two separate markets for pirated media, right under the nose of Cuban authorities.

"How do you get away with this?" I asked him.

"Well, there's no pornography or anything political or against the Revolution," he said. Dany seemed intent on assuring me that there was nothing he was doing that authorities might consider antigovernment, or anti-Castro.

"Hold on," I said, interrupting his explanation. "The government knows?"

He smiled a sheepish grin and shifted his hands in his pockets. "They're some of my best clients."

I was stunned. But I shouldn't have been. We had met on a public street in Centro Habana, where eyes were everywhere. Closed-circuit cameras dotted the buildings. Onlookers and informants scattered about side streets, leaving little chance that authorities were in the dark about the identity of Dany and his suppliers. For a country that had gotten so proficient at surveillance that it exported its services to other countries (namely Venezuela), the idea that Dany had been operating as a clandestine underground kingpin outside government monitors now seemed almost laughable. He existed because the country's powerful Interior Ministry had allowed him to. Cubans desperately wanted to be informed and entertained like everyone else, and state officials were media hungry too. Many wanted to see the latest episode of *Game of Thrones* or *Scandal* and seemed to be offering people like Dany a pass—as long as their product wasn't critical of Cuba. It was pure conjecture. But it made sense and was probably why his first comment to me had to do with what the Weekly Package *didn't* include. "No pornography or anything political or against the Revolution," he had said of his weekly deliveries. He wanted to make sure that was clear.

The rest "is just normal," Dany added, adjusting his baggy shirt before sitting down for a Bucanero. He seemed totally relaxed. His downloaded movies, documentaries, and telenovelas were all circulating, which was more than enough to get him locked up. Yet he seemed wholly unconcerned—confident, perhaps, that this sort of service had become too valuable. The Weekly Package was a window into the outside world, part of an offline Cuban internet that could deliver everything from the most recent iPhone apps to Showtime's latest miniseries. And virtually everyone seemed in on it.

Meanwhile, other tech-savvy Cubans were devising an internet of their own, stringing broadband cables between apartment buildings and connecting thousands of laptops with hundreds—if not thousands—of concealed Wi-Fi antennas across neighborhoods. The system was called SNET, or Streetnet, and allowed for a file-sharing network that mimicked the World Wide Web and could quickly spread information Cuban censors sought to suppress. It was a testament to Cuban ingenuity and the growth of its underground media, a stark contrast to the crawling internet browsing and download speeds that were officially sanctioned and censored. In 2013, an undersea fiber-optic cable strung between Venezuela and Cuba had quietly become operational, offering download speeds authorities claimed were three thousand times faster than what the island had been accustomed to, replacing costly satellite uplinks from countries such as Chile and Canada. And yet the benefits of the ALBA-1 cable remained largely restricted to official intranet use—government offices and censored hot spots—as authorities remained wary of the potentially destabilizing and mobilizing effects of social media.

Following a visit to Havana in 2014, Google executive chairman Eric Schmidt described the island's internet as "trapped in the 1990s," reliant on poor infrastructure and dominated by Chinese-made equipment. "If you wish to modernize," wrote Schmidt in a column posted by Google, "the best way to do this is to empower the citizens with smart phones and encourage freedom of expression."[2] He then advocated putting "information tools into the hands of Cubans directly." But authorities didn't seem all that eager for it. In 2010, amidst a wave of social media–inspired, prodemocracy uprisings across the Middle East and North Africa, Havana saw the Arab Spring and grew wary of a Cuban Autumn. But the X factor in Cuba was the internet, or lack thereof. It was a stopgap that protected Cuban authorities. So the kind of liberalization that Schmidt was calling for seemed unlikely. For residents, government television or state-run publications like *Granma*—Cuba's official newspaper, consisting of eight thin pages of a soft-gray recycled paper—left much to be desired.

In fact, during one of the island's many shortages, when the hunt for toilet paper reached a fever pitch, *Granma* was at times a secondary option. (It was briefly made of recycled sugarcane, but the new material quickly evoked complaints with its harder, stiffer feel.) "You can't always find it," our office housekeeper once told me of the island's toilet paper shortages and the use of a *Granma* replacement. During moments of crisis, Cubans were literally wiping their asses with the official word of the government. Safe to say, it wasn't exactly a scintillating read. The Weekly Package was a welcome reprieve.

13

LEFT BEHIND

Cuba is not Havana. I was reminded of that whenever I left for the provinces, where machete-slinging tobacco cutters in Pinar del Río and oxen-driven farmers in Camagüey seemed more than a world away. Out here, the older, more muted voices of those who had survived and grown accustomed to Castro's top-down approach now worried about another revolution that this time might leave them even further behind. I had traveled out to Matanzas, on Cuba's southern coast, to meet an old farmer named Rigoberto Campos who I had been told also shared that sentiment.

When I arrived, he was standing in his wooded yard, where a few pigs and chickens rooted in the dirt. His ruddy demeanor and callused handshake hinted at a man who'd rather be tilling his field and slugging his rum than having a camera shoved in his face. But he nonetheless welcomed me in. "Come in, come in," he grumbled, pushing open the wire fence that framed his little farm.

At just over five feet tall—shirtless and grimacing—Rigoberto hardly had the look of a man at the crossroads of history. But by many accounts, that's exactly who he was. A half a century earlier,

in April 1961, more than 1,400 CIA-trained paramilitaries landed
at the beachhead just a few miles down the road. Sharp corals filled
the jagged coastline of the Bay of Pigs, with only brief stretches of
sandy beach, which the landing crafts of those U.S.-trained forces
had hoped to use to begin the overthrow of the Castro regime. They
had sought to kick-start a counterrevolution by slipping into the
countryside and tapping into popular discontent, much like Fidel had
done just a few years earlier. But the surrounding thicket of forests
and swamps would prove impassable to an exile army unfamiliar
with the terrain, and scores perished on its beaches and in the surrounding swamps, the largest swath of wetlands in the Caribbean.
But that's only part of the reason it failed.

By most accounts, the invasion was the worst-kept secret in Cuba.
Soviet intelligence had learned of it and tipped off their counterparts
in Havana, which had already secretly deployed agents within the
ranks of the invading force. President John F. Kennedy inherited the
plan from Dwight D. Eisenhower as public pressures mounted over
fears of Soviet influence and expansionism, and he decided to carry
it out. But Kennedy remained adamant that the United States could
ill afford to be seen as directly involved in the effort. As such, he
restricted air support and moved the location of the attack from Trinidad to the Bay of Pigs, in part to allow for a more remote and theo-
retically more secretive landing. But the decision would prove costly.
Castro knew the region and enjoyed local support there, and he
benefited from a bevy of intelligence about the details of the landing.
When it finally arrived, the CIA-trained force was routed, picked
off on the beaches and in the surrounding wetlands by Cuban infantry and artillerymen, and strafed by Cuban fighter jets largely
unencumbered by the specter of American airpower. Its failure proved
a turning point, helping to consolidate the Revolution by rallying
Cubans behind its Castro government, escalating tensions between
Washington and Moscow, and thrusting Havana further into the
Soviet orbit.

Rigoberto had been there for it all.

"I was a coward," he recalled, having taken shelter from the invading force and offering instead to take the women and children to safety.[1] When the shooting stopped, what was left of the invasion force had been scattered, hundreds taking refuge in the adjacent swamps. Rigoberto had grown up in those swamps, and though loyal to the government, he believed the invaders would die if left to their own devices. And so Rigoberto ventured into the wetlands and led them out, where they were arrested and later swapped in a protracted negotiation with the United States for $53 million in medical and food assistance. For his deeds, Rigoberto received a government commendation. But he would soon be forgotten, and resumed his work at his shack on the edge of the swamp.

"I was born two kilometers away from this spot," he said, his sinewy muscles and sunbaked skin a physical testament to what it took to survive. If the Communist stereotype was that of a lethargic bureaucrat, Rigoberto was Cuba's counterpoint. "You have to work here," he said, his hands scratching against mine as we shook. Though rail thin, his body was still strong, despite the gray wisps that covered it. And he could do something most Cubans couldn't: recall a time before Fidel.

"I started working at eleven years old," he said, resting his arm at his side. But as the years elapsed and assistance from the state gradually diminished, he would grow apprehensive about the changes in subsidies and social services as the state began a pivot toward market-based reforms. "At the beginning it was OK," he said. "But right now, we're down to the lowest," a reference to the dwindling food subsidy. His country had never quite been able to feed itself, relying on foreign food imports to supply as much as 80 percent of its needs. People like Rigoberto had always leaned on a combination of price controls, government rations, and a small private supply of food he was allowed to grow for himself. Now, as the country faced a cash crunch and a reduction of subsidies, at least two kinds of people seemed destined to be left behind. The first were those like Rigoberto, who struggled to adapt. The others lacked help, through remittances, from abroad. Sometimes they were one and the same. But the divide often seemed to break down along racial lines. Just as Cuba is not Havana, sometimes Havana is not even Havana. A man named Alberto Maricosa whom I'd meet back in the capital would explain.

With a bald head and a toothy grin, Alberto was a *bicitaxi* driver and a janitor at the Calixto Garcia Hospital in the Cuban capital. And he was terribly skinny. His clothes accentuated that fact. They hung on him like they would a closet hanger. As a black man, Alberto remained statistically less likely to benefit from the "structural and conceptual reforms" Raul Castro had pursued, which offered expanded private farming and self-employment while legalizing home and car sales. Much of that relied on start-up capital from abroad, namely South Florida, where some 85 percent of Cuban Americans identified as white.[2]

Though Cuba's socialized structure had allowed for emerging classes of black professionals and politicians, they often lacked access to the kind of family money crucial to business development. In 2018, an estimated 80 percent of Cuba's private restaurants leaned on funding from abroad, and an estimated 81 percent of Cuban business owners were white.

"You're a North American?" Alberto asked me.

"Yes," I said. "A *yuma*."

He laughed a little, before straightening his posture. "Why are you here?"

"I live here," I replied.

"But you're American?" he added, cocking his head.

"It's complicated."

"Oh, *caballero*," he replied, resting his hands across the *bicitaxi*. "Everything here is complicated."

"Well, I'm a journalist," I replied.

"I see," he said. The light in his face seemed to dim at my response, and his shoulders sagged a bit lower. At fifty-one years old, Alberto had been sweeping floors at the Calixto for the past two decades. I had met him on one of Old Havana's cobblestone side streets when he offered me a ride. I obliged, hoping for an interview. And as we spoke, he seemed to reconsider. Tension thickened. He grew quiet for what seemed like minutes before speaking again.

"My brother," he murmured.

"What about him?" I replied.

He remained quiet for a moment more and pulled the *bicitaxi* off to the side. Then, lifting his head, Alberto leaned in and whispered, "I'll show you."

Cuba's searing sun had just crested above the city. Noon in Havana was usually a time for taking refuge. Women sported mesh crop tops and skintight jeans, clip-clopping their way down boulevards, while men peeled up the edges of their T-shirts and rested them atop their tanned, round bellies to allow cooler air to slip in. On the side streets, turn-of-the-century buildings offered shade. Side streets were cooler and teemed with life.

"*Oye, caballero.* It's right up here. Come with me," he said, dipping into the crowd.

I followed. Past pushcart vendors and down cobblestone streets, I pursued Alberto until we reached a crumbling gray building nestled in the heart of Old Havana. Its concrete façade bore all the hallmarks of Spanish colonial architecture, mixed with Moorish blue tile. Flecks of metal were peeling off a rusting wrought-iron door that disappeared beneath Alberto's hand as he pushed it back. He motioned for me to come inside.

"*Venga,*" he said, in a voice just above a whisper. And with that he disappeared into the darkness. Crossing from a sun-soaked street into a darkened room without windows or electricity, it took a few moments for my eyes to adjust. When they did, an old woman appeared. She was resting on a faded blue couch at the end of the foyer, her shock of white hair a stark contrast to her dark and wrinkled skin.

"Esta es mi mamá," Alberto said, his back stiffening with a measure of pride as he introduced the ninety-two-year-old woman.

Alberto's words barely seemed to register. His mother rested her chin on her hand and stared off in another direction.

"Don't mind her," he said, grabbing my shoulder. "Come this way."

We pressed farther into the house. With my eyes now dilated, I began to make out subtle details inside their cinder-block home. There were holes everywhere, poorly papered over with ill-fitting pieces of tin, plywood, and cardboard. The ceiling had more gaping holes than it seemed possible to have and still stay aloft. And during hurricane season, they became brutally apparent. "The whole place floods when the rain comes," he said, lifting his eyes with the sort of quiet resignation one might expect of a man with few options.

"Is this what you wanted to show me?" I asked.

"No. There." Alberto pointed, motioning to a small wooden door that hung on a metal hinge near the back of the foyer.

The hinge creaked as I pushed it open. Inside, there were two more people. Both were asleep. To the left lay Alberto's one-year-old daughter. Flies buzzed around her head as she lay sprawled out on a makeshift cot, seemingly impervious to the winged creatures that occasionally landed on her bare skin. One landed on her face. No response. Just the steady rise and fall of her chest against a bare mattress.

"Please be quiet," he said.

To the right lay Alberto's brother, Adolfo. "He's why I brought you here," Alberto whispered, careful not to wake either of them.

Adolfo looked like he was in his late forties: a large man with looming features, had he been standing upright. But Adolfo was instead curled in the fetal position. Wrapped in a single sheet, he barely breathed. He barely moved, save for the occasional shift of his leg, burrowing beneath the sheet's cover.

"He's diabetic," Alberto explained, pointing to Adolfo's ankles, which had swollen to at least three times their normal size. His skin was discolored, a mix of reds and greens, and it looked infected, with collecting fluids that leaked and pussed in open crevices. While medical care remained free in Cuba, medication often had to be purchased. And though subsidized, pharmacy shelves were often bare.

"The doctor says we're going to have to amputate," Alberto explained, still whispering.

The irony was that Cuba's thriving biotech sector had already developed advances in combating the effects of diabetes that much of the rest of the world coveted. Heberprot-P, one of Cuba's success stories, accelerates "healing of deep and complex ulcers, both ischemic and neuropathic, and reduces diabetes-related amputations."[3] Its success rate surpassed 80 percent in treating diabetic foot ulcers, and more than seventy thousand Cubans had received it. But like many things, it could also run in short supply. The island imported an estimated 85 percent of what its pharma sector needed to produce its lifesaving drugs, and a growing liquidity crisis reduced the island's ability to import.[4]

"Come on," Alberto whispered. "Let's let him sleep."

When we emerged and the bedroom door was pushed gently shut, Alberto pulled up a metal chair and sat down, offering for me to do the same. His head hung low. "We're in the lower class, you understand?" Alberto said, his eyebrows raised and face now drooping. "On the outside, everything is normal," he added. It was an apparent nod to his country's system of free education and health care, which remained a constitutionally protected right. Article 50 stipulated that there should be "no sick person who does not receive medical attention," and all Cubans were entitled to medical care provided by the state without regard to "color of skin, gender, religious belief, national origin and any distinction harmful to the dignity of man." But in practice, it was more complicated.

"On the inside, there are social distinctions," said Alberto.

"What do you mean?" I asked.

"White people, like you," he said, pointing to the skin on my arm. "We [black Cubans] can't afford it." There was a matter-of-factness to his words. To people like Alberto, I was not only a *yuma* but also a white man. I bore similarities to other white Cubans who enjoyed the benefits of their skin color. *Like you,* he had said. There was no distinction.

Though Fidel Castro had all but declared Cuba a postracial society following his 1959 revolution—integrating schools and neighborhoods, launching literacy campaigns, and growing the numbers of black teachers and of black Cubans in government—nearly 70 percent of the island's civic leadership identified as white, despite the fact that two-thirds of the population identified as black or mixed race. And the disparities seemed to be worsening. In a 2007 report authored by Cuban economist Esteban Morales Dominguez, researchers found that the island's black population had experienced growing impoverishment over the previous quarter century, as highly skilled jobs went to lighter-skinned Cubans. Roughly 72 percent of Cuba's scientists and technicians were considered white, while 98 percent of privately owned land was in white hands. Meanwhile, blacks maintained only 5 percent of interests in state cooperatives, while nearly two-thirds of blacks pointed to racial discrimination as a reason for their lack of opportunities in both the business community and in hiring/promotion practices, the study found. Years later under the post-Castro government of President Miguel Díaz-Canel, the state would seek to address the underrepresentation, electing black representatives for half of the six vice presidents to the presiding Council of State. Yet as new money funneled in, Cuba's egalitarian experiment seemed to be devolving into a society of haves and have-nots, which commonly broke down along racial lines.

For those like Alberto, that difference manifested beyond the workplace. "No one in Miami is sending *me* money," he told me. As new market forces converged on the island, a new and contrasting reality was emerging. Lighter-skinned Cubans were leveraging connections from abroad, and the money stream was unequal.

"More coffee?" he asked, affixing a small, silver-colored pot atop a propane flame. Shards of sunlight pouring through gaping slits in the roof cast an uneven glow across his face.

"Yes, please," I said, a bit louder than anticipated.

Alberto pressed a finger to his mouth, imploring me to keep my voice low as we spoke. "Quiet," he scolded. His brother and daughter were still asleep.

I nodded, unsure of what to say next. But Alberto would fill the momentary gap. He walked back with a small tin and half filled it with a powdery mix of coffee beans. The aroma quickly filled the room, and steaming curls twisted out of the cup as he sat down and offered it to me.

"David," Alberto said. "This is Cuba."

"I know," I replied, finishing my coffee.

We shook hands before parting ways, reopening the rusted iron door that led back into Old Havana's sun-soaked hive. As Cuba reformed and opened new doors to private business, people like Alberto and Rigoberto seemed destined to struggle. And yet he still had offered me his coffee.

14

A WAY OUT

Around the same time that Dany was building his media empire and Alberto was searching for more lucrative work, my old friend Antonina was looking for a way out. At twenty-five years old, she was a university graduate who had been working at La Fontana, my habitual haunt, on and off for the past six years. And she was bored. Having seen a steady stream of Havana's elite drift in and out of that underground bar in Miramar, she had little to show for it. People like Ricardo Alarcon and Colonel Alejandro Castro Espín were among her regulars, along with a regular crop of Miami businessmen and real estate developers. For them, La Fontana was an escape. For her, it had become a bit staid.

"In reality, there's just nothing for me here," she told me one evening.

"Then what?" I asked.

"*Yumalandia.*"

"The U.S.?"

"Why not?" she replied.

"The trip isn't like before," I said, a reference to changing migration patterns that now favored a Mexico border crossing, rather than the *balsero* (rafter) exodus across the Florida Strait of the 1990s. Whereas the strait proved more perilous, heading for Texas was far more complicated.

"I know," she answered. "But everyone wants to leave."

Obviously, that wasn't true. But enough of them did to make a statistical impact. In fact, the island's median age had risen to thirty-nine from thirty-six over the past decade as thousands, frustrated by a stagnant economy and few opportunities, followed in the path of the some 1.5 million exiles before them. Antonina was smart and curious, and Cuba suddenly seemed too small for her. Even though she had earned a degree, her most lucrative job had been refilling mojitos and offering up *tostones* to customers like me. She aspired to more. And with an aunt already in Miami, the prospect of more lucrative days in America—a wish not so subtly etched into her subconscious—was beckoning.

"Just picture, your whole life, people always tell you that there's a better place just over there," she explained, motioning with her hand as if the United States were only a few blocks down the road in a wealthier neighborhood. "I had to see for myself."

America, it seemed, was more idea than place. Though she had saved just enough money for the journey, she still had to wait. Most Cubans simply couldn't leave. Antonina had yet to secure the requisite visa, despite applying in 2010 and having waited for nearly three years. But that was about to change. And like most changes on the island, it all seemed to start with Raul.

It was the dawn of 2013, and a barrier had broken. Raul's rubber-stamp legislature had enacted a new law that on January 14 rendered the hated Cuban exit visa obsolete. For generations, this small paper card for which Antonina had so desperately waited determined which Cubans could leave the island and which couldn't.[1] But now it was gone: a major reversal of a 1961 restriction that Raul's elder brother, Fidel, had put in place to stem Cuba's "brain drain" after the Revolution. The new law meant (most) Cubans no longer had to ask permission to leave.

"These measures are truly substantial and profound," Colonel Lamberto Fraga, Cuba's deputy chief of immigration, told reporters in Havana.

The policy also extended the time citizens could remain outside the country without forfeiting their Cuban residency from eleven to twenty-four months. Cuban law permitted only *residents* to buy homes and invest in private businesses, even though many did so under the table. But as the economy stumbled and residents grew dissatisfied, Raul was not only making it easier for them to leave, he was also making the prospect of being Cuban in America more attractive.

However, there were other hurdles, namely the U.S. Antonina had applied for a visa directly with the U.S. Interests Section in Havana, waited three years, and was ultimately denied. And she didn't want to go through that again. So now the plan was to head west, travel to Mexico, and cross the border into the United States. But the process for securing a Mexico entry visa was also time-consuming and could again end in rejection. So she did what many Cubans had done. She bribed.

"I think it was two hundred dollars," Antonina told me. She shifted on the couch beside her soon-to-be husband, Carlito, who seemed eager to chime in.

"Listen," he said. "You have to understand. In Cuba, everything is corrupt. They sell an image of a certain life to the world. But it's a lie. There's cocaine. There's prostitution. There's corruption. There's everything." Then, he said something that stuck out. "It's a country, just like other countries."

That hadn't been my impression.

Compared to neighboring countries such as Mexico or Haiti, where small bribes at police checkpoints were common and a bit of "grease" was often necessary for even the most basic of transactions,

Cuba seemed comparably strict. In 2016, Transparency International ranked the island 60 out of 177 countries in its Corruption Perceptions Index, tied with Italy and relatively lower than much of the region.

But Carlito was telling me not to believe the hype. Meanwhile, Cuba's own concept of corruption was being challenged from within. Under Fidel, corruption could be defined along its traditional meaning or simply indicate a falling out of favor with the boss. But Raul publicly focused on structural reform, and pledged to combat corruption and return his country to "economic discipline." "All this [corruption] takes place right in front of our noses without inciting public condemnation and confrontation," Raul told parliament in July 2013 at its twice-yearly session. The younger Castro brother seemed to be making tackling corruption a priority.

But for those like Carlito and Antonina, a corrupt system this time worked in their favor. The couple had planned to emigrate with Carlito's parents, and yet they couldn't all get Mexican visas. So instead, the family had taken a more perilous route, flying south to Ecuador, which in 2014 did not require entry visas from Cubans. He and Antonina had planned to reunite in Mexico before making the long trek north to fulfill their American dreams. Carlito and his parents had the longer journey, so they would leave first, stuffing their pockets and suitcases with the equivalent of $3,000—earned from years of saving and the sale of their house. They then booked a $700 flight to Quito, Ecuador, and departed for Jose Marti International Airport in Havana with the hopes of soon reuniting with Antonina.

As it was for some forty-one thousand other Cubans that year, the Andean nation was a first step. For Carlito and his parents, it was an embarkation point for a treacherous five-thousand-mile trek north through Central America and across Mexico to the U.S. border. Cubans could simply—and legally—walk across it if they could get there. You can have it if you can reach it, Uncle Sam seemed to be saying. But he wouldn't say it for much longer. In 2017, the United

States would rescind the so-called wet-foot-dry-foot policy, leaving thousands in limbo across the region. But in 2014 a window to America was still open, and both Antonina and Carlito were determined to use it. Like many Cubans, he and his parents would enter the country on a commercial flight. At this point, some Cubans had stayed in Ecuador, finding odd jobs and blending into Ecuadorian society (often earning ten times what they could in Cuba); others filled their suitcases with trendy new clothes and electronics and returned, selling the coveted items on the island's black market.

Carlito, however, wasn't going back. Not now. "America or die," he said, with a glimmer in his eye. There was an earnestness in the way he spoke. "Not just the U.S.," he told me. "New York."

Still, the route was rife with hazards, and Carlito knew he had to move quickly. It was December 2014. And as Cuba and the United States normalized relations, rumors were spreading that the Cold War–era Cuban Adjustment Act, which allowed Cubans who arrived in the United States without a visa to become permanent residents, would soon disappear.

But Carlito also knew the dangers. From Ecuador, it was a journey across seven countries through hostile terrain controlled by soldiers, police, paramilitary groups, drug cartels, indigenous tribes, and armed gangs, all of whom were jostling for control. The route typically began in Quito and meandered north to the Colombian cities of Ipiales, Cali, and Medellín, where *coyotes* (people smugglers) charged up to $15,000 per trip and offered no guarantees of safe passage.

Those fortunate enough to make it through those initial checkpoints and patrols faced an even more perilous trek as they reached South America's northern tip. There, a no-man's-land lay between Colombia and Panama: sixty-six miles of roadless jungle and swampland bottlenecked into Panama in a region known as the Darien Gap. Just months before accepting my Cuba assignment in 2009, I had ventured into Darien's jungles to write a feature story about the region. And even with an experienced Embera tribesman as my guide, its crocodile waters and mosquito-infested swamps obstructed our journey while overgrown bramble obscured any sense of a trail. It was easy to get lost in a corridor known for its drug smugglers, Colombian rebel groups, indigenous tribes, and northbound migrants, many of whom weren't even from Latin America. Between 2015 and 2016, border guards reported picking up more than 2,000 Indians, 1,700 Chinese, and 1,600 Romanians, many harboring their own American dreams. Darien was indeed a lawless choke point for the undocumented. And it was fraught with peril.

But this was the way north.

Once in Quito, Carlito inquired about a *coyote* who might guide them to the U.S. border. But the numbers of Cuban migrants had swelled in Ecuador, and Colombian border guards had stepped up their own security across the country's frontier. Prospects for an illicit overland journey seemed to be shrinking. Even if Carlito's family could make it through Darien, their trek would be far from over. Nicaraguan soldiers had beefed up roadblocks, setting border checkpoints, and in some cases employing tear gas and batons to force back transiting Cuban migrants. Nicaraguan president Daniel Ortega's Sandinista administration had publicly denounced these travelers. A Central American Socialist whose country had benefited from Cuban-supported education and health care programs, he considered the refugees traitors to his ally, Cuba. Nicaragua was part of a regional alliance bent on opposing U.S. policy. Called ALBA, or more formally the Bolivarian Alternative for the Americas, its members included Cuba, Venezuela, and Bolivia, and Ortega had been pressuring Washington to end its Cuban refugee policy that encouraged dangerous cross-border migrations like the one Carlito had embarked on.

"The situation should be resolved not by Central America but by the United States," Nicaraguan deputy foreign minister Denis Moncada said in December 2015. "[The United States] is the one that has prompted many Cubans to want to try to get to it." Turns out, the Obama administration may indeed have been listening, and would soon change a 1995 revision of the Cuban Adjustment Act that had all but assured Cubans of an eventual path to citizenship should they reach U.S. soil. The clock was ticking. Carlito and Antonina would have to reach the border soon—before that preferential treatment for Cubans ended. Their permanent U.S. residency status hung in the balance.

But the obstacles were daunting. Six more countries lay in their path. Even if they made it, the journey could take months. Sometimes longer. And time was against them.

Sensing the shift, as many did, Carlito and his parents determined to find another way and instead headed for the Quito airport. Peeling back a thick stack of hundreds—all that was left after the sale of his parents' home—the slick-haired twenty-six-year-old sought to muster up the confidence he needed. Again, it was a bribe that would get them through. But unlike Havana, Quito was unfamiliar terrain.

"Discúlpeme, caballero," Carlito said in a hushed tone to an official-looking man just beyond the departures kiosk. There, he'd begin the to-and-fro negotiation that invariably accompanies a payoff. Carlito had done it before. And though nervous, here at Mariscal Sucre International Airport in Quito, it seemed less of a risk. Perhaps it was because he had already risked so much to get to this moment: His family's home had been sold. Antonina was soon scheduled to land in Mexico. And America's borders were thought to be closing. To stop now seemed inconceivable.

It worked. Patting Carlito's stack of hundreds, the agent accepted the deal and in exchange procured three phony Costa Rican passports for his family. (Costa Rica was a country from which Mexico did not require a visa.) There would be no rafting across the Florida Strait, nor an epic journey through a roadless Panamanian rain forest. Carlito had found a way to get to Antonina by simply

stepping on a Mexico-bound airplane. And together they had found
a way to reach the United States. She was due to arrive just a month
later.

Meanwhile, back in Havana, Antonina was finally geared up to
head west. She later told me she was scared. It was her first time off
the island. So when that afternoon flight she'd anticipated finally
touched down at Cancun International Airport, a trembling also
bubbled up inside her that she tried to force down. Crossing beneath
a sign that read MIGRACIÓN, Antonina entered a maze of ropes that
boxed in hundreds of other travelers. After waiting with the others
in line, she eventually pulled her luggage up to the customs kiosk,
where a serious-looking man with official-looking patches requested
her passport.

"Why are you traveling to Mexico?" he asked.

She told him about Carlito.

"What's his address?" he asked.

She didn't know.

"What's his phone number then?" the agent persisted.

Again, Antonina didn't know. The only number she had was his
old Cuban cell, which had been rendered useless since Carlito left
Havana. In fact, the pair had only sporadically talked since he left,
conversing only when each could find Wi-Fi. They had planned
to meet at the airport. She hadn't counted on needing that information. As a result, Antonina knew little about where she was going.

"You don't know?" he asked. It all was a bit foreign, a bright-light
whirl for a Cuban woman who had never seen anything but Cuba.
She knew she was undergoing the biggest risk of her life: she had
fibbed to get to Mexico and put her trust in a man she loved. But
she also knew his judgment was clouded by American dreams. They
had both wanted to leave Cuba. But Carlito wanted it more. And
now there was no going back.

After a few moments of flipping through her passport, the agent
finally looked up at her.

"Come with me," he said, motioning her to follow him to a small room adjacent to the processing area. Antonina obliged, gathering her luggage. "Please, sit down," the agent said, gesturing toward a chair. And with that, he left, shutting the door behind him and leaving her alone. She checked her phone. No service. The minutes ticked by. And her anxiety grew. What had she gotten herself into? Would she be sent back to Cuba? The questions rotated in her mind like some sort of cruel carousel. All she could do was wait.

Meanwhile, Carlito also waited. His parents had departed for the United States already. But he remained, standing at the arrivals terminal at Cancun International Airport, expecting his soon-to-be-wife to emerge. She was late. Antonina assumed he was there, but she had no way to signal to him what was happening.

Just then, the office door creaked open, slowly at first and then forcefully, with the customary vigor of an officer who'd made the same deliberative move countless times before.

"*Venga,*" he commanded, this time motioning for her to leave.

Unsure of herself, Antonina slowly gathered her things and walked toward the door, picking up speed as they walked. And that was it. As suddenly as she had been escorted to the room, Antonina was back out in the *migración* area being processed like any other traveler. Within moments, her documents had been swiped through, and she stepped into her new life, leaving Cuba and entering Mexico's unknown. Neon signs guided the way, replete with bright lights, pink faces, cargo shorts, baseball caps, and a fluttery Spanish markedly different from Havana's Caribbean roll. Though at least one thing was the same.

Carlito.

In the distance, she could see his face in the crowd. And soon he'd see hers. Smiles erupted and, at least for a moment, seemed to wash away the uncertainly that had plagued them both for so long. His embrace. Their kiss. The wrap of an arm around Antonina's slender waist. These were the first moments of their new life together

Cuban boys in Old Havana play stickball until dark. Though the popularity of other sports, such as soccer and basketball, is growing, baseball in many ways is still king in Cuba.

A *bicitaxi* rumbles through the capital's Centro Habana neighborhood.

A farmer in Cuba's Pinar Del Rio province strings up tobacco leaves for drying.

A woman rolls cigars in Havana's Cohiba Cigar Factory.

Sea-gazers gather upon Havana's Malecon seawall at sunset.

A young Cuban girl rests on an iron chair in Centro Habana.

Nightfall on Havana's Malecon seawall.

A man strolls in front of the *Capitolio* in Centro Habana.

Two drivers lean against their taxi *colectivos* in Centro Habana.

A fisherman casts his line atop the Malecon seawall at sunset.

Spanish tourists linger atop the Malecon seawall.

Young boys get ready for a sandlot game of baseball in Old Havana.

Havana resident hangs out in Old Havana.

The author on a rooftop in Old Havana.

Young boys wait their turn at bat during a stickball game in Old Havana.

and the next phase of their years-long endeavor to become American. Soon, they'd be on their way north.

Carlito shifted in his seat and gazed out the window. He and Antonina had been traveling for weeks and were now bound for Dallas. Though tired, they could hardly wait. The blurred browns and greens of Mexico's cactus-dotted landscape were like nothing either of them had seen before.

I'm going toward my future, Carlito later told me of his thoughts. *My destiny.*

Texas seemed just over the horizon. As the car rumbled north, Antonina slept. Carlito didn't. At least not much. His romanticized vision of America mirrored my own Cuba concoction, and he was still brimming with excitement.

"We're almost there," he said, nudging Antonina and wrapping his arm around her shoulder.

After all this time, the border finally came into view. A looming concrete-and-iron edifice dominated the landscape ahead. A border guard approached the car as it pulled to a slow stop.

"*Pasaportes!*" he barked in a Texan Spanish with all the patience of a man who likely yelled this all day long. Moments like these, however, were precisely when it paid to be Cuban.

"Here," Carlito said, handing the man both their booklets.

That should have been it, Carlito thought. But it didn't end there.

"Get outside," the guard barked, ordering the young couple as he inspected their travel documents. "No, over here!" he yelled. Resuming his scan of the documents, the guard returned to Carlito. "*Cubanos?*" he asked.

"*Sí, señor,*" Carlito replied.

"OK. *Vamanos,*" the guard said, waving his hand forward, acknowledging that the young migrants had legal grounds to pass into the United States. Years later, under President Trump, those guards would have very different marching orders, detaining and deporting migrants from virtually all Latin American countries in greater numbers and often separating migrant parents from their children. Carlito had reached the border just in time.

"We're free!" he said, turning to Antonina.

After years of waiting, they had finally crossed onto American soil.

Another six hours of driving would pass before they'd reach Dallas. There, they boarded a Florida-bound Greyhound bus and headed east across the Gulf Coast, stopping in Louisiana and Mississippi before finally bending south toward Miami-Dade, where Antonina's aunt and Carlito's parents were already waiting.

"Is that it?" Antonina exclaimed as the city's skyline came into view. "Is that Miami?" More than three hundred shimmering highrise apartment buildings and financial towers dotted the cityscape. It was, again, unlike anything they had ever seen. As their bus approached, Antonina and Carlito pressed against the window, eyes fixed on this southern megalopolis that was to be their new home.

"We're finally *yumas*," said Antonina with a little laugh as the bus continued its southerly bend on Interstate 95, meandering toward the city.

"America or die," Carlito said, as tears welled.

But as they approached the bright lights, the bus inexplicably kept going. As it wended south and west, the skyscrapers of Miami's wealthier Brickell district began to fade. The bus continued south, bound for a middle-class suburb in Miami-Dade County known as Kendall, where cookie-cutter homes and concrete apartment developments dotted wide-lane roadways flanked by gas stations and convenience stores. Despite the width of the roads, they were packed with vehicles, something of a novelty to anyone from Cuba.

It was in Kendall, years later in 2017, in a modest apartment just outside Miami, where I'd finally see my old friends again.

"*Oye, David!*" Antonina shouted as I approached, planting a kiss on either cheek. "*Como te vas?*"

The sharp edges of her features had grown softer and rounder, the subtle geometry of comparative abundance.

"*Bien bien, todo bien,*" I replied, exchanging greetings and staring at both of them. All I kept thinking was that they had done it. Antonina's mention of America all those years ago was now her reality, and the pair invited me in for dinner in their new Florida home.

"Are you hungry?" Antonina asked. She'd ordered Indian food. Delivery was a new phenomenon. In Cuba, restaurants were often exceedingly pricey for people on state salaries, and there was virtually no such thing as delivery. In Florida, however, residents could summon countless food choices simply by plunking down a credit card from their cell phones. Credit cards. Internet. Rent. Insurance. These were new facets of American life to which they would have to grow accustomed.

"So how did you get here?" I asked.

"*Coño*, where do I begin?" Carlito replied, launching into a detailed recall of his trip to Ecuador, the torture of waiting for Antonina in Cancun, the Texas-bound car, and their bus-bound sighting of Miami. When he finished, I took a sip of wine and asked the only question that seemed to make sense.

"Well then, what's your American dream?"

Carlito, who was now sitting next to Antonina, promptly corrected me.

"*Mi sueño, neoyorquino,*" he said. "My New Yorker dream."

The new immigrant still had Gotham on the brain. And he had both the energy and the innocence for it. Whatever he was getting into, he seemed the sort to embrace life without a full consideration of the facts. I could empathize. Antonina, by contrast, was the more sober party, and she accordingly wielded a sharper tongue.

"What *was* his dream," she responded. "We're here now."

"My dream is still New York," Carlito snapped back. "For me, the United States is New York," he said with a certain dreaminess. The way he talked about it, it seemed like he had already been there.

"It's a fantastic city," he gushed. "We've got to get there." Carlito wasn't unique in that regard.

New York, it appeared, has a special place in the minds of Cubans—and indeed across Latin America. He had been talking about Gotham in Cuba, in Ecuador as they haggled with customs agents, and in Mexico as he waited in Cancun for Antonina. When they were Texas-bound, it's all he talked about. Antonina, who was certain about Carlito but less convinced about the Big Apple, had indulged her partner.

But she now seemed more excited about Miami. Antonina had had friends and family waiting for her. And Miami, in some ways, made the transition easier. Parts of the city were entirely Spanish-speaking. With nearly 68 percent of the city self-identifying as Latinos, including more than a million Cuban American residents, culture and traditions often seemed just as Cuban as Cuba.[2] It was a new world for people like Antonina and Carlito, but it was also one they could ease into and begin to understand. Though after a few months, America's bright lights seemed to have faded.

"Everything in Miami is far," Antonina said. "Here, you need a plan to go out. In Cuba, you just go."

The town of Kendall bore few hallmarks of the island, except for the fact that about half the population identified Spanish as their first language. Still, it was an adjustment.

"The first thing I remember was the supermarket," said Antonina, recalling the drab, often-empty shelves of Cuba's state-run stores. "Here I saw big fruits and vegetables and apples and pears and onions and lettuce and everything you could ever want. And it was all perfectly clean."

In subsequent weeks, she found work, getting a job as a cashier at a local Walgreens. Carlito took up driving for Uber. The pair soon earned more in a month than they could have earned in a year in Cuba. And yet now there was also a lot more to pay for. Antonina felt a newfound weight as she thought about it all, her shoulders visibly slumping as she looked at Carlito. She turned to me.

"It's more relaxed in Cuba," she said a bit wistfully, as if the island were part of some alternate continuum in which time slows and dilates. "It's just easier to enjoy everything a bit more."

The pace of life in Florida was decidedly faster. And in some ways it was what Antonina had wanted. She had gotten married and become financially independent, no longer reliant on her family, and free to pursue the life and career that she had wanted. Here, markets were in abundance, but life seemed more solitary as many retreated into their phones. "Here, it's username, password, username and password," she said. Something was missing in those southern American suburbs. She then paused, as if choosing her words carefully, and turned to her husband. "For him, this is his American dream. But . . ." She let the word trail off. "I miss Cuba. I miss my life in Cuba, my freedom."

She missed her freedom? That struck me. Cuba was a one-party state where civil institutions were bound by Communist rule. Press and political freedoms were curtailed. Pluralism outlawed. Dissent faced intimidation and was often punishable by jail.

"What freedom?" I asked.

"Time," Antonina said simply. She missed the freedom of time that Cuba had afforded: time to socialize, to relax, and to think without the distraction of iPhone screens and taxi TVs and the anxiety of missing out or having to catch up. Freedom, of course, did not exist in the political sense. But that word can mean other things. And it never dawned on me that a Cuban would long for it after at long last reaching her freedom in the States.

"Here it's work and save if you can," she said of her new life in South Florida. "The *yuma* life."

But the pair could hardly save. Carlito's work with Uber was sporadic and Antonina's cashier job at Walgreens was often not enough to make up the difference. She picked up weekend shifts and night shifts. But they still struggled.

"It's been very hard here," she said, leaning back against her chair.

"Yes, life is very different," Carlito said, before countering his wife. "But [in Cuba] you work and you work, and there is no future, not even an opportunity for a future." He tugged at the back of his neck and all of a sudden looked uncomfortable. Both had a point. Maybe the possibility of being wrong was just too much to bear for someone who had risked so much. "You have no money. Here, life is hard," Carlito added, puffing up his chest a bit more as he spoke. "But if you work, you have a chance at something."

My own romantic visions had been adjusted amid political crackdowns, pink-faced tourists, empty shelves, and privacy-sapping bureaucrats. My picture of Cuba was different now. His of America was still intact. I could see he had pinned his hopes on that. And as we sat together in their living room in Kendall, Florida, none of it seemed clear. It was their next chapter. They had been absorbed into America's great economy, but now they had to struggle in it in a way they never had before.

15

RETURN TO GOTHAM

One must have a mind of winter
to regard the frost and the boughs.

— "The Snow Man," Wallace Stevens

It was December 2010, a year and a half since I had packed up and left for Havana. As Antonina and Carlito had begun to sort out their plans, I was doing the same. My father's health and a business school–bound fiancée had become my focus. And so I exchanged my seaside, three-bedroom house in Havana for a studio apartment on Manhattan's Upper East Side, coincidentally just as the city's sixth-largest snowstorm dumped more than two feet of snow. Welcome to New York, cold and cramped. The fresh snowy blanket had brought with it an almost magical hush over an otherwise frenetic city.

Subways stalled and streets were covered over. Indeed, Manhattan's some 3 million commuters had been forced to slow down, whether they wanted to or not. For a moment, New Yorkers seemed uncharacteristically at peace.

Though it wasn't easy. I hadn't seen a proper northeastern December in years. And the gray and ice doldrums that invariably enveloped the city's concrete and glass pillars stood in stark contrast to my old sun-kissed home in Miramar.

And yet, though I earned far less in a city that cost far more, I also had something I was never quite able to capture in Cuba. In Havana, I was a *yuma*. An outsider. But in New York, I was a New Yorker. Whether you're from here or just moved here, the city had a singular way of making people its own. There was a community to be had. Here, I had a fiancée, a father, and a sister nearby, with neighbors equipped with accents thicker than New Jersey traffic. And of course there was also Murray, a sixty-something-year-old Upper East Sider and Mets fan. I met Murray at H&H Midtown Bagel East on Second Avenue, between Eighty-First and Eighty-Second Streets. He was a regular, as I'd soon be, and he eventually took daily issue with my Yankees fandom, relishing the sort of baseball banter that the men in Havana's Central Park would appreciate.

As different as the two cities could be, baseball had a way of connecting us.

"Heya." He'd perk up over bagel, cream cheese, and a small coffee (his usual morning order) when I'd walk into H&H. "There he is."

"How ya doing, Murray?" I asked, more in greeting than a question.

We'd chat a bit, him alternating between a far more graphic description of his ailments than I had ever wanted to know and the state of his beloved Mets: the pitching, and how rough the off-season recruitment had been. Murray was retired. And as such, he was rarely in a hurry, savoring his coffee and bagel, and opining in a way I wished I had more time for. Usually we'd chat while I was waiting for my own bagel and coffee pairing, before I descended into the first of two subways that would carry me to work.

And that was it. There was a quiet comfort to it: a burgeoning love-hate relationship as the city's history, culture, and my own family ties mingled with a magic akin to those early days in Havana. Both were wrapped in a sort of golden nostalgia that could obscure their harder edges, justifying a cost of living that would otherwise seem absurd. Magnetic for different reasons, New York and Havana shared a romance that even Fidel could not resist. After his marriage in

1948 to Mirta Diaz-Balart, Castro took his new bride to New York as part of a nearly three-month-long honeymoon, moving into a small apartment on Manhattan's Upper West Side.

Years later, during Fidel's visit to the United Nations in New York, freelance journalist Jon Alpert asked the Cuban leader what he would do if he were ever to become Gotham's mayor. Visibly tired, Castro, clad in his signature olive-green fatigues, nonetheless hadn't lost his penchant for rhetoric.

"The first thing I would do is to resign," he said with a chuckle.

"Why?" asked Alpert.

"Because I think this is a city that cannot be governed," Fidel replied. Compared to the authoritarian-style rule he had grown accustomed to in Havana, he may have had a point.

But to me, it was home. It was what I had been waiting for. A sense of community in the city built by my immigrant forebearers, including Norwegian sailmakers and Italian plumbers and stonemasons. I remembered hearing stories of my great-grandfather who had toiled in construction of the Empire State Building. Now, as a journalist living and working in New York, I often pictured his silhouette teetering on narrow scaffolding as it reached skyward and reshaped the symmetry of a skyline that men like him could never afford to live under. In those first months, walking down Fifty-Ninth Street along Central Park South toward the glimmering cityscape that enveloped Columbus Circle, I often thought of them and wished they could've seen it.

But the move back to New York wasn't without its consequences. The job involved a move to the digital side of CNN, which in 2010 seemed like the afterthought of a global news network that still regarded television as its mainstay. And my salary reflected that. It was nearly halved. In Manhattan, supporting a two-person household, I'd soon find out just how little that was. The math didn't add up. And I started looking for a second job or just a better one. But in the wake of the financial crisis, much of America's economy had only begun to rebound. Stress was building. Still, we had it better than most. New York's median income in 2010 was $50,711, enough to get by in most places, except that food, gas, and health care were astronomically higher than in most places—an estimated 68 percent more than the national average.[1]

In Cuba, I never really worried about money. Now it was all I thought about. Of course, New York wasn't unique. The financial crisis had erased $11 trillion worth of home value and prompted nearly 8 million foreclosures, casting millions of new renters into the market and driving up rental prices by 5 percent in the nation's fifty largest cities. Limited inventory, population growth, and a surge of outside speculators all made for a perfect storm. Employers, meanwhile, waited out America's financial tempest and simply paid their people less. Median national incomes dropped by 5.8 percent in the decade after the crisis, adjusted for inflation.

The American dream Carlito had talked about seemed harder than ever to attain, even for Americans. In that classic grass-is-always-greener syndrome, life in Cuba—at least for a *yuma*—all of a sudden didn't seem so bad. In Cuba, I returned from work to watch the sun sink below inky-blue waves and jogged along the Malecon just before it reemerged. New York, by contrast, with its compulsory head-bobs of residents checking their phones, was a city on the clock. And the disparity in wealth had soared. By the time I returned, those in Manhattan's top 5 percent, buoyed by a resurgent financial indus-try, had extended their reach, earning nearly eighty-eight times as much as the bottom 20 percent. Still, I had assumed we were in the middle class. A police officer or teacher in New York with at least five years on the job earned up to $69,000. Wasn't that a traditional middle-class job? If asked, chances are he or she would have said yes, given that some 62 percent of Americans identify as "middle class."[2]

No one had told us the middle had shifted.

We'd eventually move to Astoria, Queens, in search of cheaper rent and more space. But the financial squeeze persisted.

Had I made a mistake?

I'd gone from what felt like a relatively important, well-paid post in the comparatively cheap city of Havana to a cog in the wheel of CNN's corporate Time Warner behemoth, nestled in the heart of a New York money pit. As the costs mounted, so did the stress—and my weight. In the coming months, amid New York's ever-open stores and bodegas, I'd pack on some thirty pounds, likely mostly courtesy of an H&H bagel shop conveniently located near my East Side subway stop. An oversize winter jacket hid the extra layers the bagels packed on in a way a *guayabera* never could. I never had to in Havana. But there was no scarcity in this city of plenty.

I missed Cuba. And New York in winter had a way of chilling the body down to its very core, so I began looking for ways to heat up.

"Do you know of any Cuban places around here?" I asked a co-worker, Rob Frehse, on CNN's New York Assignment Desk. Rob's customary fleece-vest-and-tie combination didn't exactly suggest a man plugged into the Cuban salsa scene, but the man was nonetheless resourceful. On more than one occasion he had brushed through the often frenetic deluge of information that bombards a New York newsroom, sorting the unsortable. And so I figured he might have some insights.

"I don't know if it's Cuban, but there's the Copacabana," he replied, a reference to a bygone-era nightclub once known as much for its big-name Latin stars, such as Willie Colón, as it was for its 1940s-era mob-boss underwriters, such as Frank Costello.

"Ehh, something a little more low-key," I replied.

"Well, there's another spot down on Eighth Avenue," he said. "I don't know what it's called, but it's more a restaurant."

"Perfect," I replied, grabbing my bag and bundling up before heading out the door.

The place was aptly named Guantanamera, perhaps Cuba's most widely known folk song. Composed in 1929 by Cuban songwriter Joseíto Fernández, it offered a romantic refrain of a love affair gone wrong and referenced a *guajira* (peasant woman) from Guantanamo. The tune later evolved into a patriotic melody and was required listening delivered by virtually every hotel troupe on the island. With lyrical adaptations to later include partial verses of a poem written by Cuban independence hero Jose Marti, the song drew praise for the national—though not revolutionary—pride it evoked, and eventually took on global fame when Cuban-born singer Celia Cruz did her own salsa-inspired version. From my vantage point amid wintry Midtown Manhattan, Guantanamera seemed like the perfect place to grab a bite. But when I walked in that late winter afternoon, it was virtually empty.

"How can I help you?" a bored-looking, forty-something woman at the hostess stand asked me. Her name was Lillie Granda Fernandez, and she had moved from La Vibora, Havana's most densely populated district, just a few years earlier. She had since moved to Queens and become decidedly American, getting work by helping to run this Midtown Cuban restaurant, though she had not lost that distinct Habanero accent. It was music to my ears. Turns out Guantanamera was filled with a staff virtually all from Cuba.

Though South Florida was renowned for its Cuban population and the influence it wielded, a closer look revealed Cubans settling in large numbers in other parts of the country as well, including Los Angeles, Chicago, and New York. Move over, Miami. In fact, by 2015, more than 145,000 residents who self-identified as Cuban called the New York metropolitan area home.

"Why don't you go sit at the bar?" Lillie said, motioning to an empty set of red leather high-backs. "Take your pick."

"Thanks," I said, taking a seat and resting my forearms on the polished wooden bar.

The bartender, a thirty-one-year-old guy named Vidal, approached. "What'll you have?" he said, setting a napkin.

"Give me a minute," I replied.

"Take your time," he said. "But you should try the mojitos."

I obliged and ordered a classic: white rum, mint, lime, sugar, and soda water in a highball glass, with a bit of bitters for that extra punch.

It was just the three of us, desolate as it was, but there was a certain warmth that seemed out of place for wintry Manhattan. Brightly colored murals decorated the walls and stage where Cuban musicians would jam into the evenings. During later sets, middle-of-the-room tables would be moved back so that an array of customers, from suited old men to middle-aged and youthful *salseras,* could swing their hips to rhythms that seemed right out of the cobblestone corridors of Old Havana. Waiters would dip through the crowd, wielding steaming plates of *ropa vieja, pollo asado,* and *tostones,* while open-shirted percussionists kept that all-important clave beat.

Guantanamera was a gateway into the world I had left behind: nostalgia's secondhand smoke. And I'd soon become a regular. Vidal became a familiar face.

"So what do you think about Cuba?" he asked me one evening after work.

I had fielded that question a lot recently, and always seemed to answer by saying it's "a hell of a lot different than New York." Not that I had to tell him that. Vidal had arrived in New York from Cuba via Europe and hailed from Matanzas, an industrial region whose provincial city was situated about an hour-and-a-half drive east of Havana. Matanzas was also home to the resort town of Varadero, a twelve-mile strip of beach along the Hicacos Peninsula that had grown especially popular with foreign tourists, arguably Cuba's most important industry. There, Vidal had gotten a job working in a hotel. His official salary was around $24 per month.

But there were other ways to make money. Vidal had sold his body.

"I met a lot of girls," he said. "Girls on vacation."

Sex tourism, it seemed, wasn't just for foreign men. He was poor, by tourist standards, but a natural flirt and eager to leave. "It's not like I had a set price or anything," he explained. "I just took them out and said, 'Look, we have problems here, we have necessities.'"

Out of that came an understanding, or what he called a square deal, that would net an average of $300 per week, an exorbitant sum by Cuban standards and the equivalent of more than a year's salary.

"It seems to me that you've got two systems in the world. Communism and capitalism," he said. "And if you want to live in capitalism, you've got to have capital."

Desperate to leave, he soon saw his way out: a German tourist who had traveled to the island and showed up at his hotel looking for a good time. After a few weeks, he had convinced her to marry him. She agreed. And the pair moved to Germany.

"I wouldn't have married her if she wasn't German," he acknowledged. "Deep inside myself, I don't feel bad about anything. I did what I did because it's what I had to do."

The pair soon divorced, and Vidal headed to the United States, marrying again, this time an American woman, before taking a job at the bar where we now sat. "Everybody was leaving," he explained. Marriage was a vehicle.

Eventually, Vidal would again divorce. And he would again marry, this time moving to Florida to set up a small car dealership in Miami with the money he had saved. It was an American dream, of sorts. Ownership of his own American business, born of Cuban poverty. And yet he seemed torn, describing a new affliction he had picked up after leaving Cuba.

"When you leave and go to the first world, somehow you get infected with the 'I-want-to-have-things' . . . virus," Vidal explained. "Once you get that inside you, you can't be free."

I just listened. He was the kind of guy who needed few incentives to get talking, and his story sounded familiar. So I just listened to a man who seemed to have done everything he could to leave Cuba, including selling himself. He had succeeded, building a new life with a third wife, who was also Cuban. Yet despite the successes that his adopted country had afforded him, he seemed to long for those shoe-less, lunchless days, when bohemian romance, as he called it, still lived like "it does in your movies." It was the simplicity of a country "that doesn't move." And though it remained wrapped in the very Communist cloak that had once made him leave, he now longed for it. As an American and a Miami business owner, he had been thoroughly "infected."

"The only place that I go to be free of it is to Cuba," he added. "I get there and I don't want a cell phone. I don't want anything."

And yet that was also changing. Vidal had visited the island, but he hadn't lived there in years, and its economy now showed signs of faltering. Having replaced its Soviet benefactor with a Venezuelan one, Cuba had been buoyed by Hugo Chavez's cheap fuel in exchange for its doctors and security services. But by 2014, Venezuela, once an affluent Andean nation, had grown incapable of providing for its own people, let alone Cuba's. Hyperinflation would eventually soar toward one million percent, not far off Zimbabwe's worst years, as corruption, unrest, capital controls and a global commodity bust all played into its unraveling. As that crumbling started to play out, Cuba would directly feel the effects.

In 2012, President Chavez, who was battling cancer, had turned to Cuban physicians to remove a tumor the "size of a baseball" from his pelvic area. But he died anyway. And Chavez's political heir, Nicolás Maduro, wielded only tenuous power as allegations of voter fraud and demonstrations swept the country over growing government repression, censorship, and gross mismanagement of the economy. Maduro responded with force and employed national guardsmen to break up demonstrations as tensions were growing. By early March 2014, at least twenty-one protesters had died. Many more would follow. Enmeshed in a deteriorating political and economic crisis, Cuba appeared to be a liability, and Maduro began reducing his country's subsidies to the island, which over the years had come to rely on foreign oil for roughly two-thirds of its daily consumption.

Venezuela alone delivered 130,000 barrels to Cuba every day.[3] Now, as oil prices tumbled, that seemed to be ending.

But Raul, who had seen this dance before and enacted rationing measures to blunt the effects of reduced fuel, also had a trump card Cuba never had with the Soviets: Cubans were deeply intertwined in Venezuelan affairs. Back when Chavez was alive, he had struck up a personal friendship with Fidel, often visiting him in the hospital when he grew ill. The pair had forged a close bond between their two nations. And as a result, Cuban doctors weren't the only ones who were working in Venezuela. Two sources told me that Cuban security and political officials were spread across civil society, including Venezuelan police and ministerial offices, closely advising the president and consulting his administration on security measures "at the highest levels." Meanwhile, informant networks loyal to Maduro had been devised along classic Cuban lines—and at times with direct Cuban involvement. "We have over 30,000 members of Cuba's Committees for the Defense of the Revolution in Venezuela," claimed Juan José Rabilero, who was then head of Cuba's CDR, in 2007.[4] Though the full extent of Havana's reach inside Venezuela remained unclear, many Venezuelans openly wondered whether their country would ultimately resemble Communist Cuba.

As the crisis escalated, I had to go see for myself.

16

THE BENEFACTOR

I'm sorry, sir," said a droopy-eyed waiter named Humberto as I sat in his vacant restaurant. "Ever since the violence started here, milk is hard to come by." It was March 2014, and I had left for Venezuela, entering the once-affluent Andean country during the height of its protests. Milk was just the beginning of what Venezuela—and ultimately Cuba—would lack.

At its peak, Cuba depended on Venezuela for roughly 70 percent of its energy needs.[1] But as the price of crude oil plummeted amid an American fracking boom, Venezuela—which relied on energy for 96 percent of its hard-currency revenue—felt the effects almost immediately. The heyday of $100 per barrel was gone. And as prices tumbled into the $40 range and Venezuela's debt and inflation soared, shortages gripped the country, forcing Caracas to reduce fuel deliveries to Cuba by nearly one-third. Trade with the island plummeted as Venezuela teetered on the brink of collapse.

Riots broke out, food started to run out, and rolling blackouts paralyzed the economy and added a level of fear Venezuelans had not seen in decades, if ever. By day, thousands marched under the banner of antigovernment protests. By night, a volatile mix of anarchists and protesters hurled petrol bombs at government forces, who countered with tear gas to disperse them. Caracas was a city under siege. Its air had an acrid taste, derived from the smolder of barricades and lingering wisps of spent tear gas. And yet the focus of protesters I spoke with kept tracing back to Havana.

"We don't want to be another Cuba," Maria Sanchez yelled in my direction as I interviewed her in the midst of yet another Caracas march. She was a student protester among thousands in the Venezuelan capital who wielded banners and carried flags in protest of the government. These sorts of mass demonstrations had become almost a daily occurrence. A month earlier, a student leader named Gaby Arellano had petitioned the island's ambassador to Venezuela to refuse "to allow Cubans to interfere in our affairs any longer."

"We don't want them to go on controlling the media, directing military operations or indoctrinating our children," she told the *Guardian*. Raúl Baduel, former defense minister under Chavez, told the British newspaper that Cuba's involvement in his country was "not a myth." Rather, he said, "It's the reality."

A Brookings report went further, estimating that the numbers of Cuban military and intelligence officials in Venezuela ranged from hundreds to thousands. Its soldiers had also exchanged the old U.S.-style military doctrine for a Cuban one, the report said, while Cuban officials maintained a *"sala situacional"* (situation room) for the Venezuelan president. Maduro, the former bus driver turned president, was at least in part reliant on his Cuban counterparts.[2] And yet his power—and therefore Cuba's influence—had waned in Venezuela's western reaches near the Colombia border, where student demonstrations first unfurled in the state of Táchira.

That's where I assumed I needed to go.

Here, in the once-affluent college town of San Cristóbal, some five hundred miles southwest of the capital, lay the birthplace of Venezuela's countrywide protests. And it was taking a heavy toll. Maduro could not fully dominate his country the way Raul, and Fidel before him, had dominated theirs. And so he seemed to be encouraging levels of violence for worse than any in modern-day Cuba.

Evening was approaching. I could see the weariness on the faces here, especially for those like Humberto Moncado, who was lamenting his restaurant's lack of milk.

I was his only customer.

"I'm sorry, sir," he said, after I had asked him for a splash to go with the coffee. There was none. No milk at the restaurant. No milk at the grocery store. And as far as I could tell, there didn't seem to be any milk in town.

"Don't worry," I said. "I usually take it black anyway."

He seemed to know I was lying. "Of course," Humberto replied, adjusting his beige bow tie, which he had pulled a bit too tight. Despite the crisis, he was intent on keeping up appearances, determined to keep his shop open, if only for a while. His shirt was crisp. His brass name tag looked polished. And yet for all the decorum, he couldn't mask the bags and dark circles forming under his eyes.

"We close at three p.m.," he said, wiping down my table and shuffling back to the front of the bar. "The fighting usually begins around five p.m.," he added, nonchalantly, and so he wanted to safeguard his staff by allowing them to get home before it started. "Would you like anything else?" he sighed.

"Do you have any chicken?" I asked, hungry from the journey.

"No," he replied. "I'm sorry."

"A burger?"

"Not that either," fatigue etched across his face. Perhaps it was the knowledge that there were few of the ingredients he needed for all those dishes listed on his voluminous red-leather-bound menu.

Handing the menu to customers had become his habit, even though what he could offer had dwindled so much that the choices were now easy enough to remember.

"What do you have?" I asked.

"Right now it's just coffee," he replied. "Though there may be some *arepas* in back."

His country was crumbling.

"Coffee will be fine," I said.

Venezuela's central bank would report that its economy was contracting by nearly 3 percent, while inflation soared by 64 percent.[3] And that was just the beginning. By 2016, inflation topped 800 percent as the economy lost nearly a fifth of its size. I seemed to have arrived at the start of the slide.

This is the country propping up Cuba?

Venezuela was heading for collapse, though few realized just how bad it had gotten. The Cubans, however, must have known, and they would be preparing. The Castros had a knack for sniffing out disaster.

Just then, the high pitch of a woman's voice broke my train of thought. "Are you open?" she shouted, clutching a bag and holding the hand of a little girl, no older than five. "Yes," Humberto replied, extending his hand toward the scattering of empty tables. "Just sit where you like."

"Thank you," she said, staring off under hooded eyelids before settling in to a seat directly beside mine. The woman's long, dark hair was frayed, looked greasy and unwashed, and she took her seat with a collapse of bones and body weight. Exhaustion was evident in her every movement: the extension of a hand, the turn of her head. All of it labored and slow. Still, her little girl smiled, toying with a bit of lace that hung down from the woman's shirt.

"Look. Look," she commanded, beckoning her mother's attention.

The woman turned, nodded, and then gazed off. There was plenty of space to sit, and yet the pair had chosen a table right next to me.

"Hi," I said, looking up from my mug. Our proximity required me to say *something*. "There's not much on the menu."

She turned to me, and her eyes widened, as if only now noticing that another person was beside her.

"That's OK," she exclaimed, regaining her composure. "As long as they have something."

Her name was Norlyn Mota. She was in her midthirties and worked at a clothing store just outside San Cristóbal. Though she usually prepared a mix of *arepas,* rice, and beans for her daughter after work, today had been different. Norlyn had been delayed in reaching the market to replenish her shrinking supply of food after student protesters erected a fresh crop of barricades, or *guarimbas,* on the road in. Now, few markets were open, and she figured it best to just go buy a meal and head home rather than risk staying out too late. The little girl needed her dinner.

"All the stores are closed," she told me, and we chatted there, less than a two-hour drive from the Colombian border. Meanwhile, Humberto's was about to join the ranks of those neighboring shuttered stores. It was nearly 3 p.m. In two hours, like clockwork as Humberto had warned, the violence would begin. Norlyn ordered *arepas.* No matter what shortages gripped the country, one could usually find those white corn cakes somewhere. And yet that too was changing. Soon even corn would be a luxury. She ate quickly with her daughter, but not before turning to me once more when I asked how she felt about the recent events.

"It's hard not to be a little afraid," she said.

In the city's hillside neighborhoods, where residents railed against President Nicolás Maduro, the air had a bitter taste, much like Caracas. Spent tear gas canisters littered streets and sidewalks. At least twenty-one people had been killed since the fighting broke out less than a month earlier, according to the government's official tally, though student protesters claimed the real number was far higher. Hundreds had been wounded in the clashes, and scores arrested.

"The heart of this situation is an economic crisis," a man named César Pérez Vivas, the former governor of the state of Táchira, told me over the phone. "But the government is responding with the military." He was right. Each night armored cars would smash barricades as guardsmen launched volleys of tear gas against protesters in the city's northern neighborhood where I had booked a room for the night.

I had arrived that afternoon, fresh off a trip to Puerto Cabello, Venezuela's busiest port city and a virtual lifeline to Havana, where oil production declines were most evident. There, a diesel smell remained, even though refineries, hobbled by unpaid debts, were churning out less crude to be sold on the world market. With minimum-wage public-sector workers earning the equivalent of just $12 per month, poorer Venezuelans could be seen scrounging for food in garbage piles overrun by flies. The situation had grown desperate. Many simply couldn't consume enough calories. By 2016, nearly 75 percent of the population had lost at least nineteen pounds due to the crisis.[4] And it seemed almost entirely man-made.

Back in 2002, then president Chavez had put down a series of worker strikes at the state-run oil firm Petróleos de Venezuela (PDVSA), replacing technocrats with party supporters and siphoning company funds, including a $500 million pension trust, following a failed coup. The result would prove devastating. Workers began walking off the job at a dizzying pace as their pay diminished and working conditions grew fraught. The infrastructure was collapsing, and the country's oil sector—its lifeblood, which accounted for 95 percent of Venezuela's export earnings—was in shambles.

Even as the global price of oil rebounded, production here still dropped, in large part attributed to corruption and mismanagement. As hard currency depleted, the government printed more money to fund legacy welfare and subsidy programs like the discount fuel and oil it offered Cuba. But now, with inflation rampant, cash reserves dwindling, and renewed questions over the country's oil-fueled patronage, economic crisis had engendered a political powder keg. All it needed was a spark.

And that spark came on February 2, 2014.

A university freshman was strolling through the botanical gardens of Andes University of Venezuela in San Cristóbal when she was attacked and nearly raped. Muggings and assault had grown commonplace, but news of the attempted rape spread across campus. This time was different. Students who had for more than a year called for more security on campus had had enough. Buoyed by civic groups, they took to the streets in the protest. Government forces responded with a heavy hand, beating back protesters, jailing them, and then transferring them to a prison more than four hundred miles away in the port city of Coro, far from their families. The move exacerbated tensions. Within three weeks, student protests had snowballed into nationwide demonstrations, fueled by shortages of basic goods, soaring inflation, and spiraling criminality and violence. The environment emboldened opposition leaders, claiming Venezuela's democratic institutions had been eroded and its economy mismanaged.

The crew of journalists I normally worked with were still in Caracas, and I had traveled out to that same town, San Cristóbal, alone, and found there a debris field of broken glass, rebar, and tear gas canisters. The once-affluent college haunt bore the pockmarks of a city under siege. It was now 5:00 p.m., and the streets were virtually empty. Families had hunkered down behind barricades and inside boarded-up homes, and an eerie quiet had settled over the city.

I made my way back to my hotel.

"*Hola*, David," said Rosalina, the front desk clerk, as I entered the Posada Estancia El Paraiso, a salmon-colored boutique hotel with iron gates. It was the iron gates that drew me. The place seemed relatively secure. But like Humberto's restaurant, it was empty. I had only checked in that day and Rosalina already knew my name. The feat wasn't remarkable, since I'd later find out that I was indeed her only guest.

"How is everything?" she asked, her round and almost cheery face framing the question. At first, she seemed almost blithely unaware that her hotel sat on a battleground. The electricity was out, as was the water. But Rosalina's voice had all the peppery sweetness of a bed-and-breakfast owner, and I half expected a "y'all come back now, ya hear?"

I wondered if, since the conflict was still somewhat young, it had yet to take her innocence. Or maybe this was just her method of coping with a world that had grown uncertain—indeed deadly. She reminded me of my mother in a way, a former emergency room nurse, steady and dependable in a crisis, though a woman who had a penchant for laughing when she felt anxious. Here, there was plenty of reason. Despite the fighting and having but one guest, her hotel was fully staffed with a housekeeping staff, a bellhop, and amazingly, a cook. The cook was the deciding factor in choosing El Paraiso. I needed a place that would have food stocked. Anyplace with a cook would likely have that.

"I'm well," I finally responded, turning back to Rosalina after surveying the lobby. She forced a smile. But unlike the coerced merriment Jose had exhibited back at Havana's Hotel Nacional, a deep-set fear was transparently behind hers.

Midnight explosions, gunfire, the high-pitched whine of motorbikes, the pop of tear gas, the crash of petrobombs hurled by students who shrouded their faces with scarves and sunglasses, yelling, screaming, and wailing all seemed a part of San Cristóbal's nightly cacophony, and therefore part of Rosalina's reality. But with my arrival, a new factor had been introduced. I was a journalist. And an American. That made me a target of forces loyal to President Nicolás Maduro, whose party line regarded the unrest as a product of a U.S.-hatched plot meant to destabilize his country.

"The U.S. wants to impose a unipolar world controlled from Washington," he said in a national address the same year I arrived in San Cristóbal, blaming U.S. interventionism for the emergence of the protests. It was a claim I had heard Castro's government assert countless times in Cuba. And despite its bluster, like in Cuba, the Maduro government did have some relevant recent history to lean on. In 2006, less than five months before President Hugo Chavez called President George W. Bush the devil in front of the United Nations General Assembly, diplomatic cables from the U.S. embassy in Caracas exposed at least part of the U.S. strategy.

Documents classified by political counselor Robert R. Downes, later released by WikiLeaks, called for "creative US outreach to Chavez's regional partners [that] will drive a wedge between him and them." Chavez had accused the Bush administration of backing a failed coup against him in 2002. He broke off diplomatic relations with the U.S. in September 2008 in solidarity with his ally Evo Morales, Bolivia's leftist president who had expelled America's ambassador on accusations of fomenting civil unrest. Relations were later restored under President Obama, but the distrust remained. Later, in January 2010, emails revealed U.S. secretary of state Hillary Clinton had asked her assistant secretary of state about ways to "rein in Chavez." They were hardly smoking guns, but each tidbit played into a meddling U.S. narrative that President Maduro—and Chavez before him—had cultivated. Just weeks before I arrived, Venezuela had kicked out three American diplomats on suspicions of supporting antigovernment protests. But for many across the country, including people like Rosalina, those sorts of headlines had little impact.

"It doesn't interest me," she said when I asked her about it. She just seemed to want her old life back.

Rosalina's routine was to go to work, keep her head down, and try not to make enemies. There was no going out with friends, having drinks at cafés, or heading to the theater after work. Evenings were simply too dangerous for most people to be out. If she did have to be away from home, the concrete walls and barred windows of El

Paraiso seemed like a good choice. Except now, with an American journalist holed up in her hotel as its only guest, the game had changed.

"How long will you be staying?" Rosalina asked, a feigned casualness in her tone.

"I'm not sure," I said. "It'll be at least a few days."

She smiled again, looking down toward her guest book. The power had gone out, and with no functioning computer, Rosalina was instead obliged to log my name in pencil. Rolling power outages had been an issue for more than a month, rendering this old-fashioned ledger necessary for much of that time. Yet when she showed me the pages of her guest book, mine was the only name for more than a week. It was a business without clients. But its workers kept showing up, hopeful all of this would eventually pass.

"Well, try and let me know," Rosalina added, slipping the pencil back into her mouth as she chomped down.

I smiled, picked up my bags, and headed to the room, a honeymoon suite painted pastel pink with a king-size bed. A treat of two liters of sparkling water rested atop the bedspread. At dinner, Rosalina appeared again. She also worked as the hotel waitress and served up a tray of sandwiches stuffed with a tasteless cheese and a canned mystery meat. I knew better than to ask. The bread disintegrated like sawdust on the first bite. That's also what it tasted like. Still, it was a hot meal. And I wolfed it down greedily.

"*Gracias,* Rosalina," I said as she refilled my coffee cup with the *guayoyo,* a popular espresso-like drink and the lifeblood of most Andean mornings. The ubiquitous Venezuelan coffee was in short supply, and so she reminded me to savor it.

"I'm sorry, David," she said, shoulders slumped, pouring the remnants of the pot into my cup. "Our chef has not been able to restock. This may be the last of it for a while."

"OK," I replied. What else could I say? Even the coffee supplies were dwindling, and Rosalina inexplicably felt obliged to apologize, as if it were somehow within her control. Of course, like Cubans, Venezuelans took their coffee seriously and needed their caffeine fix. Shortages of coffee, I should have realized, were a weather vane signaling even leaner times ahead.

As the crisis deepened, a government known for shipping its premium beans around the world had been obliged to buy from abroad. And the situation would grow steadily worse. In the last three months of 2014, the government imported nearly seventy thousand bags of Nicaraguan beans, a bitter pill for a country steeped in coffee tradition.[5]

Like Humberto, Rosalina was pointedly apologetic.

"I'm sorry," she said again, turning to me. "We also don't have any more milk."

There was a sadness in the way she spoke. It wasn't about the milk. Milk was just the beginning of what they all didn't have. I wanted to tell her to stop apologizing. None of this was her fault. An existential crisis had indeed transcended what she could affect, let alone ameliorate. The shortages. The violence. The isolation. The uncertainty. The diminishing chance for something better. There was nothing she could do on her own to change any of it. But I was an outsider. What right did I have to tell her how to make sense of all this? Even here, I was a *yuma,* a man who empathized though could never actually understand. I had never watched my community, or indeed my future, begin to crumble. I had never really been fearful of my neighborhood, the people in it, and those who were coming.

What could you possibly be apologizing for? I thought. I should be the one expressing sorrow.

And yet she kept at it. "I'm sorry," Rosalina said again, holding the empty coffeepot. "I'm so sorry."

And then something dawned on me. Maybe I was looking at this all wrong. Rosalina was apologizing to me, yes. But maybe it wasn't about me, but rather a statement to anyone who would listen. An utterance of self-preservation. A way to keep her spirits up and to demonstrate that amid all the turmoil and uncertainty, there was still a decorum of the old way, when shelves were stocked, guests filled the rooms, and civility had not been abandoned. By expressing an apology, she perhaps wasn't saying "I'm sorry," but rather assuring me this was not how it usually worked at her hotel, clinging to the memory of a more plentiful time, which she likely hoped would return. And yet as the weeks dragged into months and the shortages and violence grew worse, those memories seemed to be fading.

She then handed me the bill. I sucked down the *guayoyo* and reached for my pack.

Reaching for my cash, I thought about how Venezuela's currency had devalued so severely by 2014 that residents would take to carrying duffel bags full of cash, carting it around in wheelbarrows for larger transactions. As debt soared and oil prices dropped, authorities set prices and printed more money to make up for its lack of hard currency, driving up inflation and creating new incentives for corruption. An investigation by the Associated Press later discovered in 2017 that President Maduro's decision to put the military in charge of the nation's dwindling food supply had contributed to Venezuela's downward spiral. Military officials—tempted by rising consumer demands for basic items such as milk and butter—had turned food trafficking into big business. Pallets of corn flour were sold on the black market, the report found, for up to a hundred times the government-set price. One retired general is quoted as saying the military would not manage the nation's food supply "without getting their cut." As supplies dried up, desperation set in.

"My store has been empty for months," Augustín Sánchez, a local pharmacy owner, later told me, after I walked into what from the outside looked like a fairly large store. Row after row of his metal shelves were empty. "No baby formula, no nothing."

I had seen markets with empty shelves in Cuba. But nothing like this. Sánchez's white-painted shelves were not only completely bare, but they had also collected dust. His store seemed a store in name only.

Though not everyone subscribed to the opposition's call for undoing Maduro's Socialist programs, which had benefited impoverished neighborhoods still loyal to the government, the question of food would change the math. President Maduro, it seemed, was losing his grip on power. Determined to maintain control, officials turned to an old tactic of the guerilla wars of the 1960s. Pistol-wielding men, who often covered their faces and traveled into opposition neighborhoods, had begun to grow more prevalent. In San Cristóbal, their motorbikes could be heard throughout the night, inspiring terror as the sounds grew nearer. Financed by extortion and profiteering in the black-market food and drug trade, the government allowed them to exist in exchange for loyalty in repressing opposition. These grassroots militant groups were called *colectivos,* or collectives, and in some cases received military training. Though of the same name, these weren't the friendly ride shares of Havana. Instead they were armed men who acted with impunity, and who remained particularly effective in traumatizing residents, especially when coupled with national guardsmen. *Colectivos* were also a major reason why people in town, like Humberto, insisted on closing their shops early. *Colectivos* incited fear, were accused of targeting journalists, and had successfully undermined government opposition throughout the country.

But in the Andean college town of San Cristóbal, the students had decided to fight back. By midafternoon, they—alongside men from civic and labor groups—dragged sheet metal, wood, glass, and iron rebar into piles of rubble that served as barricades at major thoroughfares across the city, but mostly in San Cristóbal's hillside neighborhoods where the fighting was most intense.

"Without them [the barricades], *colectivos* would drive up to our houses with guns and start firing," a man named Ricardo Alvarez told me. Ricardo was a twenty-three-year-old native of San Cristóbal and part of the student movement rallying local opposition. With curly dark hair and excited eyes that accentuated his youth, he had the look of a young man simultaneously filled with purpose and naïveté, and thus gave off an aura of both predator and prey. "With the barricades, they have nowhere to go," Ricardo said, showing me around a series of ramshackle defenses he and a cohort of students had organized. "And we can fire back if we need to."

Though no one I saw had a gun, the students had devised an intricate system for protection. In the daylight hours, under the afternoon sun, students busily packed the city's empty milk crates with Molotov cocktails, filling dozens of glass bottles with gasoline before fashioning wicks. The empty bottles of milk Rosalina had lamented had literally been turned into weapons for battle. By nightfall, the students had equipped each block with stockpiles of petrobombs to be lit and hurled at approaching guardsmen and *colectivos*. Elder classmen manned checkpoints and coordinated movements with hand radios and cell phones, while others cemented iron spikes behind barricades, like the sharpened traffic strips at a car rental shop. All that was missing was a sign that read: DO NOT BACK UP, SEVERE TIRE DAMAGE. The barricades, meanwhile, grew larger as night wore on, with residents piling more wood, more sheet metal, and more barbed wire onto the heap that students would eventually douse in lighter fluid and set ablaze. From the elevated rise of Third Street where the El Paraiso hotel sat, more than a dozen fires could be seen burning in the surrounding hills, casting an eerie glow as darkness fell. And when it did, the whine of motorbikes and crack of gunfire inevitably echoed in the distance.

Loading a fresh battery into my Canon 5D camera, I walked east out onto Third Street as the sun dipped below the horizon and was immediately greeted by Ricardo, who grabbed me by the shoulder.

"Hey, man," he said. "I'm glad you came."

I hardly recognized him with his face wrapped in a cloth bandana that smelled of vinegar. Protesters and opposition groups had taken to soaking cloth in vinegar or diluted baking soda, then pressing the cloth against their noses and mouths, supposedly because of the blunting effects it has against tear gas. Breathing through acidified cloth offered a few extra moments to get upwind. Whether this technique actually worked was debatable, but those without respirators were all doing it.

"They're gathering," Ricardo said, pointing to the surrounding hills. "The guardsmen."

I doubted he could know that. It was just the impression of a young man gearing himself up for a fight, I figured. Though for weeks, national guardsmen along with armed paramilitary fighters on motorbikes had launched assaults. Opposition groups, to which Ricardo belonged, hid behind these homemade barricades, launching petrobombs by hand and rocks by slingshots from across the city's northern and eastern neighborhoods. The students were expecting another fight tonight. And they seemed prepared for it. Yet by the time I left the hotel and walked north, the streets had grown quiet. Even the high-pitched whine of motorbikes had disappeared. Still, dozens of students and others had remained.

"We're ready for them," said Ricardo, pointing to the crates of petrobombs stacked on street corners. He, like many of the young men of that age, was itching for a fight. No doubt a result of the crisis, he seemed to have found purpose here, and his eyes glimmered and fists clenched as he spoke, causing the sinewy lines of his forearms to throb and ripple. His fingers never stopped moving, dancing around glass bottle necks while affixing the fuses that would transform them into bombs.

"Are you going to stay?" he asked, brushing back curly hair that mopped in front of his face and lighting a cigarette.

"Yes, of course," I replied.

Meantime, others sat at checkpoints and coordinated movements by radio and cell phone, straining to see in darkness illuminated only by firelight, cigarette butts, and a few streetlamps.

But as the hours had passed from late afternoon and into the evening, virtually nothing happened. I leaned against a concrete wall of a home located beside one of the barricades, and then checked my watch.

At 11:00 p.m. Nothing. And the boys were getting weary.

By 12:00 a.m. I was barely propped up. Fatigue was settling in, and I could feel it almost wash over my bones.

By 1:00 a.m. the faces of the opposition, which had once looked youthful and energetic, had grown drawn and long as the night wore on. Few still stood upright, while others had heaved themselves onto folding chairs, battling sleep's inevitable onset. Eyelids fluttered. Some were closed. This wasn't their first late night at the barricades.

"OK," I said finally, as the clock neared 1:30 a.m. without incident. "I'm going to sleep." I gave a half-hearted wave to those who had welcomed me and promptly departed.

"OK, *chico*," I heard Ricardo say as I turned to walk south. "We'll be here."

Slinging my camera over one shoulder, I headed back to the hotel and promptly lay down. The nervous energy that once enveloped my consciousness in this surreal new scene of curfews and barricades by now had subsided. I just wanted some sleep. Little was happening anyway.

And inside those concrete walls and iron gates, sleep came easy. It was another reason I had chosen El Paraiso. It wasn't easily penetrable, at least not without an obvious warning to those inside. It was also situated on a side street just outside the fighting. Recent violence had occurred in the hills farther north and to the east of Third Street. El Paraiso was on the periphery and could serve as an effective staging point for coverage. I'd venture near the fighting should it happen, and then retreat back to the relative safety of the hotel. With few contacts and admittedly little sense of the city, it seemed like as good a plan as any. Though it didn't really matter. Nothing was going to happen tonight anyway. Despite Ricardo's prognostication of a mounting attack, the city seemed to have collectively gone to sleep.

He's just hoping for a fight, I thought, brushing my teeth with bottled water. I'll sort it out tomorrow. Then I settled in for what looked to be a few good hours of shut-eye.

What I didn't realize is that the battle lines had moved.

17

INTO CHAOS

The fight came around 3:00 a.m.

Shattered glass and metallic bangs cut through the early morning quiet. Then, an explosion rattled the pastel walls of my nearly empty hotel. Rubbing my eyes, I stumbled toward the door and grabbed the camera.

The students had struck first, lobbing petrobombs at a single armored vehicle descending from the surrounding eastern hills, probing their defenses. The sounds carried and disrupted San Cristóbal's slumbering Third Street neighborhood like a stone cast into a glassy lake. Students blew whistles, rallying others to the barricades. "David!" Rosalina yelled from outside my room. "They're coming!"

Ricardo had been right. And he was still out there, lighting a wick as I saw him, lobbing the flaming bottle at an armored vehicle approaching his flaming barricade. Just a few hours earlier, the students had set it ablaze, dousing it in lighter fluid as night fell, an effort to render it all but impenetrable to *colectivos*. And it was all that was separating government forces from the students, waves of whom were now sprinting forward, wearing those vinegar-soaked bandanas on their faces. Some passed fist-size stones to the slingers, who'd press them into the leather pouches of their homemade sling-shots before launching them over the barricade. Others moved crates of petrobombs closer to the front. Still others pressed cell phones to their ears. There seemed a practiced efficiency and coordination to the maneuvers. The students would arm, sprint to the front, launch their weapons, and retreat, only to regroup, rearm, and make another sprint frontward. But guardsmen were now returning fire, launching tear gas canisters. Metallic pops and cracks accompanied a cacophony of explosions, yelling, and car horns and the smell of gunpowder. The air had turned acrid. And it hung heavy. I had scrambled to throw on a pair of boots tucked alongside the bed.

Meanwhile, Rosalina raced to the lobby. She seemed both fran-tic and focused, trying to shutter the hotel's paneless windows in a fruitless attempt to keep the gas from seeping in. White clouds of exploded tear gas canisters had already blanketed the street as fresh canisters pierced the haze and streamed toward the youths, who were now in full retreat.

But back in the hotel, Rosalina's efforts had come too late. Two steaming canisters had landed in the small courtyard that abutted the hotel lobby. Noxious white clouds of tear gas were now pouring in, and within seconds we were both in a coughing fit. Employed in riot control, the guardsmen were firing and advancing. Rosalina and I scrambled toward the back of the hotel. I hooked around and climbed out on the roof to get a better view of the scene unfolding. From my perch, I could see a column of at least thirty guardsmen advancing in formation behind a second armored car. Both cars were painted white. Clad in protective flak jackets and wielding riot guns, the guardsmen were dressed in shiny black. They crouched as they walked behind the second armored vehicle, which had up until that point been driving slowly. But then it lurched forward and sped toward the barricade. When it struck, the grinding metal-on-metal sound of the collision echoed down Third Street and then lingered as the vehicle spun its wheels for a moment and pulled back, twisting iron rebar and scattering embers of the blaze in the process.

The flaming barricade had held. But only temporarily. And the students seemed to know it, scattering west and south down Third Street, many in a full sprint as canisters streamed overhead. The armored car had backed up and was again speeding forward. This time, the barricade gave way under its weight and momentum, clearing a path for the guardsmen, who were firing more gas and a fresh volley of rubber bullets. Third Street was disappearing under white smoke, and the guardsmen were in full advance, emboldened by their success. From my vantage point, they seemed to have won the night, scattering the opposition. I climbed down from my perch and hooked around back just as Ricardo passed by. His bandana had slipped lower on his mouth and I could now see more of his face, sweaty and enlivened.

"I told you," he said, before dipping back into the crowd of students, who were falling back, their supply of petrobombs depleted and rendered useless against the approaching armored cars.

By daybreak, it was clear that this scene was just one of several to have unfolded throughout the night. Broken glass and twisted iron filled the streets. Hundreds of spent tear gas canisters lay strewn across the city, along with a few bullet casings. One student lay dead. And the barricades were nearly all smashed.

Yet at first light, students alongside local civic groups and residents had returned. They were back at the markets, again waiting in hours-long lines. And they were again reconstructing the barricades. It was clear that it took only a few rams of an armored car to knock them down. But here they were, building them again anyway. The cycle would repeat again and again as violence gripped what was once South America's richest nation. The country was being torn apart. In an effort to blunt opposition and prop up loyalists, the Maduro government had followed Hugo Chavez in his populist approach, demonizing opposition groups and redistributing wealth, while the gradual erosion of democratic institutions drew protests nationwide. That, coupled with hyperinflation, shortages, the imprisonment of political leaders, a growing health and debt crisis, and spiraling violence, indeed seemed a recipe for the beginnings of a failed state.

Cuba might have to look for another benefactor, even though its relationship with Caracas had long been an unequal one. In 2012, Venezuela's bilateral trade with the island accounted for roughly one-fifth of Cuba's gross domestic product in exchange for doctors and security services. The country's former minister of Trade and Industry, Moisés Naím, a staunch Maduro critic, called the Venezuelan president a useful idiot for Havana, which in turn had helped preserve Maduro's power even as the Andean nation devolved into crisis.[1]

I walked out atop the rubble and again ran into Ricardo. He looked like he hadn't slept all night, and that glimmer in his eye had turned a bit manic.

"I told you," he said again with a sort of puffed-up pride as I approached. For all his bluster, Ricardo was hardly a prognosticator. This sort of clash had happened virtually every night for weeks.

"Yes, you did," I replied, walking with him for a bit. As we strolled, he pointed to a cluster of tear gas canisters the students had grouped together to be photographed with their phones and posted on social media.

"We have to let people know what's happening here," he said, making sure to call my attention to the expiration year imprinted on the canisters. Those he showed me dated 2004.

The barricades, smashed and in pieces, were still smoldering. I walked over them and noticed a young woman seated on a folding metal chair at one of the barricades' far edges. She was using a pair of pliers to twist and wrap a metal cable around a long piece of iron rebar she had presumably fished from the wreckage.

"What are you doing?" I asked.

She looked up, narrowed her eyes, and ignored me, methodically resuming her work. I asked again, and she sighed, an audible exasperation to an outsider inexplicably asking questions.

"Rebuilding," she finally replied, quickly refocusing on her work.

The rebar was to be reimplanted. And the metal cable better allowed for it to be woven in the tapestry of sheet metal, glass bottles, and other debris. The barricades were being resurrected.

The woman's name was Ani Sanchez, a twenty-four-year-old resident who had joined Ricardo in the resistance.

"Why do you keep building them?" I asked. "The barricades, I mean."

Unlike Ricardo, Ani wasn't one for bluster, nor had she been swept up in the broader politics of the opposition's now-nationwide struggle. Instead, her family and neighbors had taken up the resistance, and so she had.

"We use them for protection," she said.

"But if they destroy your barricades each night, are they really protection?" I asked.

Ani put down the iron rebar and let her hands drop, narrowing her eyes again and looking directly into mine. She didn't seem to like the question. Maybe there just wasn't an adequate answer. Or perhaps she just didn't feel like explaining. So she settled for something in between: a one-word answer that broke her pregnant pause. "*Colectivos.*"

"We build them to stop the *colectivos*," she repeated.

Though these makeshift barricades would only slow the advance of guardsmen who used their armored personnel carriers to smash their way through, they were quite effective against *colectivos* who marauded on motorbike. And it was those freewheeling armed bands of young men whom residents seemed to fear most. While the guardsmen could be and often were violent, they also seemed to play by a more formal and restrained set of rules. From what I had seen, guardsmen employed their batons liberally, emptied clips of tear gas from their riot guns, smashed barriers and sometimes homes.

Colectivos, by contrast, had ill-defined hierarchies and roamed with pistols loaded.

"I see," I said.

She brushed back her hair and seemed a bit more relaxed now, having put down her tools to enjoy an afternoon coffee from a small paper cup that an elder woman, presumably her mother, had just served her. The woman offered me one as well. I accepted and leaned against the house to sip and steal some shade from the rising Andean sun.

"Thank you," I said to the woman, whose crinkled face and tired eyes were like many here. She bobbed her head and looked toward Ani, who—with a bit of caffeine now coursing through her system— seemed more inclined to chat.

"What do you want out of all this?" I asked, taking the liberty of talking politics. Ani looked confused and then turned to me suddenly, as if the answer had just dawned on her.

"Freedom," she said.

"But what does that actually mean?" I replied. She paused again, considering the question.

"Freedom from *Chavismo.*"

Chavismo was a political ideology tied to the late Venezuelan president in which the government supported social welfare programs for the impoverished classes, nationalizing private industries and using the revenue to foot the bill. But it also clamped down on the independence of the legislature, the courts, and the media—a philosophy borrowed from Castroism. Though Ani's answer still seemed somewhat vague, I couldn't blame her. With clashes by night and growing food lines by day, where does one begin making sense of it all when food and security are the more immediate concerns? This once-powerful petro-economy, which sat on the world's largest proven oil reserves, was on the verge of collapse. And to many protesters, their country's problems increasingly mirrored Cuba's—scarcity, underinvestment, and an authoritarian government—with the added detriment of spiraling crime and violence. A growing homicide epidemic had ensued. More than seventeen thousand Venezuelans had fallen victim by official tally, though outside monitors claimed those reports were grossly underreported. The more accurate number, these groups said, was more than twenty-seven thousand killings. If true, that would place Venezuela among the world's most violent regions, with more than ninety killings per hundred thousand people each year.[2]

A student was killed my first night in San Cristóbal. And Ani knew him, as he lived only a few blocks from the barricades where the fighting so often occurred. This was Ani's community. And these were her friends, neighbors, and family members who were dying.

But Ani wasn't a leader. She wasn't even much of a protester, but rather someone inextricably caught up in the fight. And now she was talking to an American journalist amid protests that endeavored to reshape her country and determine its future. She leaned against a support beam that extended from the house.

"David?" Ani asked, taking a seat. "Why are you here?"

The question, simple and innocent, caught me off guard. It was obvious why she was here. But to many, I was just a *yuma* voyeur, a man who didn't belong. In truth, the idea had germinated one evening over beers in a Caracas bar with my fixer, or local producer, Daniel.

"You should see where [the demonstrations] all started," he said, three days into covering opposition protests that had spread across the capital and in cities such as Valencia and Puerto Cabello. I agreed and we drummed up a plan to fly out the following afternoon, traversing a lush green-and-brown countryside over hilltop roads before finally arriving in San Cristóbal before nightfall. But now I had to answer for it. Ani, who had taken a risk in speaking with me, wanted to know if it had been worth sharing her thoughts with a foreign journalist whom she correctly assumed she'd never see again.

I'd been asked this question before. And so I had a ready-made response, replete with the kind of ivory-tower back-patting one

might expect of a journeyman journalist: I was there to offer a dis-
passionate view of history; to "comfort the afflicted and afflict the
comfortable," in the well-trodden adaption of what *Chicago Evening
Post*'s Finley Peter Dunne once spouted. I didn't actually buy into
Dunne's perspective. But there was a sort of puffed-up righteousness
in the cadence of his words—polished and practiced bullshit, conveyed in popular literature that glamorizes the Hemingways, the
Faulkners, the Greenes, and their outsized roles, personalities, and
lifestyles, no matter how dubious and self-aggrandizing it all
might be. We journos have a way of buying our own hype.

I looked at Ani, ready to open my mouth and begin my spiel,
but nothing came out. The words were right there. But instead I
paused and just looked at her. Young, inexperienced, and still a student, she likely would have gobbled up whatever narrative I spewed.
But all I could do was think about the chain of events that brought
me here. Of how different our circumstances were. Ani rubbed her
face. It was ashen and dirty. The sweat from her brow matted the
front of her dark brown hair. A surgical mask rested just above her
forehead. She would pull it over her nose and mouth when the tear
gas came. Her white T-shirt and denim jeans were unwashed. She
looked both scared and ready for a fight—the harried look of an
animal caught in a snare. She was indeed caught. Between hours-
long food lines and mending barricades, something was being lost.
Her quiet mixed with the exhaustion of never getting a good night's
sleep. But at the moment, she wasn't focused on any of that. Instead,
Ani had taken a hiatus from her problems to ask me a very simple
question.

"Why are you here?"

"It's my job," I replied. It was all I could muster. The once-shining
narrative had lost its luster and now seemed transparently vain. As
a son of middle-class America—steeped in a considerable dose of
white privilege—I had license to choose the life I wanted, and I had
imagined my work contributing to the information thicket that

guided global opinion. *The right side of history.* Say those words often enough and they not only convince others, but *you* yourself start to believe.

Of course, news—especially television news—remained a business like any other. It was a numbers game. Viewership had declined in both the United States and United Kingdom by an average of 3 to 4 percent every year since 2012.[3] And news executives were well aware that their jobs relied on blunting those inevitable drops, making producers particularly eager for the next crisis—or even just the next compelling video. Once the tear gas and bullets stopped flying, the logic went, there was little reason to stick around. There was always another crisis to sate those voyeuristic appetites upon which their business models increasingly depended. Click-baited viewers needed their fix, lest they search elsewhere. And foreign news was always a tough sell. Haiti had proven that. But how could I say that to Ani? How could I tell her that while I believed in the power of good journalism, a big part of why I came here was the promise of "good pictures"? I certainly wouldn't be sticking around to see how it all wound up. When I stepped aboard that Caracas-bound flight, the work had felt important. Yet now, standing there in front of Ani, who had asked me a simple, honest question, it all seemed terribly shallow. I would barely begin to learn what there was to know about this place before it was again time to leave. And with that model, how much of an impact could any of us really make? I planned to be in San Cristóbal for a week to witness the birthplace of protests and to shine a proverbial light on the crimes and injustices I saw—the supposed antiseptic of good journalism. But I was an outsider with no real skin in the game—not a local reporter, many of whom had been sidelined or imprisoned—and was thus comparatively immune to the conflict's consequences. Venezuela was devolving. The violence had escalated. And many were beginning to starve. But I was a *yuma.* I had my story. And I would soon be leaving and heading back to Cuba.

18

TRAPPINGS OF DÉTENTE

Around the same time that Venezuela descended into chaos, President Obama was handing the pope a box of seeds. It was March 27, 2014, and the first meeting between the two leaders was underway: an American president who campaigned on his willingness to engage with almost anyone, and a popular pope, born in Buenos Aires, who wielded enormous influence across Latin America. The seeds, encased in a custom-made wooden chest, were meant to signal a fresh start after troubled past U.S. relations with the Vatican.

"These, I think, are carrots," Obama explained to a smiling Pope Francis. The two men conversed in private for more than fifty minutes. What few outsiders knew at the time was that much of that conversation had focused on Havana.[1]

"The Vatican's involvement in this policy change was crucial," Assistant Secretary of State Roberta Jacobson later explained before a 2015 Senate subcommittee hearing.[2] "The respect for this pope, because he's a Latin American, and his importance in Cuba and throughout the hemisphere is part of the reason [the process is] so well respected."

Momentum for normalization was building. And Pope Francis would prove pivotal.

Five months later, the two sides would revisit the issue on an August afternoon in Washington. This time, the pope had dispatched Havana's archbishop, Jaime Ortega. The portly, balding Cuban was in Washington officially at the invitation of Georgetown University. But Ortega, the same archbishop who had brokered the release of political prisoners in 2010, now had other motives. He was bound for a secret meeting with President Obama.

For much of Washington, Cuba was still a comparatively low U.S. priority. Yet top aides, including White House chief of staff Denis McDonough and Latin American affairs specialist Ricardo Zúñiga, greeted Ortega when he arrived that afternoon before his Rose Garden meeting with the president. Obama then arrived and the two briefly conversed, Ortega handing the president a letter from Pope Francis that reiterated the church's willingness to serve as an interlocutor.

A window for action was opening, made possible by a rare confluence of factors: An influential pope had urged détente and offered to help. Latin American leaders were demanding an end to Cuba's isolation. Fidel had stepped down, removing a decades-old lightning rod from Miami's calculus, while Fidel's brother Raul had pursued the beginnings of the kind of market-based reforms that Washington had long called for. Meanwhile, President Obama, now in his second term, benefited from a far different political landscape. As a generational shift in South Florida left older exile hard-liners weakened, polls showed residents favored a restoration of ties.[3] There still was that pesky issue of detained American contractor Alan Gross. But after the earthquake in Haiti, when Cuba and the United States found ways to collaborate in disaster response, new channels had opened up for more dialogue, eventually contributing to a breakthrough with the Cuban government that afforded Alan's wife, Judy, the ability to make regular visits to see her husband.

A second channel would emerge by way of a man named Tim Rieser. A former Vermont public defender turned veteran insider of the U.S. Senate Committee on Appropriations, Rieser was a top aide to Senator Patrick Leahy (D-VT) and over the years had earned Leahy's confidence. And both Leahy and Rieser were interested in Cuba.[4]

"I might have thought of something else, like working to help rid the ocean of plastic or some other worthwhile project," Rieser told me one evening during an interview. "But this one struck both me and Senator Leahy as actually achievable. . . . The stars had aligned in ways that they hadn't before."

Part of that alignment had to do with the ticking biological clock of the wife of an imprisoned Cuban spy. Adriana Perez was forty years old and had grown desperate for a baby. Her husband, Gerardo Hernandez, was serving two life sentences in a federal prison in California. A part of the so-called Cuban Five, an intelligence ring Fidel Castro had placed in South Florida, Hernandez was arrested for spying on exiles and U.S. military installations. Lawyers for the men sought to move the location of the trial outside Miami, where they argued an impartial jury would be nearly impossible to find in a region dominated by Cuban exiles. But the request was denied and the men were promptly convicted. In Cuba, they would become a cause célèbre, their faces plastered across billboards and their work extolled during state speeches. But as the years progressed, Adriana despaired and asked her government to intervene. Obliging, Cuban officials contacted their State Department counterparts, but to no avail.

Meanwhile, Senator Leahy and Rieser had been making trips to Cuba to see Gross, while back channeling with Havana in an effort to improve his conditions. During one such visit, the Cubans saw their chance to help the wife of their jailed hero, leading Adriana to the Havana hotel where Leahy and his wife, Marcelle Pomerleau Leahy, and Rieser were all staying.

There, Adriana made her plea.

"I think both the senator and Marcelle felt that this was a person who was genuinely desperate and that they wanted to do something to help if they could," Rieser told me. "Not as quid pro quo or anything, but because it was the right thing to do."

She wanted a baby. From there, an idea sprouted. Federal prisons do not permit conjugal visits, but there was certainly precedent for artificial insemination. Rieser, who by now had emerged as a key liaison in the exchange—routinely meeting with Alan Gross, Cuban officials, and the National Security Council—endeavored to make it possible. Vials of Gerardo's sperm were collected and transported to Adriana. The first attempt failed. But the second implantation worked. Meanwhile, Rieser pressed Cuban authorities to improve their treatment of Gross, whose health and spirits had been deteriorating. The American contractor had survived by befriending fellow detainees, Cubans whose families would bring in food to supplement the paltry diet authorities provided. But if Gross died, Leahy and Rieser surmised, it would likely mark an end to negotiations with the Cubans to improve relations, irreparably changing the political math.

At about the same time that Adriana became pregnant, Gross's situation began to improve. The lights in his detention room—which had previously remained on twenty-four hours a day—now went off at night. Cuban authorities provided Gross greater access to visitors, and they allowed Rieser and Gross's attorney, Scott Gilbert, to make regular phone calls. Each would spend hours on the phone to Havana.

These were small steps, but positive ones. "Anyone who knows the Cubans knows that Cubans don't respond well to ultimatums or threats any more than we do," Rieser told me.

Though conditions had improved, the aging contractor had lost an enormous amount of weight. If something was to be done on Cuba during President Obama's second term, it had to happen soon. Rieser scheduled a meeting at the White House. He planned to meet with staff members of the National Security Council, including Ricardo Zúñiga, then acting director of the Office of Cuban Affairs at the State Department, who had previously worked at the U.S. Interests Section in Havana. Zúñiga had experience with the Cubans and had dealt with detentions before. But negotiations were moving slowly, the inertia, perhaps, of fists clenched for so long that to release them would seem almost unnatural.

It wouldn't be easy.

Negotiations nearly broke down altogether after President Obama announced the exchange of five Taliban prisoners held at the U.S naval base at Guantanamo Bay for Sergeant Bowe Bergdahl in May 2014, as precious political capital had been expended in the deal. It remained unclear if enough was left for Gross.

The Cubans had watched the exchange from afar, and top officials assumed that this meant the United States was open to an exchange, according to those involved in negotiations. But outrage had erupted on Capitol Hill, as accusations of capitulation to a foreign enemy chipped away at the president's capacity for a similar deal with the Cubans. Then Republican presidential nominee Donald Trump called Bergdahl—who had walked off his base and been captured by the Taliban in Afghanistan—a traitor, and suggested he should be shot or thrown from an airplane for endangering those American troops who had been sent to search for him. Meanwhile, public support for prisoner swaps seemed to be fading. Leahy and Rieser had to act quickly. "We had to explain to the Cubans why [the Bergdahl situation] hurt us," Rieser told me. "They thought it was positive because there had been this prisoner trade, and they felt that was a sign that the administration would reciprocate in the case of Alan Gross. I said the Bergdahl trade was very unpopular. It meant that the administration would have to come up with a better deal."

Without more concessions from the Cubans, the political costs of another prisoner swap could be too damaging for the administration to weather. Fortunately for the prisoners, Havana was listening.

To sweeten the deal, the Cubans added Rolando Sarraff Trujillo, a double agent whom President Obama referred to as "one of the most important intelligence agents that the United States has ever had in Cuba," to the prisoner exchange. Shuttling back to Washington, Rieser continued meeting with the National Security Council staff, at one point suggesting that the goal should be for President Obama to actually go to Cuba. "It's our job to make it possible," he told the staffers during one visit, prodding and eventually appealing to that potent blend of partisanship and legacy searching that so frequently dominates Washington circles. "Why is it always Republicans that make history by going to Russia or China?" he asked.

Momentum was again building as Obama dispatched top aides Ben Rhodes and Ricardo Zúñiga to Ottawa and Toronto for a series of secret negotiations with their Cuban counterparts. Canada seemed like a safe choice.

"With Canada, it was a country where both countries had good relations," Dan Erikson told me in an interview. The former top State Department adviser explained that it was "a place where it would be possible to do this discreetly. All the negotiators had a legitimate reason to be there. So, it didn't raise any eyebrows."[5]

Knowing the sensitivity of such discussions and the baggage they carried, particularly in electoral politics, the Americans insisted on secrecy—a difficult task for a man like Rhodes, who had become increasingly known as the White House spinmaster. The Cubans obliged. And as a sign of their seriousness, one of their top negotiators would bear the Castro name. In fact, the envoy would turn out to be the very man who'd sat across from me at that Havana bar half a decade earlier. It was Alejandro Castro Espín who would negotiate détente on behalf of his government.

A lot had happened since that beer-and-rum-soaked night back in Miramar. Alejandro, the president's son, had quietly risen from obscurity to take on a role of growing importance within his father's government, advising the president on key issues much like Raul once had for Fidel, traveling to the Vatican for a meeting with Pope Francis and later to Panama City during the Summit of the Americas, witnessing the historic moment when his father shook President Obama's hand. Though Alejandro would later dismiss the idea of succeeding Raul as president in a 2015 Greek television interview, dissidents openly wondered about the extent of his power.[6] "The dauphin {in North Korea} is named Kim Jong Un; perhaps soon they will communicate to us that over here ours will be Alejandro Castro Espín," wrote Yoani Sanchez following reports of the colonel's supposed ascendance.[7]

19

THE NORMALIZATION

The news broke on a Wednesday. It was December 2014. Christmas was just eight days away, and the story I had long given up on had just landed in my inbox.

"U.S., Cuba seek to normalize relations," flashed a news alert on my cell phone.

The faint glow of the morning's rising sun had just begun to seep through my apartment's corner window, so it took me a moment to process. I rubbed my eyes and looked again.

"Normalize relations," the news alert said.

Millions of Cubans who had spent their lives waiting to hear this news had, on December 17, 2014, gotten their wish. Few knew what "normalize" actually meant, and indeed Cuba analysts would years later still be trying to decipher its full implications. But on that day none of that seemed to matter. It was a first step, the first of its kind in more than fifty years.

"Where are my glasses?" I asked aloud to no one in particular.

Old habits die hard. But unlike those early days in New York when I had just returned from Havana, I was alone. My marriage hadn't survived. We divorced just a few years after my return to the States. And my routine these days consisted mostly of work, a growing stack of partially read books, a few alcohol-soaked nights and head-throbbing early mornings, followed by that inevitable search for glasses. But this morning I was awakened to the sound of hard plastic vibrating against polished wood. My phone was ringing. Emails were flooding in. News teams were mobilizing. I knew I was heading back to Havana.

"Yeah?" I said into the phone, wiping away sleep's remnants.

"How soon can you be ready to go?" an urgent voice responded. The staccato tone of his words punctuated the priority of the question. It was Amir Ahmed, vice president of newsgathering at Al Jazeera America. He had not even referenced Cuba. By now, it was a given. I had known Amir from our days at CNN, when he was on CNN's international desk in Atlanta and I was in Havana. It seemed fitting for him to be the one calling now, after we had both taken jobs at Al Jazeera America.

"Just a few hours," I replied, pulling my passport from my top drawer.

I already kept a bag crammed full of clothes and gear tucked in my closet for just this sort of thing. But I was missing one thing. In Cuba's credit card–free economy, I needed cash—and lots of it. I phoned the network's accounting department. In Cuba, it was always better to have too much than too little. And there was still the question of a journalist visa. No matter what policy changes America made, journalists still had to be accredited by the Cuban government. Those were contacts that had to be worked in both Havana and the Cuban Interests Section in Washington, usually weeks in advance. But now there was no time. I headed for the airport and started making calls on the way, with plans to board an afternoon flight to Miami without the visa.

Somewhere in the midst of the scramble, more concrete details about the announcement were becoming clear. On December 17,

2014, roughly four years after I parted ways with an island I had then thought I'd never see again, President Obama strode up to a blue podium embossed with a gold seal in the Cabinet Room of the White House and promised to end America's estrangement from Cuba.

In exchange for imprisoned American contractor Alan Gross and U.S. spy Rolando Sarraff Trujillo, the Cubans had gotten back three of their own. But perhaps more importantly, it was a signal that the president of the United States sought to wipe clean more than fifty years of bad blood and pursue a fresh start in what many hoped to be a new post–Cold War era. After months of secret negotiations, what had begun as a prisoner swap had turned into the most historic shift in relations between the two old foes in half a century. Two nations that once sat on the brink of nuclear war were finally ending an "outdated approach," as President Obama put it, ushering in a normalization that had eluded ten previous U.S. administrations.[1] Church bells were ringing across Havana. News of the deal spread like wildfire. Talk of "what could be" filled the island. And the path toward resolution of even the most intractable issues seemed to be at hand. Yet I still wasn't certain my Cuban journalist visa would be approved.

We had arrived in Miami. The visas hadn't.

"Listen, baby," said Addy Sanchez, a resolver who also ran a travel service out of Florida and had been communicating with the Cubans on our behalf. Addy called everyone "baby." "Everybody is trying to get there."

Cuba's International Press Center had been flooded with calls. The world had again woken up to Cuba, and it would take some time to get in.

"OK," I said before making calls to my old minders myself. I still spoke with Raulito at Cuba's press center every now and again. "Keep me posted."

As we waited, our Al Jazeera crew packed up and headed for Little Havana. Surely, the exile community would be up in flames.

For generations, whenever even the hint of capitulation crossed into the American zeitgeist, residents came out in force.

Just fourteen years earlier, demonstrations had erupted in the Little Havana district after federal agents smashed their way into the home of six-year-old Elian Gonzalez to return him to his father in Cuba. The boy, whose mother had drowned after carrying him aboard a small aluminum boat as they attempted to flee Cuba across the Florida Strait, had somehow survived and was saved on Thanksgiving Day in 1999 by two Florida fishermen who handed him over to the U.S. Coast Guard. An impassioned international custody battle ensued. Elian's relatives in South Florida insisted he stay with them, while his father in Cuba demanded the boy's return. At the urging of those like U.S. senator Patrick Leahy, President Bill Clinton, and Attorney General Janet Reno, federal agents ultimately sided with the father, but not before the struggle to keep the boy had become a cause célèbre in South Florida. When federal agents raided the Little Havana home and forcibly extracted the child at gunpoint, protesters spilled into the streets, setting more than two hundred fires and burning tires and trash in a show of anger.[2] They would make the Democrats pay for it.

Though Cuban Americans in Florida typically voted Republican, Clinton had managed to secure 35 percent of their vote in the 1996 election, helping him edge out Bob Dole. But that was before Elian. Four years later, in the 2000 presidential race against then Texas governor George W. Bush, Vice President Al Gore would draw less than 20 percent of the Cuban vote, narrowly losing the state. Residents called it *el voto castigo,* or the punishment vote, and it was largely over a custodial battle.[3]

Now, the stakes were far higher. And President Obama had gone much further.

Surely, Miami's Little Havana would again erupt.

As I walked down Eighth Street, I had expected to see another mass demonstration like the one in 2000. Local and national news crews had already descended from across the country with the same idea. Demonstrations. Marches. Fires. Something. But fourteen years is a long time. Long enough for a hotbed to cool. And by noon on December 18, 2014, just one day after Obama's announcement, the number of journalists out on Miami streets seemed to rival the number of demonstrators. Versailles Restaurant, a traditional rallying spot, had given way to a handful of retirees sipping their *cafecitos,* as tourists ogled brightly adorned TV news anchors and their accompanying satellite trucks.

"Obama is a traitor!" yelled Miguel Saavedra, his well-coiffed gray hair unmoving despite his wild gesticulations. Saavedra was the president of a right-wing exile group called Vigilia Mambisa, loosely translated as Patriotic Watch, which still advocated the violent overthrow of the Castro regime. Flanked by a handful of aging Cuban Americans wielding signs and shouting anti-Castro, anti-Obama slogans, they did their best to make a stir. But they didn't quite have the numbers of yesteryear. Opinions of the younger generation of Cuban Americans were shifting, likely a factor in Obama's decision to normalize relations. And the polling supported it. In fact, a 2014 poll commissioned by the Atlantic Council found that 63 percent of adult respondents living in Florida actually favored improved relations with Cuba. The risks politicians once faced in crossing powerful lobbyists like the late Jorge Mas Canosa seemed to have died along with him, as demographic shifts engendered new political priorities. We were there for what we assumed would be the inevitable Miami reaction, but times had changed. Still, the old hard-liners seemed intent on making up the difference.

"We got nothing," Saavedra told me, referencing the deal that ushered in détente.[4] "They got everything."

In some ways, he was right. President Obama had essentially handed President Raul Castro a major policy shift that allowed for new financing, investment, and tourism dollars without securing any commitments to democratic reforms. Though Castro had released

Gross and Trujillo, there were virtually no structural concessions the U.S. administration could identify that might blunt the swell of criticism. Aside from the prisoner swap, to many it seemed like a giveaway. And the hard-liners were incensed. Doing business in Cuba was expected to get a whole lot easier. And in the coming months, President Obama would double down, instructing his Treasury Department to carry out what were perhaps the most comprehensive changes to Cuba trade and investment in more than half a century. Twenty-seven pages of new regulations authorized American entrepreneurs to engage with Cuban government–owned companies as well as the more than two hundred categories of independently licensed businesses on the island, essentially promising to open the door to companies such as FedEx, John Deere, and Microsoft, which had all expressed interest in both opening offices in Havana and hiring Cuban employees.

"This isn't an end run around the embargo," John Kavulich, the president of the U.S.-Cuba Trade and Economic Council, told me in an interview shortly after the announcement. "It's a full-frontal assault."

The regulatory shift also eased restrictions on travel, provided a framework for financial institutions, expanded general licenses for telecommunications and internet services, and did away with restrictions on the money sent to Cuba from relatives abroad. I thought of Alberto, and of how this new policy wouldn't likely help him and other black Cubans nearly as much as it would help their white counterparts. In 2014, remittances exceeded $2 billion, and U.S. residents could send $2,000 maximum per quarter, upon which about two-thirds of Cuban households and 90 percent of its private retail market relied. Now, the tap was open, and a crescendo of microfinancing came with it. Born largely of U.S. paychecks, the new funding source filled the pockets of Cuban restaurateurs and bed-and-breakfast owners, many of whom for the first time had the capital they needed to upgrade and expand.

The embargo was indeed loosening, the island overtaken by the prospect of new investment and the chatter of change. Lifting sanctions required an act of Congress, but the executive branch enjoyed a certain degree of leeway in how those sanctions were interpreted and applied.

"The embargo has more holes than Swiss cheese," said Pedro Freyre, chairman of Akerman LLP, a law practice that focused on Cuba-related matters. In fact, an often overlooked regulatory exemption allowed U.S. companies to sell agricultural goods and medical supplies to the island. Though the relationship was not reciprocal, and Cuba could not buy on credit, trade between the two countries had nonetheless made the United States the island's fourth-largest trading partner. Now, with the 2014 détente, American companies hoped for much more. The administration boasted about the prospect of "more than $6 billion in trade," expecting companies to make use of the 490 new Cuba licenses its treasury department had granted.

But granting of licenses is not quite the same thing as doing business. In fact, a closer look revealed that despite the improved relations and the flood of microfinancing on a person-to-person level, Cuba and U.S. companies were actually trading less than usual. In 2007, U.S. agricultural exports to Cuba accounted for approximately $710 million in trade. But by the end of 2014, following détente, the figure had dropped to just $291 million, notably in foodstuffs such as corn and soya.[5] Sure, falling commodity prices made the value of such exports cheaper, but that couldn't account for the more than 240 percent drop.

It didn't make sense. Wouldn't improved relations foster more trade, not less? The island certainly needed the cash. Despite an 80 percent increase in U.S. visitors, Cuba remained cash-strapped, as low commodity prices and the lingering effects of drought and hurricanes left it unable to pay down its debts. It seemed logical for Havana to be eager for new investment, especially from a natural trading partner just ninety miles from its shores. But in Castro's Cuba, decisions were rarely based purely on economics.

Trade was a political tool. And for the past decade, a state-owned Cuban food-trading company known as ALIMPORT, which oversaw all food imports to the island, had been courting U.S. farm lobbyists while gradually increasing food purchases from states such as Virginia, Louisiana, Wisconsin, and California, which the USDA predicted would "likely see significant gains from lifting restrictions on trade."[6] It all seemed a part of Castro's inside-outside strategy, railing against the U.S. embargo from far away, while looking for pressure points from within. And yet after years of pressure, U.S. sanctions against Cuba remained. Havana had tried the carrot, whetting American farm industry appetites. Why not try the stick? So when détente unfolded in 2014, the island was already reducing its food purchases from U.S. farmers, a punishment of sorts for the lack of action. On the one thing that really mattered. Normalization was nice, but an end to sanctions was the prize.

There was also another reason for the drop, and it followed the same marketing strategy that guided the island's exorbitantly priced car dealerships: bait. The United States could be used to attract foreign investors. The thinking went that a normalized relationship with Washington would improve perceptions of Cuba's investment climate, which many foreign companies avoided due to U.S. sanctions and restrictive labor policies. Détente might encourage new deals with other investors, preferably those with whom Havana had often done business, such as the Chinese and Russians. The fewer strings attached the better. Cuban leaders seemed to prefer dealing with countries that didn't scold their own lack of democracy or set terms over Cuba's record on human rights. In other words, Havana wanted the kind of investment that normalization with the United States might bring, just not necessarily American investment. Besides, there was just too much history with Washington to ignore.

"I don't trust the policy of the United States," Fidel Castro declared in January 2015, following détente.[7] A half century of estrangement couldn't simply be flicked away by an Obama speech, no matter how welcoming its language. Cuba's old guard was still wary of reengagement and the specter of American meddling. No, this had to be a deal brokered from a position of strength. Raul needed the cash. Foreign investment goals now routinely missed their mark, while more than $1 billion in unpaid commercial debt stacked ever higher. But the old Communist wasn't about to sign on to anything at the expense of his country's autonomy. This was still a government born of revolution.

"Their sole goal is to lessen conditionality with everything," Kavulich told me in an interview. "Commercial relations, economic relations, political relations. It's to get as much as they can out of everyone by doing as little as possible."

Meanwhile, entrepreneurs in Florida were lining up. Miami International Airport had long been a way station of sorts for families waiting to board dozens of flights to cities across Latin America. And Terminal D, where charter companies ferry passengers on the forty-minute flight to Havana, always seemed to have the longest lines. Addy had come through. And with a Cuban journalist visa now in hand, I was about to join them.

"OK, baby," she said, handing me a white packet of forms. Staring out across those heaps of clear-blue-plastic-wrapped luggage of Havana-bound travelers, we were all enmeshed in the throes of real change.

When our plane touched down at Jose Marti International Airport, there was a lightness to the city that I had never experienced. An almost unbridled enthusiasm swept the island, infectious to even the most hardened skeptics. This time, after four generations of starts and stops, Cuba and the United States had finally crossed the Rubicon. Or so it seemed.

"One year, the embargo will be lifted," one woman told me, her exuberance lifted by a bottle of rum she shared with a group of friends who were still celebrating on Havana's Malecon. "We're going to erect a statue to Obama here," said another.

They then danced into the night, seemingly forgetting our conversation, so wrapped up were they in the promise of détente and what it could mean. After a half century of sanctions, even rumors of their lifting could spawn a rum-soaked catharsis that was practically palpable.

While Cuban officials seemed to welcome the news, that sort of revelry likely also made them squirm. A popular American president presented a potential danger to graying Cuban leadership that would soon experience its own transition as Raul prepared to step down from the presidency. In fact, a 2014 poll determined that 80 percent of Cuban respondents held a positive view of President Obama, while 79 percent said they were "not too satisfied" or "not at all satisfied" with Cuba's economic system. Another 49 percent lamented the "lack of freedom," while 58 percent gave their country's Communist Party a negative rating.[8] Polling is extremely difficult in a country that fiercely guards its information. Pollsters are compelled to travel in secret, without authorization, which raises questions about the veracity of the findings and whether methods adopted by clandestine pollsters could yield reliable results. Yet the report seemed to reinforce what many in government had feared: a budding crisis of confidence just as Cuba's biggest political transition approached.

THE OLD GUARD

I imagine Raul Castro woke up that Wednesday morning on December 17, 2014, pulled himself out of bed, and walked over to his wardrobe. It was a big day to be sure. His deputies, including his son, had just spearheaded the closing of a negotiated prisoner exchange that would bring home Cuba's captured spies and solidify a deal to normalize relations with the United States. All Raul had given up were an aging American contractor and a spy. Now all that was left to do was to tell his country about it on state television. But like most big days, there still was the question of what to wear. Raul, a discreet pragmatist, reluctant in his role—quite the opposite of his showman brother—didn't seem like the kind of man to have his clothes laid out for him. Still, this appearance would likely be choreographed. There would be theatrics, and his words would be only part of the performance. Since assuming the office of the presidency, Raul had often taken to wearing dark suits or the more casual white *guayabera,* depending upon the occasion, as opposed to the green military fatigues to which he had grown accustomed as head of the Cuban Revolutionary Armed Forces. The clothes often set the tone.

That morning, President Barack Obama wore a dark blue suit. But Raul would not return the favor. Instead, he reverted to his revolutionary roots and donned the green fatigues, likely a nod to his country's old hard-liners, who remained skeptical of the intentions of the comparatively young American president. It was a message both to the island's residents and the world at large: Cuba may welcome détente, but it wasn't about to let its guard down.

Still, President Castro thanked President Obama and acknowledged that Cuba had "embarked on the task of updating our economic model in order to build a prosperous and sustainable Socialism."[1] Indeed, he had. In 2011, Raul had launched a series of belt-tightening measures, unveiling plans to phase out one-fifth of Cuba's workforce over the coming years, reduce its social welfare programs, and expand its private sector.

"We have to erase forever the notion that Cuba is the only country in the world in which people can live without working," he said during an August speech to the National Assembly in which he pressed cooperative-based agriculture and self-employment in the hopes of absorbing Cuba's newly unemployed.[2]

Careful to avoid using the word "privatize" lest he provoke others in the old Communist guard, Raul's reforms nonetheless bucked the Soviet-style system, where at least 80 percent of the population worked. With Fidel sidelined, Raul enjoyed a degree of leeway to exercise his more pragmatist side. And Cuba needed that. For decades, even professions considered relatively autonomous, such as plumbers and carpenters, were employed by the state and paid through third-party government intermediaries. The effect tamped down wages and created few incentives for growth. Now, by legalizing home and car sales and granting new business licenses—stoking the potential for higher earnings—Raul hoped to breathe new life into the Cuban economy.

To some extent, it worked. Between 2010 and 2013, the number of Cubans working in small, privately owned businesses or who were self-employed more than doubled, from 160,000 to 390,000.[3] Following détente, private sector opportunity increased, and the number of private restaurants (*paladares*) and family-stays (*casas particulares*) swelled to 2,000 and 22,000 respectively.

But with a flood of new American investment, Cuba's old guard, skeptical of Obama's motivations, fretted about a less egalitarian society. Two basic camps were emerging. The first, filled with Cuba's gerontocracy, sought to preserve the island's paternalistic structure, in which decisions remained hierarchical and Communism-centric. The second seemed to recognize that life couldn't continue as is and that market reforms had to occur if Cuba were to survive, especially now that Venezuela's help had weakened. The Americans were forcing Havana's hand, but Havana wasn't so sure it wanted a Starbucks on every corner, let alone the kind of disruptive economic transformation that brought chaos to Russia following the collapse of the Soviet Union. Cuban officials seemed to be dragging their feet.

Meanwhile, Cubans I spoke with had long grumbled of two embargoes: one imposed by Washington and the other self-inflicted by the island's Soviet-style command economy. Raul had shrunken state payrolls and encouraged more than half a million self-employed workers, slimming Cuba's bloated public sector; yet income inequality was now rising, with foreign investors again hopeful of regaining influence. Few outside observers would have accused Raul of moving too quickly. But in a country that for generations had relied on the state's paternalistic structure, even a hint of liberalizing reform could raise concerns among the party faithful that Cuba's bulwark against American-style capitalism was wearing thin. So Raul slowed it all down, suspending the issuing of new business licenses and agriculture reforms. Cuba was changing. But the reforms would be slow and proceed on Cuba's terms, at least so long as the Castros remained in power.

Meanwhile, U.S. State Department officials seemed intent on placating concerns over its Cuba policy, at least in part to curry greater influence in a region that was drawing new attention from America's old adversaries. China had been expanding its Latin America investments at a dizzying pace, drawing up plans for a shipping canal in Nicaragua, rail transport in Mexico, and energy exploration in Ecuador. From 2000 to 2012, Chinese–Latin American trade had increased from $10 billion to $270 billion, and the region had emerged as its second-largest foreign investment destination, second only to Europe.[4]

Then there was Russia. Keen on getting back in the game, the Kremlin had forgiven 90 percent of Cuba's $35 billion debt, much of it dating back to the 1980s; had helped Bolivia with "peaceful nuclear research"; and was pushing its state-owned energy giants Gazprom and Rosneft into Argentina and Brazil. Meanwhile, leaders in much of Latin America, including Argentina, Brazil, Venezuela, Bolivia, and Ecuador, had all recently come off leftist electoral wins atop platforms sympathetic toward Cuba, and many seemed intent on strengthening their own bargaining power. A South American trade bloc known as Mercosur allowed its members to raise tariffs up to 35 percent on imports from countries outside the bloc.[5] Washington had taken notice, but eight years of strained relations under the Bush administration had reduced American leverage. President Obama seemed to make changing that a priority.

Days before the April 2009 Summit of the Americas in Trinidad, the White House announced an easing of restrictions on remittances and travel for Cuban Americans. Just months before the arrest of Alan Gross, Obama had promised "a new beginning" in relations with Havana. Raul responded by saying he was ready to put "everything" on the table, including "human rights, freedom of the press [and] political prisoners."[6] The Latin left was now listening, including Venezuela's populist president Hugo Chavez, who shook Obama's hand on the sidelines of the summit and expressed a desire to "reset" relations. You could almost feel the love, along with a newfound desire to change the status quo.

Of course, that was then.

Three years later at the 2012 summit in Cartagena, Colombia, the region's leaders, no longer swooning over Obama's rhetoric, now wanted action. But the summit wouldn't quite go according to plan, as a sex scandal involving a U.S. Secret Service agent and a twenty-four-year-old Colombian prostitute cast a shadow on events that were meant to hone global attention on issues such as climate change, the region's drug wars, and immigration. Senior White House staff were infuriated. Yet on the sidelines, during private conversations between officials that so often prove to be the real value of these summits, the State Department team had also learned something that would guide their new American policy in Latin America, and quietly prove a precursor to détente. All roads traced back to Havana. To improve relations in the region, Cuba had to be addressed.

"After Cartagena, when we were meeting with the countries that were essentially friendly to us, Cuba was still such a thorny issue," Daniel Erikson told me in an interview. As a State Department and White House adviser on Latin America, Erikson was directly involved in the normalization. "The president decided that it was time to move forward, to be much more forward-leaning on that. And so I think that three-year window to operate was very important."

Deputy national security adviser Ben Rhodes and White House special assistant Ricardo Zúñiga would lay the groundwork, meeting with both Cuban and U.S. legislative officials as well as legal experts from across Washington to determine just how far they could go. Their goal was to make headway before they reached the next regional summit—slated to happen three years later in 2015—in Panama City, Panama. But there still was the issue of Alan Gross, the detained American contractor. America's initial warming toward Cuba had all but halted in the aftermath of his arrest. And yet a resolution all of a sudden seemed possible.

21

ALAN GROSS

It was a cool fall morning in late October 2017 when my cell phone rang. It registered an unknown caller from Washington, D.C. Likely a telemarketer, but I picked up anyway.

Life was different now. My employer, the Qatar-funded Al Jazeera America news network, had collapsed. And after a series of jobs that spanned New York and Washington, I had returned to Manhattan as the managing editor of a news start-up called Brut. I had also gotten married again, to a fellow journalist, and had become a stepfather. In other words, my priorities had shifted.

But that fall morning, I was focused on an edit when the phone's ring broke through the early quiet. "Hello," I finally answered, moments before voicemail engaged.

"Hi," said a gravelly voice on the other end of the line. "This is Alan Gross."

Gross's words hung in the air a moment before I could answer. For nearly eight years I had been reporting on and hearing about this man who had been at the very crossroads of U.S.-Cuban relations. He was practically the reason negotiations fell apart in 2009, when all signs pointed to a warming. And his release five years later, on December 17, 2014, may have done more to improve U.S.-Cuba relations than any effort of ten previous U.S. administrations. Obama acknowledged his administration had over the course of "many months . . . held discussions with the Cuban government about Alan's case and other aspects of our relationship." After some five years in detention, the wide-eyed Maryland native whose shock of white hair and broken teeth later revealed the torment of his imprisonment had finally been set free. It had taken eighteen months of back channeling and intense negotiations, but when it happened, his release paved the way for détente. And up until this moment, he had never returned my calls.

"Hello?" The phone crackled and seemed to briefly cut out.

"Alan!" I exclaimed. "It's so good to hear from you."

"Well, I got your voicemail."

Gross was fresh off a lawsuit, receiving a $3.2 million settlement involving USAID and his old employer, a Bethesda-based consultancy and government contractor called Development Alternatives Incorporated (DAI). The company was already under intense scrutiny after USAID auditors raised serious doubts about its poppy eradication program in Afghanistan.[1] But miraculously, business for the firm still seemed quite good. In 2009, the firm netted approximately three-quarters of its yearly revenue from USAID contracts and had hired Gross as part of a $6 million contract intended to bypass internet restrictions in Cuba. The focus of his efforts was to establish satellite internet connections among Jewish communities in Havana, Santiago, and Camagüey, reportedly earning him $590,000 over the course of a year and a half.[2] He had done this sort of development work before, in countries such as Gambia and Kenya. But the gear he brought to Cuba was designed to avoid detection, and included prohibited high-tech SIM cards, unavailable to most civilian consumers, which scrambled satellite transmission to obscure the signal. The technology masked the source of the broadcast "so that its GPS location cannot [be] pinpointed to within 400km."[3]

The Cubans, unsurprisingly, caught on and arrested him.

"Did you realize how dangerous that was?" I asked, trying my best not to reveal my sense of What-the-hell-were-you-thinking?

"Well, not at first," Gross replied. "But with each trip, I grew more anxious." He then paused, as if to reflect on his thinking during that time, and sighed with a sort of chuckle. "In Cuba, things are not as they appear."

No shit, I thought.

Though Gross had spent roughly two decades setting up communications equipment for relief agencies, he seemed more naïve adventurer than hardened spy. Yet he had acknowledged in a report prior to his arrest that the discovery of BGAN (a global satellite positioning terminal) equipment by Cuban authorities "would be catastrophic."[4] It appeared Gross knew exactly the extent of the risks he was taking. If he were an intelligence operative, he seemed just about the worst possible choice: a white-haired, wide-eyed Marylander who barely spoke Spanish and had no experience in Cuba or even a family connection that would make his entry more seamless. He was an aging American white guy: a quintessential *yuma.* And he looked it.

"I had no investment in Cuba," he told me. "But I invested a lot in democracy." In many ways, I could relate to Gross. We were there for different reasons. My job was transparent: to document and inform. His was not: to covertly spread democracy. The Cuban government wasn't exactly thrilled about either of us. But the difference was authorities likely perceived some sort of marginal use for me. Though accredited U.S. journalists in Havana were a relatively new phenomenon, Fidel was by no means a media novice. His courtships with the press dated back to before the Revolution.

In fact, it was a journalist from the *New York Times* who may have lent the credibility Fidel initially needed to grab power. In 1957, veteran columnist and reporter Herbert L. Matthews scored a journalistic coup—an interview with Fidel himself, then a rebel leader who had for months been presumed dead. Fidel's fledgling force had been all but routed by Fulgencio Batista's superior numbers, and he had fled into the heights of Cuba's Sierra Maestra mountain range to regroup. Though Batista's forces had set up checkpoints across the region, Matthews evaded detection by traveling in a car with his wife, posing as rich American tourists.[5] Once beyond Batista's guards, he slipped into the mountains to meet Fidel. There, the Cuban leader captivated Matthews, tapping into his penchant for romantic narrative, which prompted the veteran journalist to pen a glowing front-page story for the *Times* that described Fidel as a man "fighting for a democratic Cuba."[6] Naïveté from abroad was hardly a new phenomenon in Cuba. And Matthews's articles quickly filtered back to the island, enraging Batista and adding to Fidel's growing legend. It was a lesson the Castro brothers would likely not forget: the press could be harnessed and used. That was likely a big reason why the government allowed foreign news bureaus to set up shop in Havana in the first place. But as for Gross, there was little utility in having someone like him roaming free.

The Friday he was supposed to return from his latest trip to the island, his wife, Judy, sat waiting in their kitchen. But when his flight landed in Dulles, she was informed that Alan wasn't on it. It was the beginning of their five-year saga.

Following Gross's arrest on December 3, 2009, John Kerry, then chairman of the U.S. Senate Committee on Foreign Relations, "put a hold" on the multimillion-dollar Cuban initiative that was run through USAID, at least temporarily; the agency had been employing contractors and subcontractors such as Gross to carry out its initiatives, rather than deploy its own people from State.[7]

A man with a closely cropped haircut and vise grip of a handshake named Fulton Armstrong was in large part behind that effort. "This is how they do business now," he told me over beers one afternoon in a Dupont Circle bar. A former CIA official who had served in Cuba, Armstrong explained that "the State Department doesn't engage in certain policy areas anymore for a reason. They contract out to third-party companies, so there's no paper trail beyond State's front door."

Armstrong, who later worked for the Senate Foreign Relations Committee, said he often asked for contract documentation of activities in countries where the groups were operating. "There just wasn't any written record that they would share with Congress," he said. "What they did write down stayed in the files of the 'contractors' and 'grantees' as proprietary information beyond the reach of U.S. taxpayers and their representatives."

In the case of DAI, the company had hired Gross to travel to Cuba and "implement activities in support of the rule of law and human rights." DAI president Jim Boomgard said as much in a written statement, though he refused to further explain the company's efforts in Cuba except that it was to foster "political competition, and consensus building, and to strengthen civil society in support of just and democratic governance."[8] Whether Alan understood the extent of those risks was never really clear, but he and his wife successfully sued both USAID and DAI for failing to adequately train him or "take basic remedial measures to protect" himself. Yet during his third trip, Gross seemed to acknowledge the risk of what he was doing, describing his work as "very risky business in no uncertain terms."[9]

Now the former subcontractor seemed almost magnanimous. "I had a great relationship with DAI," Gross told me. "Though I don't know that I'd do it again." He then chuckled over his own gallows humor.

"What else was DAI involved with in Cuba?" I asked. Gross then paused, drawing a breath as if to carefully choose his words.

"DAI had a problematic group within it," he said.

"What do you mean by that?"

"Listen," he said. "I can't say any more without affecting the terms of my settlement."

U.S. law prohibited USAID from engaging in covert actions, so these efforts were instead labeled "discreet" actions. But an eighteen-page Cuban court document said Gross had covertly sought to avoid detection and entered the country using a tourist visa. To Cuba, he was just another part of a $20 million effort by Washington to undermine its government, and it had become increasingly aware of his activities. For Gross, the money was good and the cause seemed important. So he kept going. On his last visit, he checked into a four-star hotel called the Hotel Presidente in Havana before Cuban authorities closed in.

"They came to my hotel room," he said, referencing state security agents. Gross wouldn't see his old home for another five years.

"What was it like," I asked, "being locked up for so many years?"

"I thought about Bill Murray a lot," he replied with another chuckle. "You know, from the movie *Groundhog Day*. There was just no differentiation between the days."

Each morning, he would rise in his room and pace back and forth to stay in shape. In addition to daily interrogations, the lights in his room were initially left on for twenty-four hours a day. When he was finally released, he had teeth missing and looked frail. Judy said he had shed more than a hundred pounds and suffered chronic pains. Yet on his release late in 2014, he appeared in good spirits and seemed to harbor no ill will toward the Cuban authorities. Gross called the shift in relations "a game changer, which I support." Speaking to me three years after his release, some ten months after President Donald Trump assumed office, Gross openly wondered where U.S. policy was headed, drawing on his experience in Cuba as a cautionary tale.

"I'm just really disappointed," he expressed of the new American president. "He's a megalomaniac, just like Fidel Castro, just not as well read."

Eight years after his arrest, the U.S. State Department under Trump's secretary of state Rex Tillerson announced that it was again assembling a task force to assess ways to support independent media (i.e., bloggers) and to promote information access (i.e., the internet) in Cuba—potentially paving the way for another jailed American contractor. Meet the new boss. Same as the old boss. "We are supposed to learn from our mistakes," sighed Gross when he learned of the announcement. But that decision was yet to be. Obama was still in office. And Secretary of State John Kerry had a flag to raise in Havana.

22

RETURN OF THE EMBASSIES

It was summer of 2015. The fishmongers were out. Their morning beckons alerted neighbors of their latest catch, which these days signaled the break of dawn as much as that old rooster's crow.

"*Pesce!*" one yelled, looking vaguely in my direction. Whatever could be snared using wooden boats, inner tube rafts, and inflated condoms, which kept the bait high in the water and allowed it to drift farther out to sea where the bigger fish lurked, would be hocked in state-run stores and on Havana streets throughout the morning.

"No, *gracias,*" I replied, making my way through Vedado, a commercial district situated just a few miles west of the old city. Columns of diesel smoke had just begun belching from exhaust pipes as commuters flagged down *colectivos,* the vintage ride shares that puttered along their morning routes. Others waited for Chinese-made buses, the *guaguas,* at various stops. Back in 2005, as the economy rebounded, then buoyed by Venezuelan subsidies, the Castros began importing them to replace Cuba's *camellos,* or camels, the tractor-trailer inventions that spewed a blackened smoke and were as much known for their humped backs as they were for their uncomfortable rides. Today, *camellos* seemed relics of the past as the city woke up to a much different future.

As for me, I was walking, bound for the city's concrete coastline. The salty air had yet to give way to its acrid patina, which invariably envelops Havana by midafternoon. As of now, it still smelled fresh, despite the fish vendors, which somehow paired well with the tiny paper cup of *cafecito* I had just scored from a bandana-clad woman working the counter of a local bodega.

It felt like just another Friday—but it wasn't.

Cuba was awaiting a visitor of historic proportions. It was August 14, 2015, and John Kerry, the first U.S. secretary of state to visit the island since 1945, was about to arrive. Accompanied by three retired U.S. Marines, he would preside over a flag-raising ceremony at the newly minted U.S. embassy in Havana. For decades, it had served as an Interests Section under the auspices of the Swiss. Nearly fifty-five years had passed since the same three marines lowered the American flag at the embassy in Havana. That was January 1961, and President Dwight D. Eisenhower had ordered American personnel to leave their embassy following a collapse in relations. Lance Corporal Larry C. Morris and then Corporal Francis East joined Sergeant Jim Tracy to wade through a gathering crowd of Cubans to lower the flag. Concerned about the prospect of violence, a noncommissioned officer in charge requested volunteers, and said he was looking for "the biggest, ugliest Marines you can find."[1] Morris, East, and Tracy had taken their chances. Now, they were waiting to present an American flag that would again be raised in the very place where they had removed it.

Standing on a platform, within the small compound of that seven-story building, it was one of those history-making moments I never thought I'd see. The gesture, though largely symbolic, seemed to put a stamp on a normalization process that was gaining steam. And yet as we stood there, both sides were taking their sweet time. The August sun has a way of making even the most fervent advocates of pomp and formality quickly reevaluate their priorities. And with a dark blazer that collected heat like a solar panel hiding a white dress shirt that by now was sweatier than the inside of a shin pad, I was getting impatient. By early afternoon, temperatures had not abated, soaring into the nineties and forcing many of us to shed superfluous clothing or huddle beneath the few umbrellas that were scattered atop an otherwise shadeless platform.

And yet those just outside the embassy walls didn't seem at all fazed. Hundreds of Cubans had gathered to watch American marines hoist America's flag up the pole. When it finally happened, a brass band played both the Cuban and American national anthems. Tears streamed down the faces of many who looked on as residents hung over apartment balconies, anxious to steal a glimpse of the ceremony, draping Cuban and American flags down the buildings. Many I spoke to openly wondered what it meant for them. As journalists debated the big picture, a man I met named Yoani Naveda had more practical concerns, hoping that this latest development would speed up the visa process so that he could finally see his father in Miami. "From today," he told me, following the ceremony, "it's been three years."

In a green space adjacent to the embassy with a few concrete benches, Cubans like Yoani gathered most weekday mornings, often awaiting processing at the U.S. embassy. Families often visibly aged in the time that they waited. The space was colloquially known as the "park of life and death," life referring to the American-inspired chance to travel north. Many were circumspect, wary of the past vicissitudes in U.S.-Cuba relations.

Clad in a straw fedora, sunglasses, and yellow cutoff T-shirt, Miguel Sanchez, like many Cubans, had learned by experience not to let hope cloud what experience had always told him.

"You know changes, they don't always benefit everyone," he said in an interview a day after the U.S. Marines hoisted Old Glory back atop its embassy flagpole. "In my opinion, there's still a lot missing."

Despite the zeal of the moment, the scope of the shift was still not clear. Sure, a U.S. embassy had returned to the Cuban capital. But its predecessor, the U.S. Interests Section, had already long functioned as an embassy in all but name. Yes, commerce and travel restrictions had been eased, but regime change was still inscribed in the language that governed the U.S. trade embargo. Six interlocking American laws determined how sanctions were applied, from the Trading with the Enemy Act of 1917 to the Trade Sanctions Reform and Export Enhancement Act of 2000, but it was the 1996 Helms-Burton Act (which prohibited recognition of even a democratic government in Cuba) that would allow for sanctions relief if Fidel or Raul Castro were in any way still in power. Helms-Burton was still on the books. So one could forgive Cuban officials for not jumping for joy during a flag raising.

Even Secretary Kerry's speech at the new U.S. embassy in Havana threw a few barbs at the Cuban government, saying its people "would be best served by a genuine democracy, where people are free to choose their leaders." Despite détente, Washington had hardly unclenched its fists.

Still, this fraught relationship was changing. Less than a year after Kerry arrived, President Obama showed the world that Cuba was a priority when Air Force One touched down at Jose Marti International Airport in Havana. To many of us, it seemed that the final chapter of this decades-long saga was finally being written. And though the usual suspects criticized the move, there seemed less to risk now—a popular majority in Florida supported a full restoration of diplomatic ties. Critics called it legacy hunting, but the significance of the U.S. commander in chief traveling to Cuba and shaking the hand of a Castro in Cuba could hardly be overstated. If there were a Berlin Wall equivalent, surely it happened on March 22, 2016, when President Obama strolled through Old Havana and into the majestic Grand Theatre to deliver his vision for the future. With Cuban president Raul Castro seated in the balcony directly across from him, Obama told an island of more than 11 million Cubans that he was there "to bury the last remnant of the Cold War in the Americas."[2] "This is not just a policy of normalizing relations with the Cuban government," he continued. "The United States of America is normalizing relations with the Cuban people."

And there it was. By focusing on "the Cuban people" throughout the speech, the American president had made a direct appeal to Cuban civil society. To Cuban authorities, it was both the olive branch and the arrows. "What changes come will depend upon the Cuban people," Obama said to an enamored audience. The reaction was immediate as Cubans wondered about their future. But two days later, the Cuban government struck back. Many suspected a Faustian bargain.

"We don't need the empire to give us anything," wrote Fidel Castro in a letter published in the state-run *Granma* newspaper, blasting the visiting U.S. leader.[3] To hard-liners, this was the same old United States, whose goal was what it always had been: regime change. To some, in his call to empower Cuban civil society, President Obama had signaled that he hadn't quite abandoned regime change.

"My modest suggestion is that [Obama] reflects and doesn't try to develop theories about Cuban politics," wrote Fidel, still sounding the alarms. Of course, the two brothers hadn't always agreed. During a 1959 meeting at a Houston hotel, as Fidel toured the United States in hopes of ginning up support for the Revolution, Raul urged his brother to turn toward Moscow. And those ties would grow, traced to a man named Nikolai Leonov, a KGB officer and Latin American expert whom Raul first befriended during a cruise to Mexico following a 1953 youth festival in Vienna. He met Leonov again in 1955 when Leonov was stationed in Mexico for Soviet intelligence. When they spoke, Raul relayed the seriousness of increasingly bellicose talk toward Cuba by leading voices in the United States such as Nelson Rockefeller, who a year earlier had become New York governor and was already vying for a spot in the

White House. Those like Leo A. Hoegh, then director of the U.S. Office of Civil and Defense Mobilization, openly proclaimed that "the U.S. should charge that the Monroe Doctrine had been violated and should go in and take over." That doctrine, formulated in 1823 by President James Monroe in an address to Congress, warned European powers against further colonization in the Western Hemisphere, essentially claiming the region as America's sphere of influence. It would quickly become a template for U.S. intervention across Latin America. And fears abounded among Cuban leadership that the doctrine would be used as a pretext for invasion.

In Prague, during a summer of 1960 tour of Czechoslovakia, during which time KGB agents actively sought to contact him, Raul expressed his concerns of a growing U.S. menace. "The Cuban revolution has entered its most critical moment of development," he reportedly told Leonov in an apparent plea for Soviet protection.[4] The Kremlin seemed only too happy to oblige. And on July 9, 1960, Soviet premier Nikita Khrushchev raised the stakes, promising to "speak up in defense of Cuba." In a speech he gave to the R.F.S.R. Teacher's Congress in Moscow, Khrushchev laid out a bold new Soviet position that would come to define the framework for Kremlin-Castro relations:

> Figuratively speaking, if need be, Soviet artillerymen can support the Cuban people with their rocket fire, should the aggressive forces in the Pentagon dare to start intervention against Cuba. And the Pentagon would be well advised not to forget that, as has been shown by the latest tests, we have rockets which land accurately in a predetermined square target 13,000 kilometres [about 8,000 miles] away. This, if you wish, is a warning to those who might like to solve international problems by force and riot by reason.

Moscow's stance could hardly be more clear. Fidel dispatched Raul to Moscow to publicly express "gratitude for Nikita Khrushchev's comments on Cuba." When he arrived eight days later, the young defense minister was assured of additional military supplies and support. Soviet marshal Matvei Zakharov furnished Cuba with a hundred thousand automatic rifles and a fleet of tanks. Raul, fresh from burnishing his Communist credentials in Prague, reportedly replied to his Soviet counterparts that "we believed that your military assistance would not come in time, before the large U.S. intervention."[5]

"After Khrushchev's statement the situation changed," Raul added. "The Americans no longer dared attack us." And it hadn't cost Havana a thing. The Kremlin did not require Cuba to pay for the arms shipments. Perhaps more importantly, Raul had moved closer to the Soviet orbit. And over time (by 1980) more than 70 percent of Cuban trade would route through the USSR, which subsidized fuel imports and paid above-market prices for the island's sugar exports, all while furnishing weapons, training, and logistical support. Raul helped oversee it all. Over the years, he became close friends with Leonov, who would eventually author Raul's biography, entitled *Raul Castro: A Man in Revolution.* Together, they had been "able to make history."[6] Even after the Soviet collapse in late December 1991, the relationship remained close. It seemed unlikely that he would throw all of that away.

But two decades later, Raul was at Cuba's helm and charting a new path to improve U.S. relations. Yet could Washington be trusted? Was American financing, its U.S. telecommunications deals (which offered the promise of greater internet access), and its appeal to civil society merely an Obama Trojan horse, aimed at pursuing the same regime-change goals of his predecessors? Wary of past intervention (with those from the Kremlin still whispering in Cuban ears), Havana was hardly moving fast.

"Fifty years have shown that isolation hasn't worked," Obama said during his December 17 announcement. "It's time for a new approach." The approach had indeed changed, but had the goal? Cuba's aging elite were unconvinced. "That was a mistake to appeal to civil society," Carlos Alzugaray, a former Cuban diplomat to the European Union, told me during an interview. "He shouldn't have done that."

President Obama had mentioned "democracy" six times in that speech, claiming telecommunications deals would "do more to empower the Cuban people." Havana's reaction in both public and private seemed the same: don't interfere.

"Change will take place and the changes will have to have Cuban characteristics," Alzugaray told me.

Was he right? Was an absence of U.S. influence and American-style institutions even possible during a transition happening just ninety miles from American shores? In the years since the Castros grabbed power, private property had been seized, opposition jailed, free speech stymied, and hundreds of thousands of Cuban citizens had fled as political refugees. Meanwhile, a multimillion-dollar anti-Castro industry had cropped up and wielded influence at the highest levels of U.S. government. Could all of that really be worked out? After more than half a century, reconciliation advocates such as James Williams, president of Engage Cuba, a coalition of private American companies, seemed to think so and were making a case for it.

"People touched the stove and realized it wasn't too hot to touch," Williams told me in an interview.[7] America's business community was mobilizing. The U.S. Treasury had relaxed export restrictions. Verizon and Sprint began operating on the island, and Airbnb exploded, pouring newfound cash into residents' pockets. The company called Cuba "Airbnb's fastest-growing country in the world," pouring an annual average of $2,700 into the pockets of Cuban hosts, or ninety-six times their yearly salary. More than half of those hosts (58 percent) were women, empowering a new and emerging crop of female entrepreneurs. Meanwhile, America's more established hospitality companies were setting their sights on Cuba, as Starwood Hotels and Resorts inked a deal that gave it part management of three Havana hotels, the first for an American hotel company in nearly sixty years.

Investment, however, is a two-way street. And Cuba was still hedging its bets, simultaneously courting America's rivals. In July 2014—the same year that Presidents Obama and Castro announced their historic détente—Russian president Vladimir Putin began a six-day tour of Latin America. His initial stop was Havana, where Putin inked a series of new accords in energy, infrastructure, and health care, writing off $32 billion in Cuban debt and discussing plans to reopen the Lourdes spy base, a sprawling twenty-eight-square-mile facility just 150 miles from the Florida coast that was once among the Soviets' most extensive intelligence facilities in the West. A year later, Raul made a third trip to Moscow, discussing Russian oil-drilling plans in the Caribbean and strengthening Havana's air defense systems. Despite Cuba's fresh start with the United States, the old Cold War seemed to still be alive and kicking. President Obama's moves were historic and substantive, but they still hadn't addressed the core issue of more than fifty-five years of distrust: lost property and business claims.

The American land, homes, and companies that Fidel had seized at the onset of the Cuban Revolution—which prompted U.S. sanctions against Cuba—now accounted for more than $7 billion in value (with accruing interest). Those certified claims had to be resolved if there were to be any meaningful path toward reconciliation. Congress had made it a stipulation for the lifting of sanctions. Normalization seemed hollow without some sort of resolution on this issue. But it wouldn't be easy. There were nearly six thousand U.S. property claims on what Fidel had seized, and many more claims by Cuban exiles who were not American citizens at the time of seizure. As far as sanctions go, it was the American claims that really mattered. But decades later, they weren't easy to keep track of. Many had changed hands, having been sold and resold over the years. Half a century later, the claimants hadn't forgotten. Even though some of the companies no longer existed, descendants of the owners still had those claims on the books. And they were bad for Cuba in at least two ways: not only did they impede the lifting of U.S. sanctions, but they also stymied the kind of investment Havana needed.

"Large reputable foreign companies don't want to get jammed up in a property subject to an outstanding and unresolved claim," Robert L. Muse, a Washington lawyer who specializes in claimants, told me during an interview in a subterranean Washington, D.C., restaurant. "It's bad business."

The problem, however, was twofold. First, Cuba didn't really have the money to pay them off. The island was both cash-strapped and indebted. Though the Cuban government does not publish current data on its outstanding obligations, a European creditor group estimates its $1.4 billion worth of Cuban debt accounts for about half of the island's private sector balance. And that was *after* a restructuring effort in which Mexico, France, Italy, Australia, Canada, Japan, and Russia all wrote off hundreds of millions of dollars in debt dating back to the 1970s. The new repayment schedule pushed out to 2033, but with the economy in recession, even that seemed unlikely. There are, of course, other ways to settle a bill. Economists have long proposed tax holidays and investment incentives, such as debt-for-equity swaps in development projects as ways to generate payment, though Cuba's command economy has long been wary of relinquishing control.

Thing is, Havana said the United States actually owed *it*, presenting counterclaims for roughly $1 trillion in damages from the embargo and U.S.-sponsored attacks over the decades, most notably the CIA-planned Bay of Pigs invasion. For the Americans, that was a nonstarter. "When you walk into a negotiation and the other side says, 'You owe me a trillion dollars,' what's the other side supposed to say?" posed Muse.

The United States and Cuba were talking past each other. Still, this was their opportunity to try. The clock was ticking. Yet by many accounts, officials from each country were in no rush to get any of this sorted. Two years after normalization, the two sides had met only twice in regard to those certified claims.

"Everything began [with the claims], and it's important that everything end with those issues being resolved," said John Kavulich, the U.S.-Cuba Trade and Economic Council president. "But they didn't bother to do that." The Obama administration had taken its victory laps. But the thornier details—from direct correspondence between U.S. and Cuban banks to those problematic and decades-old claims—had been largely left for the next administration. That was the hard stuff. Figuring out how to reach an agreement on the very issues that brought about the fissure in U.S.-Cuba relations was key to any real path toward normalization. But claims weren't headline-grabbers. What's more, they were enormously complicated. Best to leave the rest to the next administration. After all, it was almost certain to be another Democrat in the White House. Hillary Clinton seemed a shoo-in for the presidency. Virtually all the polls said so.

23

THE BOOM YEARS

There was a moment—roughly a two-year window after Obama's December 2014 détente and just before Trump's June 2017 speech in Miami—where everything seemed to be speeding up. Home sales and rentals surged in Cuba as new investment and tourism dollars poured into the country. New restaurants opened, and old ones expanded, offering menus in both English and Spanish. Chanel held its first show in Havana, where beret-clad models sashayed their way down Paseo de Prado, a main city thoroughfare, to the flashes and rapid-fire clicks of foreign fashion photographers. Google made plans to deploy its first servers. U.S. cruise ships steamed into Havana ports, and media of all kinds descended.

Cuba was open for business.

And in the island's east-central city of Camagüey, a thirty-one-year-old mother named Yanet planned to cash in. She and her husband had been scraping by on government salaries of just $24 per month, while also raising a baby. After détente, as new investment began to flood the Cuban capital, they knew they had to leave Camagüey for the opportunities in Havana, where tourists more often descended. Of course, it wasn't that simple. A 1997 Cuban law known as Decree 217 restricted rural-to-urban migration and was designed to prevent overcrowding in infrastructure-poor cities like Havana. Transit police could often be seen checking IDs, verifying addresses, and deporting Cubans who were missing the proper residency status back to the provinces. In other words, undocumented Cuban migrants were considered illegal in their own country and Yanet needed to be careful. To get around this, she sold what she could and worked out an arrangement with a departing Cuban family, bound for Miami, in which she'd take over their apartment in Centro Habana, rent out its rooms to visiting foreigners, and split the money with its absentee owners.

"It was just more economical," she told me. "We needed the extra money."

And the money, she said, started to pour in, supplementing a salary on which it would otherwise be difficult to subsist. After chatting a bit more, we parted ways and I hopped into a '49 Plymouth cab and headed for Old Havana, where I had rented an Airbnb apartment with a balcony overlooking the city for around $40 per night. The driver, a squat-statured twenty-something named Enrique, put the chrome rattler into gear and clattered east.

"*Suave*," he said as I climbed in and pulled the door shut. As more Americans descended, that sort of warning had become even more a custom. "*Adónde vas?*" Enrique asked.

"Plaza San Francisco," I replied, referencing one of the area's four main cobblestone squares that date back to the seventeenth century. This one was named for a Franciscan convent that sat at the southern edge of the plaza, which abuts Havana Harbor and the main roadway where taxis could easily pull off. It was about as close as I could get.

As Enrique shifted gears, he opened his window to rest his arm, allowing a salty rush of cool air to pour into the cab. And I started to talk. I always found cabdrivers to be among the city's most well informed, and—like barbers and bartenders—usually up for a chat. Enrique was no different. Turned out, he was from Santiago, and like Yanet had seen opportunity in Havana following the normalization. Enrique had done the math and figured he could earn upward of 200 CUC per month driving his old cab here, which he shared with a friend. But unlike Yanet, he had no place to live.

"I didn't know anyone here," Enrique told me. So, he did what many Cubans do: he got married. "My wife is fifty-five years old," he told me with a bit of a grimace. "But she has a house here in Vedado district." Their marriage gave him Havana residency and a better chance to earn, while his wife got a young new partner. In fact, stories like Yanet's and Enrique's unfurled across the capital as new shops and storefronts emerged alongside car and home sales, and residents invented new and innovative ways to better their circumstances. Trappings of a Cuba-styled, and yet market-based, system were gaining ground.

Meanwhile, American media powerhouses, including late-night comedian Conan O'Brien and the Showtime series *House of Lies,* wanted in. And that was just the beginning. Cuban authorities were all of sudden allowing in productions they rarely had in the past, and the pace of change quickened. But the pièce de résistance may have been Vin Diesel. A more than one-hundred-person Hollywood film crew somehow secured permissions to shut down a wide swath of the Malecon to film the eighth installment of the *Fast and the Furious* movie franchise. And the excitement was palpable. Cubans gathered as production trucks packed with film equipment clogged streets and spawned rare traffic jams. "They even blocked an entrance to the [Hermanos Ameijeiras] hospital," said Abel Gonzalez, a Havana resident. "And no one seemed to care."

Of course, that wasn't really true. While some were enamored with Hollywood's glitz and welcomed this new outside world, others weren't so sure. Cuba's egalitarian structure made for prickly bedfellows with commercial financiers. And many of the island's older guard remained wary of foreign businessmen who sought to use the island as a tropical backdrop for their action movies and fashion shows.

The country's old-timers had seen this act before. In the years prior to the Revolution, Cuba was touted as the "brothel of the Western Hemisphere," replete with crime, prostitution, and gambling. Fueled by sugar exports and a hotel-and-casino industry that catered to rich foreigners, it had become a playground for American socialites and mobsters. "Havana is a mistress of pleasure," declared a 1956 edition of the tourism magazine *Cabaret Quarterly*. "The lush and opulent goddess of delights."

Havana also enjoyed a large upper-middle class, with literacy rates as high as 76 percent (literacy rates were far lower in the provinces). Though Cubans were comparatively better off than much of the region in terms of relative earnings and access to education, "daily life had developed into a relentless degradation," wrote historian Louis Perez in his 1999 book *On Becoming Cuban,* "with the complicity of political leaders and public officials who operated at the behest of American interests." Now, as the spigot turned back on, those old fears resurfaced among those who had spent their lives resisting what Fidelists derided as the market-driven basis for U.S. "imperialism."

Cuban art critic Desiderio Navarro may have best captured that sentiment in an interview with Michael Weissenstein of the Associated Press. "It's very important that we don't give the 'Ugly American' reason to come back," he said.[1] Cubans wanted *yuma* cash and investment, but not necessarily the *yumas*. Was one possible without the other? That seemed precisely the line Raul was trying to walk. And yet as Vin Diesel sauntered on set and a helicopter circled overhead, it seemed the Malecon's once-lazy scene of sun-bedraggled fishermen and guitar-toting *caballeros* had been displaced. Cuba's old way was being challenged, and the backlash reverberated across the capital. Securing visas and permissions soon proved onerous, especially for the mediaverse, which had quickly reacquired its taste for all things Cuba. Havana was hot. Visits by Jay-Z and Beyoncé only seemed to reinforce that. And even as its leaders tapped the brakes, Cuba remained in the throes of real change. The genie was out of the bottle.

But this time, my foray into Cuba was only a visit. I had met my fiancée, Stephanie, while working at Al Jazeera America, and its collapse had left us both unemployed and with a bit of extra time to water a budding romance. As changes swept over my old island home, I wanted her to see it.

So we went.

It was 2016. We arrived April 22, landing at Jose Marti International Airport that morning. Stephanie clutched my arm as we approached. But I had mixed feelings about that gray-and-blue airport, where straight-faced officials in tan uniforms process a steady stream of the Cuba-curious. Yet, once we arrived, Havana's rose-tinted romance inevitably resurfaced. Seen through Stephanie's eyes as we strolled the Malecon, loitered in the old city, and traipsed up the spiraling marble staircase of La Guarida—a privately owned restaurant in Centro Habana—Cuba seemed to again work its magic. Cliché-ridden illusions dispelled, I was returning with a woman whose wide-eyed wonderment forced me to remember Havana's sultry side—and its romance.

But the following morning I received an email from an address I didn't immediately recognize. I had returned to Cuba nearly every year since 2010, though I had never seen the island outside the rigor of assignments and deployments. Each trip had been about sources, spies, stories, and stocking up, with the tacit knowledge that authorities were keeping tabs. But this time was different. At least I thought as much until I checked my email.

"Hi David," it read. "How are you?"

The greeting came from Yisette, the woman from La Roca whom

I had briefly dated in those first months in Havana. And though it fizzled out long before the end of summer 2009, every once in a while she'd send me a message. But it had been ages since I had last heard from her. Now, just hours into our first morning in Havana, this email was sitting in my inbox.

Did she know I was here? If not, the timing was remarkably co-incidental. Had she been a government plant all along? What had I told her back then? A slew of unanswerable questions rushed in—along with that familiar sense of paranoia.

I deleted the email, refocused, and thought of Stephanie. To show her and to see this country now, all these years later—that's why I returned. The conspiracy theories would have to wait.

But Havana was a bit different now. It wasn't quite as crumbling as I remembered it. Restoration projects were underway across the city, particularly in Old Havana, where an effort to preserve its architectural heritage was ongoing. Larger structures such as the old Presidential Palace and the Capitolio were also under construction, scaffolding surrounding its dome. Meanwhile, there were far more *paladares* than I had remembered. Those that had been there, such as La Guarida, had also clearly benefited from a surge in new investment. The restaurant had added an additional floor of seating and a rooftop bar with fluorescent purple-and-blue lighting, attracting a more Euro-hip clientele than I remembered. But like many things in Cuba, the veneer of cool masked a darker past. The building that housed La Guarida, known as La Mansión Camagüey, was a location for the Oscar-nominated film *Fresa y Chocolate (Strawberry and Chocolate)*, known for its groundbreaking social commentary that included the famous quote: "Welcome to La Guarida, a place where not everybody is welcome." The film—released in 1993—was trail-blazing in its examination of gay culture (and homophobia) in a place that only a few decades earlier had placed homosexuals in labor camps. They were considered "a bourgeois perversion," as Castro put it, and a pariah in the eyes of the law. Article 303(a) of the penal code outlawed "publicly manifested" homosexuality, along with "persistently bothering others with homosexual amorous advances." Before committing suicide, Cuban writer Reinaldo Arenas authored a damning political memoir entitled *Before Night Falls,* which criticized a system that had allowed for "a permanent 'collar'" around Cuba's gay community.

Yet that, too, was changing, spearheaded by none other than the Castro matriarchs. Vilma Espín, wife of President Raul Castro, had urged for a softer government stance toward the gay community. And their daughter Mariela would grow up to become the director of the country's National Center for Sex Education. At her urging, the government in 2008 began allowing the island's doctors to perform gender-reassignment surgery and would revise its labor codes to offer new LGBT protections. Though discrimination and a machismo culture persisted, much of the old way seemed to be fading.

Stephanie and I would travel to Cuba again a year later, booking an apartment with our friends Grant and Celine through Airbnb. We rented an absurdly small car before traveling east to the Spanish colonial city of Trinidad. With a four-hour drive ahead of us and virtually no trunk, the four of us were comically yet quintessentially *yuma*. Firing the ignition and rolling down the rear windows in *Beverly Hillbillies* style so that the luggage could fit, we pulled out onto the Autopista Nacional and headed east on the open road, where a few cars and buses rumbled past a steady crop of hitchhikers who did their best to flag us down. In a country with limited cars and public transport, hitchhiking had become a national pastime. Cubans across the island could be seen with outstretched thumbs even on national highways, piecing together their journeys through the goodwill of vehicled travelers. On occasion, I'd pick up one or two of these side-of-the-road *campesinos* and chat about the weather and the latest harvest, hoping to glean greater insights into how the island's murky economy actually functioned out in the provinces. Supplies were a recurring concern. And many discussed the shortages they experienced openly. Out here, there seemed fewer concerns about the overseeing eyes of the state. As the car bore down on the open road, I could see a few stragglers in the distance. But on this trip, with luggage poking out from our windows, there simply wasn't space.

Still, it felt good to leave Havana. The air was fresher in the countryside and a welcome reprieve from the capital's muggy, diesel-laden atmosphere. Havana was to Cuba what New York was to the rest of the United States: comparatively expensive and bustling, with a near-constant hustle that carved sharper edges among its people. I often relished those chances to get out and meet tobacco farmers in Pinar del Rio, fishermen in Matanzas, or shopkeepers in Santiago, where Raul had planned to retire. The tendency was to think what was happening in Havana had been replicated across the country. But much of Cuba had not experienced the kind of invest-ment boom that accompanied détente in the capital. Trinidad might have been the exception. A UNESCO World Heritage site on the is-land's southern coast known for its sugar mills, cobblestone streets, and lively salsa bands, its economy now heavily leaned on tourism, evidenced by row after row of *casas particulares.*

"Another hour or so and we'll be there," I yelled into the back seat, resting my arm on the driver's-side door. The idea was to make it to Trinidad before nightfall, check into a *casa particular,* and ex-plore the city on fresh legs and fresh coffee. I pictured the pastel wash of Spanish colonials abutting turquoise waters that lapped Cuba's southern shore. But there was something in the distance. I could see in the dim twilight of dusk that something had stopped on the road ahead. It was a police car. The officer had gotten out of his car and was flagging us down. I obliged, and he approached.

"Documents," the officer barked into my open window.

"Excuse me?" I replied.

"Your documents," he repeated. "License. Passport. Your documents."

"OK. Sure," I said, pulling a stack of rental agreements from the glove compartment.

His gloved hands accepted our papers, glancing at them only briefly before leaning in again.

"You know you were speeding."

"No, *caballero*," I replied flatly.

"Listen," he said. "Pay me sixty CUC and that'll be fine."

I just looked at him. It was a good old-fashioned shakedown, not uncommon elsewhere in Latin America. But this was Cuba.

"*En serio?*" I replied, blankly looking at the officer, who now seemed unsure of himself, looking down and away and eventually allowing a sheepish grin to creep across his face. It was the look of a man who didn't intend to follow through. Maybe this was all a bit new for him.

"No, it's fine," the officer finally said, returning the documents. "Just drive more slowly."

And with that, we resumed our travels, leaving him a fading gray-and-blue speck in the rearview mirror. Trinidad was less than an hour's drive away. But night had now fallen and we'd be making our way into town without the benefit of twilight.

Still, the mood in our packed little car was light as the conversation had focused on where to eat. Trinidad boasted the island's largest per capita concentration of *paladares* as the economy shifted toward tourism. Over the years, everything from small homes to Spanish mansions had been converted into eateries, serving up fresh rock lobster, roast pork, frothy piña coladas, and stiff mojitos with fresh mint to wash it all down. My stomach stirred just thinking about it.

And yet I wondered about that police officer, his checkpoint, and his lack of follow-through. In a system of centralized planning, corruption and bribery seemed natural offshoots. Police officers were known at times to pull over drivers to siphon off cash or even barter after minor traffic offenses. But I had never personally experienced a roadside shakedown here. Though just because I hadn't experienced it before didn't mean much, still, it seemed a new shift was underway.

The problem was data—or lack thereof. Polling and other data collection methods consistent with more open and transparent societies were only sporadically published in state media or read aloud during committee speeches. As a result, there seemed an overreliance on anecdotal information, which invariably led to oversimplifications and, at times, gross mischaracterizations of trends in Cuba. Everything from the health and education systems to the numbers of jailed dissidents languishing in Cuban prisons was frequently based on loosely cobbled-together information that elsewhere would seem woefully insufficient. But in Cuba, official figures were often flat-out unavailable. What's more, Cuban authorities' reluctance to answer our questions did little to combat our own cognitive bias. Their silence reinforced our worst assumptions, whether or not they were accurate. It was maddening: the government had its side of the story to tell, but for years their officials rarely spoke to the press. That was especially true under Raul, who, unlike Fidel, hardly ever gave interviews. What broader information was available dribbled out in heavily censored state media. That meant deciphering trends was especially difficult, if not impossible.

One example was the mystery of corruption. What I did know is that Raul seemed to make combating it a top priority. In 2009, he created a special Comptroller General Office to audit and investigate the state's multifaceted bureaucracy, adding a new level of oversight unseen during his brother's reign. And the arrests soon followed. Everything from the state's cigar monopoly to new development efforts at the Port of Mariel was under new scrutiny. But he wasn't done. Two years later, during a National Assembly meeting,

Raul went further, saying he was "convinced that corruption is cur-rently one of the principal enemies of the Revolution . . . far more damaging than the subversive and interventionist activity of the United States government."[2] Uncle Sam was no longer enemy num-ber one. It was groundbreaking.

Tackling corruption had quickly become a defining aspect of his presidency, even though critics alleged the Castros had been among its greatest beneficiaries. But beginning in 2010, as the economy wobbled and the government looked to attract new investors, Raul decided to clamp down. A public fight against corruption would be helpful in promoting at least the perception of a business-friendly climate. Yet even after Cuba's kumbaya moment with Washington, foreign business leaders were still hedging their bets.

"It's early days, obviously," Marriott CEO Ursula Burns told CNBC in March 2016. "We need to understand more as early as pos-sible so we can be ready, more ready, to partner up with the Cubans as they open up their markets." Marriott currently operates a Shera-ton Four Points in my old neighborhood, Miramar, as well as the famed Inglaterra, considered Cuba's oldest hotel, which dates back to 1875. Those deals, however, were struck through Cuba's Armed Forces Enterprises Group (GAESA), headed by Raul's powerful ex-son-in-law, General Luis Alberto Rodriguez Lopez-Callejas, who in-volved himself in virtually all major investment negotiations within the Cuban economy. In other words, the military under Raul still ran the shop. And that, at least in part, made foreign investment in Cuba a risky business—still too treacherous for several business lead-ers I spoke to.

"The risks are still greater than the opportunities," Andy Gómez, founder of the University of Miami's Institute for Cuban and Cuban-American Studies, told me over the phone during an interview. "Twofold."

Despite the bait of a newly minted American embassy, Cuba was still falling short of its foreign investment goals, tallying an estimated $1.3 billion in investments—hardly a quarter of its target. The math just didn't add up. And now, with President Trump in office, the United States was again turning the screws, tightening travel restrictions in an effort to dampen one of Cuba's few bright spots: tourism.

The to-and-fro of the Cold War had yet to be retired. Raul, on the other hand, was ready to. In 2013, he declared that his second term as president would be his last, building himself a retirement compound in the eastern city of Santiago. Insiders postulated that the aging revolutionary wanted some time off, perhaps to revel more in his role as grandfather, but he remained concerned about his hopes for a seamless political transition.

"I think he wants to make sure his family's place in Cuba is secure once he dies," said veteran Cuba analyst Robert Muse during an interview. Raul and his wife, Vilma Espín, "were much more than Fidel . . . the ones concerned about the Castro family as a family," according to a June 2007 State Department cable released by WikiLeaks.

"He is the most reluctant dictator we've ever known," former CIA analyst Fulton Armstrong later told me, noting that family always appeared a priority.

When Raul's wife, Vilma, a chemical engineer with whom he had four children, died in 2007, the toll was evident, Raul openly weeping at her funeral. In subsequent years, it seemed clear that he was intent on both consolidating power—replacing top government posts with army brass—and protecting the future of his clan. To critics, it had the markings of imperial consolidation. Raulistas (people loyal to Raul) were spread across key positions in the economy, military, and politburo, with much of Havana's inner circle tracing back to the president. His former son-in-law Luis Alberto Rodriguez Lopez-Callejas had given Raul two grandchildren and seemed to be in the president's good graces despite an estrangement from Raul's eldest daughter, Deborah. Raul had tapped Lopez-Callejas as president of GAESA, a powerful holding company that governed the military's wide-reaching business interests. Foreign companies, like Marriott, were usually required to partner with GAESA should they pursue major business interests on the island. A gatekeeper to investors, Lopez-Callejas became among the island's most influential men.

Still, the man I sat across from at that Miramar bar all those years ago posed the bigger mystery. Since those first heady Havana days back in 2010, Raul's eldest son, Alejandro Castro Espín, had been cultivating a public image abroad, writing books, negotiating with Washington, and accompanying his father on diplomatic trips overseas. He had also been promoted to head of the National Defense and Security Commission and ranked high with the country's powerful Interior Ministry. And yet just months before his father's official handover of power, Alejandro had not been named to the Council of State or promoted to general, considered first steps if he were indeed being groomed for power.

"He might rise higher, but not immediately," former diplomat Carlos Alzugaray told me during an interview. The more pressing concern, however, was the transition. Raul retained his position atop the Communist Party, which oversaw government policy. But day-to-day governing was left to his successor in Havana, a fifty-seven-year-old party-line faithful named Miguel Díaz-Canel, first vice president of the Council of State and Council of Ministers. "I am sure that something like this might have happened," posited Alzugaray. "Raul says, 'OK, Díaz-Canel, you're going to take over.' Probably Raul's going to tell him: 'Listen, from now on governmental decisions are your purview. Some things we are going to discuss at the politburo—you bring them to the politburo, we discuss them at the politburo. But on the day-to-day and on the politics, you are going to be the top guy. And don't come very often to consult me.'"

As Díaz-Canel settled in, the country seemed poised for greater reform, including constitutional reform. Just as Raul had embarked on a series of market-oriented moves, he had also laid the groundwork for something much more visible: El Capitolio. Once an emblem of Cuban democracy, it would again return as a building where meaningful government business would be done. Erected the very year Fidel Castro was born in 1926, it was among Cuba's tallest buildings and bore a striking resemblance to the U.S. Capitol in Washington, D.C. Vacated in 1959 after being considered an icon of American excess, its granite and marble halls had been repurposed as the main office for the Academy of Sciences. But now Cuba's old capital building was to again be home to the national legislature. The size of its 614-member body, considered a rubber-stamp congress, was also reduced, paving the way for a potentially more powerful assembly. After more than half a century, the faint whisper of democratic institutions was again seeping into the stone and iron of that century-old structure. And the jockeying for power had already begun. For decades, Cuba's stability had largely been taken for granted, its leadership traced straight to the top. But in a post-Fidel, post-Raul Cuba, the real power would lie in the shadows.

24

COLD WAR GAMES

After Barack Obama became the first sitting American president since Calvin Coolidge to travel to Havana; after Donald Trump shocked virtually everyone by winning the 2016 U.S. presidential election; and after Fidel Castro, Cuba's longtime leader who once pushed the world to the brink of nuclear war, died at the ripe old age of ninety, an old Cuban spy came to visit me and offered what seemed like a remarkable question.

"Do you really think so much has changed?" asked the former senior Cuban intelligence officer. The man, whom I'll call Roberto, had initially okayed the use of his real name in this book. But just weeks before it was to be typeset in the summer of 2018, he got cold feet and asked that I use a pseudonym out of fear of government repercussions.

This is Cuba.

I knew I should oblige. Roberto had much to lose. And if he was asking for cover now, he likely had good reason. The new administration under Díaz-Canel was only a few months old. And though Raul Castro retained leadership of the Communist Party and the military, he would not hold it forever. The balance of power was shifting. And the path ahead was a murky one for the island's old Cold Warriors.

Roberto had for years served as a frontline spy for the Castro government, recruiting intelligence assets across the globe on behalf of a revolution that regarded the United States as its most pressing existential threat—and it still did. As a young man, Roberto had joined the Directorate of Intelligence (DGI), the island's most powerful spy agency, to prevent his government from being toppled in the way CIA efforts had helped undo Cuba's neighbors, including in Guatemala in 1954, the Dominican Republic in 1961, Brazil in 1964, and Chile in 1973. Born in the rough-and-tumble days of the Cold War, his interests and those of his government aligned. Intelligence was a top priority.

With the onset of U.S. sanctions against Cuba in 1960, and assassination plots against its leadership increasingly emanating from Langley, then prime minister Fidel Castro in 1962 decided to send his agents to Moscow for training by the KGB. Cuba's spy network grew as its operatives "benefitted from the advice of at least five Soviet intelligence experts from the very beginning," according to a declassified 1968 CIA report. After the Kremlin's initial tutelage, Cuban spies eventually would be forged into a highly active, world-class intelligence agency, tasked with identifying and neutralizing potential threats to Fidel's hold on power. And the agency quickly (and quietly) found success. Its spies fanned out across the United States, Latin America, and Europe, as well as Cuba itself, infiltrating exile and dissident groups alike. It penetrated the highest levels of the U.S. government by slipping into meetings of the Joint Chiefs of Staff and the National Security Council, then funneled untold secrets back to Havana.[1] By the time Roberto joined its ranks, the DGI had been "molded into a highly professional intelligence organization along classic Soviet lines."[2] There, Roberto thrived. Impressing his superiors with almost an innate knack for the craft, he was promoted several times. When it came to intelligence matters, Fidel had a particular habit of personally handling operational details, down to the man. Fidel was "a supreme, unchallenged spy master," according to Brian Latell, a retired CIA analyst, and he often chose operatives himself—especially the harder-edged boys, who often lacked formal education. "Castro wanted them to be uncontaminated by the old Cuba," Latell wrote. "He wanted them to be malleable and enthusiastic."[3] That was the environment in which Roberto mastered his spycraft, and over time he would become not only a powerful player within Cuban intelligence services but also, according to U.S. intelligence sources, an adversary respected by his American counterparts at Langley.[4]

One might not know it by looking at him. Hardly a Cuban James Bond, Roberto had an everyman's appearance and demeanor, with an affable smile and a lightness to his character that masked his dark past.

I liked Roberto immediately. After years of meetings in which he appeared to be sussing out whether he could trust me, Roberto finally agreed to explain how this intelligence game was played.

It had been months since we had last spoken. Conversing by telephone had its limitations. In-person meetings seemed like the only means acceptable, so we settled on a location outside the capital. I arrived first, though I didn't have to wait long.

"Roberto," I exclaimed as he arrived, and offered him a hearty handshake. "It's good to see you." He replied in kind and clasped my extended hand with both of his before we made our way into the building and sat down near an open terrace. Roberto seemed in good spirits, though he kept a close eye on me and our surroundings. It all seemed a bit surreal. "Where do we begin?" I asked.

I wasn't certain where our conversation would take us, so it was tricky to know where to start. But with tensions again ramping up between Washington and Havana, a series of what then appeared to be sonic attacks against U.S. embassy personnel seemed as good a place as any.

Between November 2016 and August 2017, U.S. and Canadian diplomats reported a variety of concussion-like symptoms. The cause remained unclear, but as reporters gradually learned more about the incident during the spring and summer of 2017, conspiracy theories abounded, in part fed by rhetoric from Washington. By summer's end, the incident had spiraled into a full-fledged diplomatic crisis. U.S. officials called it a "sonic attack," and some seventy diplomats were tested for a series of symptoms, including hearing loss, concussions, and nausea. Secretary of State Rex Tillerson referred to the incident as "deliberate attacks" in an interview with the Associated Press, while New Jersey senator Bob Menendez referred to it as "brazen and vicious attacks," even as federal investigators expressed their doubts.[5] An FBI report in January said it identified the symptoms but found no evidence that sound waves were responsible. The neurological impacts, which included mild traumatic brain damage of twenty-four embassy officials, were further investigated by a team of physicians at the University of Pennsylvania, who later published their findings in the *Journal of the American Medical Association*.[6] The team concurred with the assessment of concussion-like symptoms, and also downplayed the likelihood of sonic attacks, poison, or mass hysteria. But without definitive answers, rumors swirled—it was the Castros, rogue Cuban hard-liners, the Russians, the North Koreans, or anti-Castro factions in Miami bent on undermining the détente. Everyone had a theory. And virtually all of them emanated from a Cold War mind-set that had kept these neighboring countries at odds.

"Roberto," I said, deliberatively. "What can you tell me about what's happening now?"

He knew what I was asking and sighed. The relaxed look evident earlier was gone. "David," he replied, mirroring my own deliberative tone. "I've dedicated my life to do whatever I could to harm your country." By now Roberto seemed more a convivial spirit than a hardened spy. He grinned again, pausing a moment before finishing his sentence. "But in the last few years, I've done whatever I can to improve relations," he added. "I did both, thinking that it's better for my country."

When it came to those so-called sonic attacks, however, Roberto seemed just as bewildered as the rest of us. "Nobody knows," he told me. That seemed implausible. Not a leaf falls in Havana, as the saying goes, without a Castro knowing it. Of course, by May 2018, reports of a similar incident surfaced on the other side of the globe in Guangzhou, China, when a U.S. State Department worker complained of "abnormal sensations of sound and pressure." Secretary of State Mike Pompeo described it as "very similar" to what had occurred in Cuba. The phenomenon was no longer unique to Havana, and the revelation further muddied the waters as to whether Cuba had ever intentionally launched any such attack. By August 2018, Douglas Smith, a lead author of the JAMA study, said that his team now considered an attack by use of microwaves among the leading suspects in the case. The technology, first tested in the early 1960s at Cornell University, could produce acoustic effects by concentrating the focus of the beams. The U.S. Defense Intelligence Agency cautioned in 1976 that Soviet researchers had expressed "a fairly high degree of interest and a genuine desire to pursue these investigations." Now, as Cuba cozied up to Washington, was it possible that Russia's hand was again quietly at work, putting the brakes on any further U.S. détente with the Kremlin's old Caribbean ally? It would be hard to prove.[7] The government in Havana, meanwhile, remained adamant that it wasn't responsible.

"What else?" he asked.

The room was small, and hardly accommodating. Roberto wasn't likely to stay long. So I transitioned my questions and stumbled more generally through the recent diplomatic changes and rapprochement between Havana and Washington.

"From the looks of it," I said, "it had seemed like this old spy war between these two countries was finally coming to an end."

Roberto just looked at me. He said nothing. "But now I don't know if that's still true, or if that were ever true," I continued. Roberto took a slow sip of juice that had been resting atop the end table beside his chair. Then, taking a deep breath, another smile cracked his face, thus betraying his thoughts before he could answer.

"That never was really true," he said with a husky laugh. "It will go on. That never will stop."

The spy-fueled inertia of the Cold War's quid pro quo, steeped as it was in seven decades of mistrust, was not subject to the flip of a switch. It couldn't just be turned off. Roberto had over the years cultivated what he described as a "very extensive" intelligence apparatus. Many were still players in the spy game. It was all they knew.

"Did you personally cultivate assets?" I asked, trying to reorient the conversation.

"Of course," he replied.

"How did you do it?"

He again shifted in his seat. "There are many ways," he said. One was blackmail. "We have many women who work for us," he said as the same puckish smile again crept in. I thought of Dalia, along with that miraculously timed email from the woman I had briefly dated in Havana. I would almost certainly never know their motives for sure. My mind trailed off, wondering what I may have unwittingly compromised. Perhaps Roberto's comments merely inspired a bit of unfounded paranoia. Both were possible.

"There's another way," he said, his croaky voice bringing me back to the present. Spies would at times pay for intelligence, or recruit assets under "a third flag," he added, misrepresenting which government they actually worked for. "A man who worked for us might say he worked for the CIA," he said, clarifying his point. The effect, if done well, rendered potential assets vulnerable to manipulation.

But those methods were not the most effective, Roberto explained. The best way, in fact, was through ideology. "Convince them," he said, leaning back in his chair. "When you go to recruit somebody, you have to be sure. First, you've been friends with this person for months or years. And then you know how he thinks. How he behaves. And then you know what to tell him. How you can, as we say, enter him." It was a process that took considerably more time than blackmail, payment, or misdirection. But according to Roberto, it yielded far more dependable results.

In the case of Ana Montes, that strategy was particularly effective. For seventeen years, the former Cuba analyst at the U.S. Defense Intelligence Agency seemed motivated by neither money nor blackmail to betray her country at the behest of Cuban intelligence. Montes, who hailed from Kansas and Iowa, with Puerto Rican roots, behaved like a "quiet, frugal and unassuming neighbor," while routinely sitting in on highly classified U.S. intelligence briefings. But she was routing information back to Havana, memorizing reports while actively attempting to steer U.S. action on Cuba. In 2001, she was found out and arrested for espionage—and sentenced to twenty-five years in prison.

But what got her there began decades earlier, in 1984, during a causal conversation with a student at Johns Hopkins University. The student was a Cuban intelligence officer, and apparently sensed something in Montes that suggested she was ripe to be turned. A 2005 Defense Department report further explained her alleged motives: "In her view, Cuba was victimized by U.S. repression and [she] concluded that she had the 'moral right' to provide information to Cuba," investigators wrote in their report. "Throughout her career as a clandestine agent, she believed that 'destiny was offering me an opportunity to do everything that I could do to help Cuba.' She often exclaimed, 'I couldn't give up on the people I was helping.' In sum, she indicated that she 'felt morally rewarded.'"[8]

And there you have it. With few financial resources, Cuba had proven extraordinarily successful in extending its spies' reach through those like Montes, while frustrated U.S. officials complained that American senior intelligence officials weren't taking these formidable Cuban counterparts seriously.

"The Cubans have bested us so many times because we systematically think they're stupid," explained Fulton Armstrong, a former top CIA analyst for Latin America. Armstrong had served in the U.S. Interests Section in Havana and in 2010 had joined Senator John Kerry's staff on the Senate Foreign Relations Committee. "If you have an existential threat, you take it seriously and you put your best people on it," he told me during an interview. "To think that some goofball Cuban American, some goofball neocon from NED [National Endowment for Democracy], or some goofball from IRI [International Republican Institute] is going to recruit entire classes of people with phrases like 'the regime doesn't love you, so you should hate the regime.' The naïveté is immense."

There is no apparent evidence to suggest Roberto was involved in the recruitment of Montes. But to senior U.S. intelligence officials focused on Cuba, such as Armstrong, that was almost beside the point. The island just didn't rate when it came to national security priorities. The Soviet threat was over. And to many Americans, Cuba's best days were behind it. Cuba seemed an afterthought, hardly a primary focus in Washington, save for a dedicated group of Florida and New Jersey lawmakers and lobbyists.

The mind-set in Havana couldn't have been more different. To Cuban authorities, the intelligence game remained a fight for their very survival. They took it seriously. America's leaders had had ample time to learn this by now. Their first real wake-up call had come years earlier with a man named Florentino Aspillaga Lombard, a senior Cuban intelligence officer working in the Slovakian capital of Bratislava. Recruited at age sixteen, Aspillaga had spent nearly a quarter of a century working in Cuban intelligence. But on June 6, 1987, he had had enough and simply got in a car and drove across the border to Austria, presenting himself to U.S. diplomats.

Once with the Americans, Aspillaga offered at least two shock-ing disclosures. The first referenced President John F. Kennedy and what the Cubans may have actually known about his assassination. The revelation surfaced during an interview with former CIA ana-lyst Brian Latell, who had served as U.S. national intelligence officer for Latin America. According to Latell, on the morning of Novem-ber 22, 1963, Aspillaga's supervisor asked him to redirect his anten-nas away from South Florida and instead home in on Texas. Shortly after noon that same day, President Kennedy sat in his motorcade in Dallas, Texas, as gunfire rained down across Dealey Plaza. The American president was pronounced dead less than an hour later. Latell theorized—based on his interviews with Aspillaga, more than a dozen defectors, and CIA officers, plus a review of declassified intel-ligence documents—that the Cubans were "complicit in Kennedy's death." That said, their "involvement fell short of an organized as-sassination plot."[9]

"It was [Lee Harvey Oswald's] plan and his rifle, not theirs," wrote Latell.

Oswald had indeed expressed sympathy for the Cuban cause, according to the Warren Commission report, which determined Oswald had "expressed strong admiration for Fidel Castro and an interest in joining the Cuban Army." Fidel, who called Kennedy's assassination "a plot against peace, a sinister conspiracy," also ac-knowledged in a November 27, 1963, speech at the University of Havana that Oswald, whom U.S. investigators believed Cuba to be monitoring, had traveled to the Cuban consulate in Mexico.[10]

What's more, a declassified cable from 1967 detailed a conversa-tion between two Cuban intelligence officers in Mexico discussing Oswald. Concerned the United States would blame Cuba for Ken-nedy's death, one officer remarked, "Oswald must have been a good shot." The other, a man named Abreu, replied, "Oh, he was quite good." Asked how he knew this, Abreu responded, "I knew him."[11]

Still, there was no direct evidence to support the idea that

Oswald had ever been working for Fidel, who by 1963 was engaged in the beginnings of secret negotiations with Kennedy. Those dealings began following a botched CIA-inspired invasion at the Bay of Pigs, when Attorney General Robert Kennedy dispatched a New York lawyer named James Donovan to negotiate the release of the remaining exile paramilitaries, who were by then imprisoned in Cuba. Successful, Donovan reached an agreement that swapped more than 1,100 prisoners for $62 million in food and medicine. The exchange appeared to lay the groundwork for future negotiations, despite the efforts of American intelligence: the CIA had tried to use Donovan as an unwitting assassin, lacing a wet suit he prepared to give Fidel with poison, according to a 1975 Senate report. But Donovan gave Fidel a different wet suit, and the encounter, despite CIA efforts, inspired a modicum of confidence between Cuba and the United States. "I'm in the business of negotiation, not assassination," his daughter, Mary Ellen Donovan Fuller, reportedly recalled her father saying.[12] Unlike Cuba, the United States was not speaking with one voice. Nevertheless, the standoff suddenly seemed surmountable.

Momentum was building. An April 22, 1963, trip to Havana by ABC reporter Lisa Howard—who interviewed Fidel, Raul, and Che Guevara—punctuated a growing sense that Cuba was ready to talk. When Howard returned, CIA deputy director Richard Helms debriefed her, and, according to his declassified report, she told him that "Fidel Castro is looking for a way to reach rapprochement with the United States."

By November, President Kennedy had dispatched to Cuba a French journalist named Jean Daniel to serve as a secret intermediary with the Cuban leader. An avenue for normalization was opening. But his efforts would be for naught. On the afternoon of November 22, as Daniel and Fidel lunched in the popular beach town of Varadero, the news of Kennedy's assassination was delivered.

"This is terrible," Fidel reportedly told Daniel.[13] "There goes your mission of peace." The young Castro then predicted: "They are going to say we did it."

And yet a recently declassified staff report from the House Select Committee on Assassinations revealed that many in Washington scarcely believed that was true. "The Committee does not believe Castro would have assassinated President Kennedy," the report said. "Because such an act, if discovered, would have afforded the United States the excuse to destroy Cuba. The risk would not have been worth it."[14]

CIA-inspired attempts to kill the Cuban leader would nonetheless continue, employing everything from "the use of underworld figures" and poison pills to deadly bacterial powders and "other devices which strain the imagination."[15] Nothing worked. The Cuban leader always seemed to be one step ahead.

Decades later, Aspillaga's revelations would help explain how. During a series of top-secret briefings following his defection, Aspillaga divulged what may have been among Fidel's greatest secrets: when it came to Cuba, the CIA's sources were not their own. "Aspillaga said that every asset that CIA had recruited was a double," said former CIA analyst Fulton Armstrong, who was formerly stationed in Havana.[16] Long before Montes, Cuban intelligence had already penetrated the firewall of American espionage, according to the Cuban defector. Four dozen assets the CIA had recruited, dating back to the early 1960s, were actually loyal to Fidel.

The ways in which the aging Castro had managed to avoid assassination all these years were becoming more clear.

BALTIMORE
BACK CHANNEL

My cabdriver eased his yellow taxi left and ascended a sloping asphalt path that led to the estate of a man named Alvin B. Krongard. "Buzzy" for short, he was a former investment banker and CEO at Alex Brown and Sons, the nation's oldest investment bank. In 1997, Bankers Trust purchased the bank, netting the Baltimore son $71 million in stock and helping cement his fortune.

"Just drive up," I told the driver, who gave a nod, though he looked uncertain about it. When we pulled in, a pair of large German shepherds came trotting over, circling the cab. I had only once seen dogs even remotely this big, and that was during a reporting stint at Marine Corps barracks in southern Afghanistan. A moment later they retreated. Krongard had just walked out of his mansion.

"Come on inside," he said, shaking my hand with a vise-like grip. Once inside, a scene of old-world opulence unfolded, replete with eighteenth-century oil paintings hung over a display of brass medals inscribed by the CIA for valor and service. I surveyed the scene, giving it my best nonchalant look, before taking a seat. Tough, with a martial arts background, Krongard had the conservative look of a banker. During his tenure at Alex Brown, the bank specialized in financial services, health care, and technology—including biotechnology.

Biotechnology was at least one sector in which the Cubans seemed to be making real strides. Though the Soviet Union collapse had prompted major food, cash, and fuel shortages on the island, out of the despair emerged the sort of MacGyver-like ingenuity that had kept those old cars running—only this time, in pharmaceuticals. Cuban biochemists were making knockoff drugs and had gotten quite adept at it. Since at least 1991, just around the time Wall Street interest in biotech was surging, they had been running clinical trials on cancer vaccines and other drugs that would eventually yield results.

A Cuban-engineered drug called CimaVax showed in clinical trials that it targeted a growth factor in metastatic cancer cells and could reduce the spread of the disease. And it would eventually bear fruit. In an August 2016 trial, which had an accompanying study published in the peer-reviewed *Clinical Cancer Research* journal, researchers determined that patients receiving the treatment (following chemotherapy) survived an average of three to five months longer than those who did not. Those diagnosed with elevated levels of a protein called epidermal growth factor, which CimaVax was designed to arrest, were found to live significantly longer.[1]

But as Cuba steered toward a cancer cure, it faced American headwinds. The trade embargo restricted both U.S. companies and their foreign subsidiaries from trading with the island, a law that had become increasingly problematic for Cuba as the industry consolidated. "You'd have a supplier for several years, and suddenly you'd get a letter from the company saying, 'We can't supply you anymore because our firm was bought by an American transnational,'" Ismael Clark, president of the Cuban Academy of Sciences, reportedly said.[2]

But as Castro aged, investors looked to Cuba with growing interest, and they became more vocal about U.S. restrictions. "Americans are losing lives because they can't access the scientific development in Cuba," wrote billionaire entrepreneur Richard Branson, "while Cubans are losing opportunities for further advancements through collaboration with the U.S."[3]

Krongard seemed ahead of the game, traveling to Cuba throughout the 1990s and expressing interest in its burgeoning biotech sector, and grew close to the highest echelons of the Cuban government. Should the embargo ever be lifted, the Maryland banker would be well positioned.

But Krongard also had other interests. After the sale of Alex Brown and Sons in 1997, he consulted for George Tenet, then director of the CIA. It's not clear if he had done intelligence work prior to that point, but it did seem clear that Krongard's service as an infantry officer in the U.S. Marine Corps left him with a taste for the kind of work the CIA promised. In 2001, Tenet, looking to breathe new life into his agency, gave Krongard the position he wanted, naming him executive director. It was the agency's third-highest position, allowing Krongard to streamline its practices and consolidate personnel. (He held that position at the agency during the time of its controversial detention and interrogation program at secret black sites across the globe.) Meanwhile, Krongard forged a working relationship with Erik Prince, and was later listed as an adviser to Prince's security company, formerly known as Blackwater. And when we talked, the conversation often veered back to Afghanistan.

"Anything else?" he asked.

It was a Wednesday afternoon in November 2017.

Foreign investors were still eyeing Cuba. Détente had whet investor appetites, and a reinstated American embassy spurred investor confidence. And Krongard still had occasion to travel to Cuba, heading to Havana for a meeting that same year to meet with "the highest levels of Cuban government." But this time it was for potential collaboration, he told me. Tucked into a twelve-page Obama-era directive on trade and travel, the U.S. Office of the Director of

National Intelligence called for ways "to find opportunities for engagement on areas of common interest," for the purpose of combating "mutual threats."[4] America's spies were to work with the very men and women who had spent their careers infiltrating U.S. intelligence.

There was reason to be skeptical.

In fact, in February 2016, James Clapper, then U.S. director of national intelligence, listed Cuba as among the nation's greatest counterintelligence threats, behind Russia and China, and on par with Iran, in a statement he made at the Dirksen Senate Office Building in Washington.[5] But Krongard, who was no longer in an official capacity in government, was determined to see how feasible collaboration really was. With the U.S. embassy restored, trade and travel restrictions reduced, and the prospect of greater state-to-state cooperation on issues as serious as security, a relationship once defined by distrust and antagonism seemed to be warming.

And yet by the summer of 2017, amid the fallout from those alleged sonic attacks, that had all come to a grinding halt.

Maybe Roberto was right. Maybe things hadn't actually changed so much. This is Cuba, after all, where conspiracy thinking is incubated and elevated into policy. Evidence for the sonic attacks, however, was inconclusive. Investigators produced fourteen recordings of the sound, which some diplomats first attributed to cicadas. As the U.S. embassy pulled staff and issued warnings, the Canadians initially seemed less concerned. Their diplomats had also been affected, but the rationale for an attack against them seemed less clear. Cuba-Canada relations had never suffered the way the U.S.-Cuba relationship had. And Prime Minister Justin Trudeau announced in June that his country was still conducting "business as usual" with Havana, though he later instructed the families of Canadian diplomats to return home as a safety precaution.

Raul, however, appeared shaken. Channeling through intermediaries, Cuban authorities asked Krongard to visit Havana to discuss the controversy as part of a series of discussions that included a rare in-person meeting with America's top Havana diplomat, Jeffrey DeLaurentis.

"If they're acting, they deserve an award," said Krongard, inclined to believe top Cuban authorities, who seemed desperate to get the issue resolved. Unlike at prior meetings, there was no denying something had happened. But the Cubans were adamant that they weren't the ones behind it.

In a sign of just how seriously Raul took the charge, he invited American investigators to Havana and deployed some two thousand officials of Cuba's own to investigate, offering the rare gesture of making his deputies available to the media. "I can guarantee you that this is completely false," Colonel Ramiro Ramirez, chief of diplomatic security for the Cuban Interior Ministry, told NBC's Andrea Mitchell. Even President Castro weighed in publicly, predictably denying responsibility, while his daughter Mariela Castro blamed rogue groups in the United States for trying to "vandalize" Cuba's reputation.[6]

Meanwhile, researchers in the United States were busy trying to unravel the mystery. In March 2018, scientists at the University of Michigan said they believed the incident might have actually been the result of a poorly engineered eavesdropping effort. Researchers claimed they were able to reverse engineer the sound diplomats heard, referred to as "intermodulation distortion," created when ultrasound listening devices are placed too close together. "A malfunctioning device that was supposed to inaudibly steal information or eavesdrop on conversation with ultrasonic transmission seems more plausible than a sonic weapon," said Kevin Fu, chief scientist at Virta Laboratories and associate professor at the University of Michigan. "That said, our results do not rule out other potential causes."[7]

Whether or not the Cubans were responsible, the effects were clear: the Trump administration had made permanent cuts to its embassy staff, reducing personnel to just ten people, diminishing Washington's influence and obscuring its perspective at the precise moment of economic reforms and political transition. For the first time in decades, a man whose name wasn't Castro was about to assume the presidency, and America's diplomats had in large part left. "This would be a moment where the United States would want to be very present," said Dan Erikson, a former top State Department aide on Latin American affairs. "Both to monitor and help interpret events there, as well as some sort of role in engaging with the government."

And yet for once the alleged sonic attacks gave Cuba's hard-liners, who remained wary of normalization, and Miami's hard-line exiles, who viewed détente as appeasement to a dictator, something that seemed to benefit them both: a breakdown in U.S.-Cuba relations. For Miami, it served as a reminder to think again to those who had considered the Cold War over. For Cuba's hard-liners, it offered some breathing space at a critical juncture. Did they really want engagement with their old enemy at such a precarious time in their country's transition? Raul was pursuing a series of market reforms and anticorruption efforts to gradually wean his country off a Marxist-Leninist system that even Fidel said "doesn't even work for us anymore." In the process, he had also laid the groundwork for a delicate transition of leadership, whereby a man without revolutionary credentials had taken the helm. The process was delicate. And Cuban officials cautioned me that it was hardly set in stone.

"I know you guys all think this is all well established and thought out already," former Cuban diplomat Carlos Alzugaray told me over the phone. "But this is a long process of negotiation inside the elites. Who's going to be who, and where." The Cubans were hedging their bets. And though President Obama had promised to "bury the last remnant" of the Cold War, calls for democracy had only reinforced old suspicions. Now, with President Trump in office, and his apparent modus vivendi with Miami hard-liner Senator Marco Rubio (FL-R) in full view, Washington looked as if it was back to its old tricks.

Castro likely hadn't trusted Obama, but he may have calculated the benefits of playing along. Trump was a far different calculation. The former real estate mogul seemed like Republican presidents of the past who had usually taken the fight to Cuba. Entrenchment was back en vogue.

"What an interesting thing this international chess game is," Fidel Castro in 1960 told his treasury minister Rufo Lopez Frequet about the possibility of normalizing relations with the United States. Six decades later, what Havana and Washington actually meant by "normal" is still being hashed out.

The chess game continues.

EPILOGUE

A revolution is a struggle to the death between the future
and the past.

—Fidel Castro, January 1961,
Revolution Plaza, Havana, Cuba

The bar where I had met Alejandro Castro Espín was gone. Nine
years after I first strolled into La Fontana, its dank subterranean saloon where late-night patrons puffed Cohibas and sipped Habana
Club had been built over and moved to a swank aboveground location, replete with koi fish ponds, shiny glass fixtures, and pricey new
menus. It was all part of a modernizing effort by its owners, Horacio Reyes-Lovio and Ernesto Blanco, who enjoyed a surge in cash during the investment boom of those waning Obama years.

"Not just foreigners here," Ernesto told me, referencing the sort
of clientele to whom he catered. "Cubans also dine and drink."

The surge of investment had been a boon for the island's Ernes-
tos, with thousands capitalizing on the opening. Official state salaries still hovered just under $25 per month, but a torrent of
remittances and new private enterprise buoyed incomes and swelled
business opportunities. In a 2016 multiprovince survey, 73 percent
of Cuban respondents reported they were at least doubling their
official state salaries. The good news, however, was tempered by

Cuban leadership in no mood to rush things. The old Communists, wary of moving too fast, still held some sway. Having watched the pendulum swing back following the Soviet collapse, as market capitalization and reconciliation with the West ushered in Russian chaos and violence, they seemed loath to relinquish control. Havana still preferred its old client model, accepting donations rather than invoices, as John Kavulich put it, while failing to adopt the kind of far-reaching macroeconomic reforms that other former centrally planned economies, such as Vietnam, had enacted.

Yet as the country's leadership inched toward change, Cuban entrepreneurs who earned too much too quickly faced the risk of being shut down. Ernesto had always worried about that. Two nearby restaurants, the Dolce Vita and the Lungo Mare, allegedly suffered the ire of the island's overseers. The Mare's owner was reportedly accused of money laundering and ties to drug traffickers, though his neighbors surmised that he might have simply been too ambitious. Cuba was very much still Communist. And authorities wanted everyone to know it.

In a series of updated economic guidelines, the National Assembly, wary perhaps of growing inequalities, declared that a "concentration of property and financial and material wealth" would be prohibited. And yet in the wake of plummeting Venezuelan subsidies, government coffers were running low. The Cuban economy had dipped into recession and faced yawning deficits and the lingering devastation wrought by Hurricane Irma in 2017. Without another Moscow- or Caracas-like benefactor, even senior leadership privately acknowledged that their country would need more profound market-based reforms if it were to survive. Perhaps a generational shift in leadership would mark the beginning of that trend as the island's aging gerontocracy faded away. But little was certain.

When I returned to Havana in April 2018, Cubans were again fretting about their future: not because of who occupied the presidency in Havana, but because of who sat in the Oval Office in Washington. At first, the change seemed marginal. In November 2017, a clear reading of Trump's actual Cuba policy indicated that it reflected only a partial change from the Obama-era directive. Under Obama, officials had relaxed travel rules and permitted Americans to go to Cuba provided they fit into one of twelve categories. By law, the president had the authority to lift neither travel restrictions nor economic sanctions. But Obama-inspired interpretations of those sanctions allowed for new commerce in banking and telecommunications, while affording Americans the right to travel, provided that their trips were not *entirely* for tourism purposes. The new policy reflected a new and gaping hole in the U.S. trade embargo and seemed tantamount to a White House wink and a nod that gave Americans the green light to go smoke Cohibas, sip rum, and ride around in the vintage cars of their childhoods.

Cut off for more than half a century, Cuba again seemed open for business. And private restaurateurs, hoteliers, and cabdrivers, such as Ernesto, Yanet, and Enrique, all seemed to benefit from the surge by refurbishing their businesses or starting new ones.

But that would begin to change under Trump. Under the new administration guidelines, trade and commerce with businesses owned by the Cuban military were restricted. The individual "people-to-people" exchange—enjoyed by American travelers—was also circumscribed. Those who ignored the new rules faced potential fines, prompting visitors to Cuba to book travel through cruise lines or licensed tour operators, rather than simply go on their own.

And yet a curious thing happened. The year 2017 turned out to be a banner year for Cuban tourism, with nearly 5 million travelers breathing $3 billion of life into the island's moribund economy. Foreign appetites had been whet by the opening, and travelers were coming anyway, hoping to catch a glimpse of the old time capsule "before it all changes." Some six hundred thousand American travelers (without Cuban family ties) arrived: nearly seven times the annual Bush-era levels that the island's infrastructure and hotels struggled to accommodate.

Cuba had capitalized on its old-world allure and nostalgia's secondhand smoke. Yet much of the money seemed to be flowing toward the very place Trump intended to avoid: government coffers. Cruise liners and tour operators offered more self-contained travel, booking state-run hotels and riding in government-run tour buses. Meanwhile, many of the bed-and-breakfast owners I spoke to reported a drop in their numbers of clients. By the first quarter of 2018, the effects of the Trump policy had more firmly taken hold. Non–Cuban American travel to the island had dropped by almost 60 percent as disenchantment filtered through the island's some six hundred thousand *cuentapropistas* (self-employed).

"We had a mini boom," Yanet told me one afternoon in April 2018 while sitting in her Centro Habana apartment, a reference to the more bustling years of 2015 and 2016 when her three extra rooms were commonly filled with visiting tourists. Now they were often vacant. "That boom has ended," she said with resignation, shifting in her seat.

As Washington and Havana squabbled, the Cuban people had once again been the ones to suffer. Despite Obama's overtures, Washington had again changed course. To the island's old guard, it was vindication, their experience teaching them American foreign policy was a fickle hydra, subject to the whims of money and politics. No matter what the promises of presidents like Kennedy, Carter, Ford, and Obama had been, the prospect of a succeeding administration undoing what had been done perpetually dampened island optimism. And yet Cuban leadership also did itself no favors. That, of course, may have been the point all along.

For instance, when in February 1996, Fidel ordered his air force to shoot down Cuban American pilots after their repeated incursions into Cuban airspace to drop anti-Castro leaflets, the attack fueled congressional momentum "that would make it very difficult for any president to lift the embargo alone," Hillary Clinton told the Council on Foreign Relations. In fact, her husband, who as president strengthened U.S. sanctions against Cuba in the wake of those attacks, later wondered about those events in his autobiography, *My Life.* "It almost appeared that Castro was trying to force us to maintain the embargo as an excuse for the economic failures of his regime," wrote Bill Clinton.

"Cuba is not opposed to finding a solution to its historical differences with the United States," Fidel had proclaimed in a December 1980 speech to Communist Party officials. "But no one should expect Cuba to change its position or yield in its principles."

Nearly four decades later, Havana's position hardly had changed. And with Trump's election, relations seemed to have devolved back to the old playbook. In April 2018, the American president was noticeably absent from the Summit of the Americas in Lima, Peru—a meeting historically employed to mend fences between regional leaders. Enmeshed in his own legal battles at home, he instead dispatched Vice President Mike Pence to head the U.S. delegation. But the rhetoric of the former Indiana governor seemed more Miami hard-liner than U.S. diplomat as he condemned Cuba as a "tired Communist regime," and then promptly walked out before Cuban foreign minister Bruno Rodriguez could respond.

"He couldn't take it and left," Raul said following the encounter, as mutual distrust reemerged from the shadows.

Old habits die hard.

Meanwhile, the aftermath of those mysterious so-called sonic attacks against U.S. and Canadian diplomats brought new hardships. By May 2018, America's diplomatic presence had dwindled to ten staff members, its lowest number in decades. The U.S. mission that Fidel once denounced as a "nest of spies" was by now virtually empty, much to the chagrin of thousands of Cubans waiting to be processed to visit their families in the States. In the absence of a functioning

U.S. consular office in Havana, Cubans were obliged to make the costly trip to Guyana to apply for U.S. visas. With Cuba's traditional relief valves of emigration shut, it embarked on perhaps its most precarious moment of transition.

Fidel was dead. Raul had left office. And as a fifty-seven-year-old bureaucrat named Díaz-Canel assumed power, the fate of the Revolution never seemed so uncertain. Yet the U.S. State Department, which had spent three generations of blood and treasure in anticipation of this very moment, had all but disengaged. The old Communist guard, men like Ramiro Valdes and Jose Machado Ventura, who had spent their careers in defiance of yanqui capitalists, were likely unnerved by Raul's absence, and yet it was hard not to picture them raising a glass to America's sudden absenteeism.

Raul, of course, wasn't really gone. He had retained his position as first secretary of the Communist Party as well as head of the army, the island's two most powerful institutions. And the new president, Díaz-Canel, seemed to know that while he wielded new power and responsibilities, the real political muscle still resided with Raul.

"I affirm to this assembly that comrade Raul will head the decisions for the present and the future of the nation," Díaz-Canel acknowledged in his assembly remarks. A former engineer who had worked in a series of provincial party posts before assuming the presidency, he had a reputation for not rocking the boat. In fact, it may have been precisely because he eschewed the limelight that he had ascended where others had failed. A relative youngster compared to party stalwarts, Díaz-Canel had been perceived as malleable, even though he had on more than one occasion made controversial calls to improve his country's internet access. Still, he was "a good Communist," according to those who knew him, charged with continuity.

"His election is not by chance," Raul said on April 19, 2018 before assembly lawmakers, affirming what most likely already knew: the new president had been handpicked, and his power would remain limited. Yet that, too, was anticipated to change. During a more than hour-long speech before the National Assembly, Raul declared that he expected his successor to serve two five-year terms as president, pledging to hand him the reins as Communist Party head when Raul more fully retired in 2021.

"From that point on, I will be just another soldier defending this revolution," the aging Castro told lawmakers. (That, of course, seemed unlikely. Raul's overseeing hand was expected to mirror that of his late brother—between 1959 and 1976, Fidel ran Cuba while a man named Osvaldo Dorticós technically held the title of Cuban president.) Still, he seemed a hands-on type of leader. In his first real test of leadership following a passenger jet crash in Havana in May 2018 that left at least 112 people dead, Díaz-Canel appeared at the scene of the still smoking wreckage to speak with aviation officials, later visiting the morgue and consoling family members of the deceased. In the provinces, he had earned that sort of reputation, and observers now looked for signs of continuity in his presidency. Indeed, in those first months in office he had kept a hectic schedule, which included hosting the UN Economic Commission for Latin America and the Caribbean, and traveling out to a waste management site where he said he learned about the city's truck shortages and supply problems.[1]

These were not the sort of issues Raul still wanted to handle. Those who knew him said he relished the idea of retirement. And yet as longtime manager of Castro family matters, he also likely recognized that the stakes were simply too high to just bow out. He had been deliberate in avoiding a blood lineage transition. But the legitimacy of the new president—a man born one year after the Revolution—would likely remain tenuous without Raul's implicit backing, as would the power of Raul's children. His daughter, Mariela, was an outspoken member of the National Assembly, and had been instrumental in promoting LGBT rights and AIDS prevention, but held comparatively little political influence without him. Raul's ex-son-in-law, Lopez-Callejas, wielded far more power, but it remained unclear how that authority would ultimately play out without Raul's expressed support. Then there was his thirty-two-year-old grandson, Raulito, who worked as Raul's bodyguard, a position that had a track record for success. Cuban president Díaz-Canel had once held the same job. But again, Raul was key.

Finally, there was Alejandro.

Eight years after he slouched across from me, arms draped atop that polished Miramar bar, the powers and prestige of Raul's only son had strengthened. He now oversaw intelligence services for both Cuba's armed forces and its Interior Ministry. Yet his absence on the nominating list of the National Assembly of People's Power meant the Castros could not be likened to the dynastic succession of North Korea's Kim family. Despite a growing profile both at home and abroad, Alejandro had remained quiet and out of politics. For now, the Castro clan seemed content to rule behind the scenes.

But they would all face mounting problems—an economy hobbled by falling subsidies, an aging, shrinking population, and a dual-currency system that warped prices and rendered state-run monopolies inefficient. To foreign investors, these bloated bureaucracies were the Kafkaesque goo that slowed the gears of the Cuban economy and kept their money away. If Raul had endeavored to fashion himself a Cuban Deng Xiaoping, he had fallen far short. The island's Soviet-style system had only flirted with market reforms, trimming state payrolls, and encouraging private sector growth, but it had never fully committed. Meanwhile, renewed antagonism with Washington only seemed to validate the old-timers' reluctance to change. Cuba had offered these men free health care, education, and, perhaps more importantly, a sense of purpose: a Cuban David to an American Goliath.

But now Cuba's benefactors in Moscow and Caracas were either gone or slipping away, as housing, food, and medicine shortages gripped the island. Yet unlike the so-called special period of the

1990s, the Castro revolutionaries were largely gone. It was now up to Díaz-Canel to stem the bleeding. It remained unclear whether he had the clout for it. A crisis of confidence was building.

Still, those at La Fontana would likely weather the storm.

"It was good to see you again," an old waiter named Alduanis said as I made my way to the door, pushing it open with a creak. His angular face looked only vaguely familiar. Eight years earlier, Alduanis had occasionally welcomed me through that very door before I encamped for a bit of writing, eating, and sipping Habana Club. Only now did I begin to remember. In the years that had elapsed between us, his island had experienced seismic shifts, but he looked the same, with a crisp white shirt tucked into black pants as he welcomed patrons and bussed tables. Some things hadn't changed. And Alduanis, like many Cubans, had a long memory.

ACKNOWLEDGMENTS

This book was technically nine years in the making. But in reality, it was put together over the course of one year of mostly late nights and weekends—which wouldn't have been possible without the support of my wife and enduring love, Stephanie. She, who helped edit this book and put up with me in the process, deserves as much credit as anyone. To my stepdaughter, Bel, sister, Elizabeth, and mother and father—you have been my pillars. I'm forever grateful to have such good, strong, and caring people to call family.

I would also like to thank Peter Riva, who took a chance by signing an unknown author writing his first book. I can't thank you enough, Peter. Your guidance and knowledge throughout this process were invaluable, and I consider myself lucky to call you a friend.

To Laura Apperson, Alan Bradshaw, Bill Warhop, and Karen Wolny at St. Martin's Press. Your excitement about this project, attention to detail in editing, and persistent willingness to help is something I won't forget. Thank you all so very much.

(Teall, Brian, Jim, Dan, and Neil—you're buying!)

NOTES

1.

1. Alejandro Castro Espín, *El Imperio del Terror* (Cuba, 2009).
2. Interview with former Cuban diplomat Carlos Alzugaray, December 2017.
3. "The *Time* 100," Yoani Sánchez, May 12, 2008.
4. Interview with Yoani Sánchez, Havana, Cuba, November 7, 2009.
5. Dispatches and biographies pulled from *Chicago Tribune*—Profiles, http://www.chicagotribune.com/chi-gary-marx-staff.html; BBC / The Guardian, March 2017, https://www.theguardian.com/profile/stephengibb. *El Universal*, February 2007, http://archivo.eluniversal.com.mx/notas/408395.html.
6. CPJ condemns Cuba's decision to ban three foreign correspondents, February 23, 2007, https://cpj.org/2007/02/cpj-condemns-cubas-decision-to-ban-three-foreign-c.php.
7. Fidel Castro, *Fidel, Bolivia and Something More* (Cuba, 2008), prologue.
8. John Rice, "Cuban Official Defends Internet Controls," Associated Press, February 15, 2007.
9. WikiLeaks: U.S.-Cuba Chill Exaggerated, But Old Ways Threaten Progress, January 6, 2010, https://wikileaks.org/plusd/cables/10HAVANA9_a.html & Juan O. Tamayo, "U.S. expresses outrage over 'assault' on Cuban blogger Yoani Sánchez," *Miami Herald*, November 11, 2009, link: http://www.latinamericanstudies.org/human-rights/yoani-assault.htm.
10. U.S. president Barack Obama's response to dissident blogger Yoani Sanchez, New York, November 2009.
11. Jeff Franks, "Dissidents have little support in Cuba: WikiLeaks," December 17, 2010, https://www.reuters.com/article/us-cuba-dissidents-wikileaks-idUSTRE6BG1NJ20101217.
12. NPR, "We Said No Car Pictures," *Weekend Edition*, June 28, 2014.

2.

1. Donald Trump tweet, November 25, 2016.
2. Conversation with Parisa Khosravi, CNN senior vice president for international newsgathering, June 2009.
3. Donald P. Baker, "Their Woman in Havana," *Washington Post,* March 20, 1997, https://www.washingtonpost.com/archive/lifestyle/1997/03/20/their-woman-in -havana/54d3a03e-5416-4ef3-826f-8db3d96d599c/.
4. Paul Colford, "AP's Long History of Reporting from Cuba," Associated Press, December 22, 2014, https://blog.ap.org/behind-the-news/aps-long-history-of -reporting-from-cuba.
5. National Center for Biotechnology Information (NCBI), *Health Consequences of Cuba's Special Period,* July 2008, 179 (3): 257.
6. Robert Cribb, Jenifer Quinn, Julian Sher, and Juan O. Tamayo, "How Cuba Became the Newest Hotbed for Tourists Craving Sex with Minors," *Miami Herald,* March 16, 2013.
7. U.S. State Department, Trafficking in Persons Report 2009, June 2009, https:// www.state.gov/j/tip/rls/tiprpt/2009/.
8. MI5 Center for the Protection of National Infrastructure, *The Threat from Chinese Espionage,* 2008.

3.

1. Will Weissert, "Called the Great Sofa, There's Nothing Sleepy about Havana's Malecon," Associated Press, July 28, 2007.
2. John Taliaferro, *All the Great Prizes: The Life of John Hay, from Lincoln to Roosevelt* (New York: Simon and Schuster, 2013).
3. T. J. English, *Havana Nocturne: How the Mob Owned Cuba and Then Lost It to the Revolution* (New York: HarperCollins, 2008).
4. Hillary Rodham Clinton, *Hard Choices* (New York: Simon and Schuster, 2014).
5. Marian Leonardo Lawson, *USAID's Office of Transition Initiatives After 15 Years: Issues for Congress* (Congressional Research Service, May 27, 2009), https://www .everycrsreport.com/files/20090527_R40600_92252119ff05220fd70aadb14edec a632184f42c.pdf.
6. Interview with Fulton Armstrong, Washington, D.C., November 2017.
7. Michael W. Cornebise, *The Social Construction of Tourism in Cuba: A Geographic Analysis of the Representations of Gender and Race During the Special Period, 1995–1997* (Knoxville, TN: University of Tennessee, 2003).
8. U.S. Ambassador Hugo Llorens, "Open and Shut: The Case of the Honduran Coup," U.S. diplomatic cable, July 24, 2009, Wikileaks, https://wikileaks.org /plusd/cables/09TEGUCIGALPA645_a.html.

9. "Transcript: Hillary Clinton Meets with the *Daily News* Editorial Board," *New York Daily News,* April 11, 2016, http://www.nydailynews.com/opinion/transcript -hillary-clinton-meets-news-editorial-board-article-1.2596292.

4.

1. Natasha Geiling, "Before the Revolution: Socialites and Celebrities Flocked to Cuba in the 1950s," *Smithsonian,* July 31, 2007, https://www.smithsonianmag.com /history/before-the-revolution-159682020/.
2. Arthur M. Schlesinger, *The Dynamics of World Power: A Documentary History of the United States Foreign Policy* (New York: Chelsea House Publishers,1973).
3. Interviews with Cuban fishermen, Havana, Cuba, 2010.
4. Archibald R. M. Ritter, "Cuba's Underground Economy," Economics and International Affairs, Carleton University, Canada, January 14, 2005, https:// carleton.ca/economics/wp-content/uploads/cep04-12.pdf.

5.

1. W. Martin James, *Historical Dictionary of Angola* (Lanham, MD: Rowman and Littlefield, 2018).
2. Michael Ware interview of Senen, *Uncensored with Michael Ware,* National Geographic Channel, September 2016.
3. "Attempt to unify Cuba's dual currencies 'a headache,' Castro says," Reuters, May 19, 2018, https://www.reuters.com/article/us-cuba-politics-currency/attempt -to-unify-cubas-dual-currencies-a-headache-castro-says-idUSKBN1HQ2EK.
4. Interview with John S. Kavulich, president of the U.S.-Cuba Trade and Economic Council, New York, September 2017.

6.

1. Cuba National Statistics Office, 2009.
2. David Ariosto, "Cuba's Quiet Revolution," CNN, June 1, 2010, http://www.cnn .com/2010/WORLD/americas/05/31/cuba.farms/index.html.
3. President Raul Castro, address to the National Assembly, August 1, 2010.
4. Ibid.
5. Jade Garrett, "Quieten Down! Manic Neighbours Refuse to Tolerate Noisy Rehearsals," *Independent,* June 26, 2001, https://www.independent.co.uk/news/uk /this-britain/quieten-down-manic-neighbours-refuse-to-tolerate-noisy -rehearsals-9169483.html.

7.

1. Eric Nunez, "Captain Contradicts El Duque's Escape," Associated Press, December 6, 1998.

2. Roberto González Echevarría, *The Pride of Havana: A History of Cuban Baseball* (New York: Oxford University Press, 2001).

3. William M. LeoGrande and Peter Kornbluh, *Back Channel to Cuba: The Hidden History of Negotiations between Washington and Havana* (Chapel Hill, NC: University of North Carolina Press, 2015).

8.

1. K. Bolender, *Cuba under Siege: American Policy, the Revolution and Its People* (New York: Palgrave Macmillan, 2012).

2. Cuban Democracy Act of 1992, Pub. L. No. 102–484, 106 Stat. 2315 (1992); and Helms-Burton Act of 1996, Pub. L. No. 104–114, 110 Stat. 785 (1996).

3. U.S. Government Accountability Office (hereafter GAO), *U.S. Democracy Assistance for Cuba Needs Better Management and Oversight*, GAO-07-147, November 15, 2006, publicly released November 15, 2006, https://www.gao.gov/products/GAO-07-147.

4. GAO, *Broadcasting to Cuba: Actions Are Needed to Improve Strategy and Operations*, GAO-09-127, February 5, 2009.

5. Interview with Carlos Garcia-Perez, director of the U.S. Office of Cuba Broadcasting, Miami, Florida, 2015.

6. Desmond Butler, Michael Weissenstein, Laura Wides-Munoz, and Andrea Rodriguez, "USAID Op Undermines Cuba's Hip-Hop Protest Scene," Associated Press, December 12, 2014, https://apnews.com/7c275c134f1b4a0ca3428929fcece82d.

7. GAO, *Cuba Democracy Assistance: USAID's Program Is Improved, but State Could Better Monitor Its Implementing Partners*, GAO-13-285, January 2013.

9.

1. Eduardo Fierro and Cynthia Perry, *Preliminary Reconnaissance Report—12 January 2010 Haiti Earthquake* (Pacific Earthquake Engineering Research Center, January 12, 2010).

2. Interview with Haiti government spokesman, Port-au-Prince, Haiti, 2010.

3. Barack Obama, address, Washington, D.C., January 14, 2010.

4. Tom Brown, "Haiti Aid Effort Marred by Slow UN Response," *Telegraph,* February 26, 2010.

5. Manuel Franco, Usama Bilal, Pedro Ordunez, Mikhail Benet, Alain Morejon, Benjamin Caballero, Joan F. Kennelly, and Richard S. Cooper, "Population-Wide Weight Loss and Regain in Relation to Diabetes Burden and Cardiovascular Mortality in Cuba, 1980–2010," *British Medical Journal* 346, no. 1515 (2013), https://www.bmj.com/content/346/bmj.f1515#ref-40.

6. Ibid.

7. Ministry of Health, *Medicina: Cambios en el sistema de Salud de la Isla*, December 4, 2010.
8. UN Secretary-General, "Secretary-General Hails Cuba for Training Medical 'Miracle Workers,' Being on Frontlines of Global Health," press release, January 28, 2014, https://www.un.org/press/en/2014/sgsm15619.doc.htm.
9. Interview with Dr. Carlos Alberto Garcia, January 2010.
10. Josefina Vidal, Cuban Foreign Ministry, official communiqué, Havana, Cuba, 2010.
11. Interview with Dr. Jorge Fran Martinez, January 2010.

10.

1. *Cuba: Restrictions on Freedom of Expression in Cuba*, Amnesty International, June 30, 2010, https://www.amnesty.org/en/documents/amr25/005/2010/en/.
2. Jonathan Farrar, "Request for HRDF Funds for Cuban Organizations," July 31, 2008, WikiLeaks, https://wikileaks.org/plusd/cables/08HAVANA613_a.html.
3. Jeff Franks, "Dissidents Have Little Support in Cuba: Wikileaks," Reuters, December 17, 2010, https://www.reuters.com/article/us-cuba-dissidents-wikileaks-idUSTRE6BG1NJ20101217.
4. "2007 Country Reports on Human Rights Practices: Cuba," Bureau of Democracy, Human Rights, and Labor, March 11, 2008, https://www.state.gov/j/drl/rls/hrrpt/2007/100635.htm.
5. Shasta Darlington, "Cuban Dissidents Kept from Political Prisoner's Funeral, Activists Say," CNN, March 10, 2010, http://www.cnn.com/2010/WORLD/americas/02/24/cuba.dissidents/index.html.

11.

1. Bendixen and Amandi International, "Poll for Univision/Fusion in Collaboration with the *Washington Post*: Final Results, April 2015," Univision Noticias, http://www.cubastudygroup.org/index.cfm/files/serve?File_id=0e6dcc83-cdfb-4b62-9bea-d121f0b72a0d.
2. Interview with Havana resident Isabel Fuentes, Havana, Cuba, December 2009.
3. Karl Marx, *Critique of Hegel's Philosophy of Right* (1843). "Religion is the sigh of the oppressed creature, the heart of a heartless world, and the soul of soulless conditions. It is the opium of the people."
4. John Paul II, address to the Fiftieth General Assembly of the United Nations, October 5, 1995.
5. Pope John Paul II, address during his welcome ceremony in Havana, Cuba, January 21, 1998.
6. David Ariosto, "Jailed Cuban Dissident Released to Serve House Arrest," CNN, June 5, 2010.

12.

1. "Cuba Internet Penetration," Ding, 2017.
2. Eric Schmidt, Google executive chairman, memo posted by Google, October 2014.

13.

1. Michael Ware and David Ariosto, interview of Rigoberto Campos, *Uncensored with Michael Ware*, National Geographic Channel, September 2016.
2. 2010 U.S. Census.
3. J. Berlanga, J. Fernandez, E. Lopez, P. Lopez, A. de Rio, C. Valezuela, C. Baldomero, V. Muzio, M. Raices, R. Silva, B. Acevedo, and L. Herrera, *Heberprot-P: A Novel Product for Treating Advanced Diabetic Foot Ulcer,* NCBI and Cuba Center for Genetic Engineering and Biotechnology, January 2013, https://www.ncbi.nlm .nih.gov/pubmed/23396236.
4. "Cuba Battling Medicine Shortages in Wake of Cash Crunch," Reuters, December 1, 2017.

14.

1. *Granma*, October 16, 2012.
2. Pew Research Center 2013 survey of Hispanics.

15.

1. Census Bureau, "American Community Survey," U.S. Bureau of Economic Analysis, 2015.
2. "Middle-Class Identification in U.S. at Pre-Recession Levels," Gallup, June 21, 2017.
3. 2014 oil and gas report, Petróleos de Venezuela.
4. Carnegie Endowment for International Peace, "Cuba Fed a President's Fears and Took Over Venezuela," *Financial Times*, April 15, 2014.

16.

1. *The United Nations Comtrade Annual Report*, May 2017.
2. Brookings Institution 2014 report, Venezuela.
3. Venezuela Central Bank report, January 2015.
4. Venezuela's Living Conditions Survey, 2016: ENCOVI-Central University of Venezuela, Andrés Bello Catholic University, Simón Bolívar University.
5. Luc Cohen and Ivan Castro, "As Venezuela Coffee Output Sinks, It Swaps Oil to Import Nicaraguan Beans," Reuters, March 1, 2015.

17.

1. Moisés Naím, "Nicolás Maduro Doesn't Really Control Venezuela," *Atlantic,* May 25, 2017.

2. Venezuelan Violence Observatory, December 2017 annual report, https://observatoriodeviolencia.org.ve/.

3. *What Is Happening to Television News?* Reuters Institute, University of Oxford, Digital News Project, 2016, https://reutersinstitute.politics.ox.ac.uk/our-research/what-happening-television-news.

18.

1. Nick Squires, "Capitalism and Carrots: When the Pope Met Barack Obama," *Telegraph,* March 27, 2014.

2. 2015 U.S. Senate subcommittee hearing, Roberta Jacobson, assistant U.S. secretary of state, Washington, D.C.

3. Pew Research Center, "After Decades of GOP Support, Cubans Shifting Toward the Democratic Party," June 24, 2014.

4. Interview with Tim Rieser, senior foreign policy aide to Senator Patrick Leahy, December 2017.

5. Interview with Dan Erikson, top State Department adviser and White House special adviser to the vice president, November 2017.

6. Alejandro Castro Espín, interviewed by television reporter Iazonas Pipinis Velasco, the Acropolis, Athens, Greece, February 24, 2015.

7. Yoani Sanchez, "Kim Jong Un and Alejandro Castro Espín: Destined by Blood to Be Dictators?" *Huffington Post,* December 20, 2011, https://www.huffingtonpost.com/yoani-sanchez/kim-jongun-and-alejandro-_b_1159614.html?guccounter=1.

19.

1. President Barack Obama, statement on Cuba policy changes, White House, Washington, D.C., December 17, 2014.

2. Sue Anne Pressley, "Solemnly This Time, Miamians Protest over Elian," *Washington Post,* April 30, 2000.

3. Willian Schneider, "Elian Gonzalez Defeated Al Gore," *Atlantic,* May 1, 2001.

4. Interview with Miguel Saavedra, president of Vigilia Mambisa, December 2014, Miami, Florida.

5. U.S.-Cuba Trade and Economic Council, interview with council president John Kavulich, December 2017.

6. U.S. International Trade Commission, "Overview of Cuban Imports of Goods and Services and Effects of U.S. Restrictions," March 2016.

7. Fidel Castro, letter published in *Granma,* January 27, 2015.

8. *Bendixen and Amandi International, survey of 1,200 Cubans, Univision, Fusion, and the Washington Post, 2014.*

20.

1. President Raul Castro, televised statement, Havana, Cuba, December 17, 2014.
2. President Raul Castro, speech to Cuban National Assembly, August 2010.
3. Cuban government estimates, CPI, August 2012.
4. Ted Piccone, *The Geopolitics of China's Rise in Latin America,* Brookings Institution report, November 2016.
5. Claire Felter and Danielle Renwick, *Mercosur: South America's Fractious Trade Bloc,* Council on Foreign Relations, December 26, 2017.
6. Raul Castro, statement at Summit of the Americas, Trinidad, April 17, 2009.

21.

1. *Audit of USAID/Afghanistan's local governance and community development project in southern and eastern regions of Afghanistan,* Audit Report No. 5-306-09-003-P, Office of Inspector General, May 11, 2009, https://oig.usaid.gov/sites/default /files/audit-reports/5-306-09-003-p.pdf.
2. "Who Is Alan Gross and What Did He Do?" Reuters, December 17, 2014.
3. "DAI Proposed Expansion of Scope of Work," Case: 1:12-cv-01860-JEB, September 17, 2009, https://www.scribd.com/document/122217008/Alan-Gross-Lawsuit.
4. Case 1:12-cv-01860, document 10-15, filed January 15, 2016, page 7, George Washington University, September 2009, https://nsarchive2.gwu.edu/NSAEBB /NSAEBB411/docs/daigross-memo.pdf.
5. Anthony DePalma, *The Man Who Invented Fidel: Castro, Cuba, and Herbert L. Matthews of the* New York Times (New York: PublicAffairs, 2006).
6. Herbert L. Matthews, "Cuba Rebel Is Visited in Hideout: Castro Is Still Alive and Still Fighting in Mountains," *New York Times,* February 24, 1957.
7. Interview with Fulton Armstrong, December 2017.
8. Jim Boomgard, president of Development Alternatives Inc., statement following the arrest of Alan Gross, 2010.
9. Alan Gross and Judith Gross v. Development Alternatives, Case 1:12-cv-01860, U.S. District Court for the District of Columbia, filed November 16, 2012, https://www.documentcloud.org/documents/1383798-grosssuit.html.

22.

1. Dan Lamothe, "These Marines Took Down the U.S. Flag in Cuba in 1961. Today, They Watched It Rise Again," *Washington Post,* August 14, 2015.
2. President Barack Obama, speech delivered at the Grand Theatre, Havana, Cuba, March 22, 2016.

3. Fidel Castro, letter published in *Granma,* March 28, 2016.
4. Timothy Naftali and Aleksandr Fursenko, *One Hell of a Gamble: Khrushchev, Castro, and Kennedy 1958–1964* (New York: W. W. Norton & Company, Inc., 1998).
5. Ibid.
6. Nikolai Leonov, *Raul Castro: A Man in Revolution* (Corporativo V y T, 2015).
7. Interview with James Williams, president of Engage Cuba, Washington, D.C., November 2017.

23.

1. Michael Weissenstein, "Vin Diesel, Chanel Spark Cultural Backlash in Cuba," Associated Press, May 20, 2016.
2. President Raul Castro, closing remarks to the Cuban National Assembly, December 2011.

24.

1. Terrence McCoy, "Cuba Deal Reveals New Clues in Case of Ana Montes, 'The Most Important Spy You've Never Heard Of,'" *Washington Post,* December 18, 2014.
2. Directorate of Intelligence, *Cuban Subversive Activities in Latin America: 1959–1968, Special Report,* Washington, D.C., February 16, 1968.
3. Brian Latell, *Castro's Secrets: The CIA and Cuba's Intelligence Machine* (New York: Palgrave Macmillan, 2012).
4. Interviews with former CIA officials, 2017.
5. Josh Lederman and Matthew Lee, "Tillerson Tells AP Cuba Still Risky; FBI Doubts Sonic Attacks," Associated Press, January 8, 2018.
6. Randel L. Swanson, Stephen Hampton, and Judith Green-McKenzie, "Neurological Manifestations Among US Government Personnel Reporting Directional Audible and Sensory Phenomena in Havana, Cuba," *Journal of the American Medical Association,* March 20, 2018, https://jamanetwork.com/journals/jama/article-abstract/2673168.
7. William J. Broad, "Microwave Weapons Are Prime Suspects in Ills of U.S. Embassy Workers," *New York Times,* Sept. 1, 2018; Defense Intelligence Agency: Biological Effects of Electromagnetic Radiation (Radiowaves and Microwaves) Eurasian Communist Countries, March 1976, DST-1810S-074-76.
8. McCoy, "Cuban Deal Reveals New Clues."
9. Brian Latell, *Castro's Secrets.*
10. *Report of the President's Commission on the Assassination of President John F. Kennedy* (Warren Commission Report), September 24, 1964, 11.
11. JFK declassified document, FBI, record #124-10158-1058, Lee Harvey Oswald, Internal Security—Russia-Cuba.

12. Jonathan Wolfe, "What James Donovan Did After the Bridge of Spies," *New York Times,* November 25, 2015.

13. William M. LeoGrande and Peter Kornbluh, *Back Channel to Cuba: The Hidden History of Negotiations between Washington and Havana* (Chapel Hill, NC University of North Carolina Press, 2014).

14. Declassified U.S. House Select Committee on Assassinations report.

15. Senate intelligence report.

16. Interview with Fulton Armstrong, Washington, D.C., November 2017.

25.

1. *Clinical Cancer Research,* August 2016.

2. Douglas Starr, "The Cuban Biotech Revolution," *Wired,* December 1, 2004.

3. Richard Branson, "Visiting Cuba and Scientific Advancements," *Virgin,* November 14, 2017.

4. U.S. Office of the Director of National Intelligence, *Presidential Policy Directive— United States–Cuba Normalization,* October 14, 2016.

5. James R. Clapper, director of national intelligence, remarks, Dirksen Senate Office Building, Washington, D.C., February 9, 2016, https://www.dni.gov /files/documents/2016-02-09SASC_open_threat_hearing_transcript.pdf; Senate Armed Services Committee Hearing, "IC's Worldwide Threat Assessment, Opening Statement, Tuesday, Dirksen Senate Office Building," Washington, D.C., February 9, 2016.

6. Karina Martin, "Raul Castro's Daughter Mocks Sonic Attacks That Injured US Diplomats with Star Wars Joke," *Pan Am Post*, October 2, 2017.

7. Chen Yan, Kevin Fu, and Wenyuan Xu, "On Cuba, Diplomats, Ultrasound, and Intermodulation Distortion," University of Michigan Tech Report, March 1, 2018.

Epilogue

1. Mimi Whitefield, "Cuba's New Leader Just Faced His First Crisis. It Gave Us a Glimpse of His Governing Style," *Miami Herald,* May 24, 2018.

INDEX